Hunting and the Politics of Violence
before the English Civil War

A major contribution to debates about the origins of the Civil War, this study of English forests and hunting from the late sixteenth century to the early 1640s explores their significance in the symbolism and effective power of royalty and the nobility in early modern England. Blending social, cultural, and political history, Daniel Beaver examines the interrelationships among four local communities to explain the violent political conflicts in the forests in the years leading up to the Civil War. Adopting a micro-historical approach, the book explores how local politics became bound up with national political and ideological divisions. The author argues that, from the early seventeenth century, a politics of land use in forests and other hunting reserves involved its participants in a sophisticated political discourse, touching on the principles of law and justice, the authority of the crown, and the nature of a commonwealth.

DANIEL C. BEAVER is Associate Professor at the Department of History, Pennsylvania State University. He is the author of *Parish Communities and Religious Conflict in the Vale of Gloucester, 1590–1690* (1998).

Cambridge Studies in Early Modern British History

Series editors

ANTHONY FLETCHER
Emeritus Professor of English Social History, University of London

JOHN MORRILL
*Professor of English and Irish History, University of Cambridge,
and Fellow of Selwyn College*

ETHAN SHAGAN
Associate Professor of History, University of California, Berkeley

ALEXANDRA WALSHAM
Professor of Reformation History, University of Exeter

This is a series of monographs and studies covering many aspects of the history of the British Isles between the late fifteenth century and the early eighteenth century. It includes the work of established scholars and pioneering work by a new generation of scholars. It includes both reviews and revisions of major topics and books which open up new historical terrain or which reveal startling new perspectives on familiar subjects. All the volumes set detailed research into our broader perspectives, and the books are intended for the use of students as well as of their teachers.

For a list of titles in the series, see end of book.

HUNTING AND THE POLITICS OF VIOLENCE BEFORE THE ENGLISH CIVIL WAR

DANIEL C. BEAVER

Pennsylvania State University

CAMBRIDGE
UNIVERSITY PRESS

CAMBRIDGE UNIVERSITY PRESS
Cambridge, New York, Melbourne, Madrid, Cape Town, Singapore, São Paulo

Cambridge University Press
The Edinburgh Building, Cambridge CB2 8RU, UK

Published in the United States of America by Cambridge University Press, New York

www.cambridge.org
Information on this title: www.cambridge.org/9780521878531

First published 2008

Printed in the United Kingdom at the University Press, Cambridge

A catalog record for this publication is available from the British Library

ISBN 978-0-521-87853-1 hardback

For Nina and Anna

At last my drim of love has came true.
George Herriman

CONTENTS

MAPS

ACKNOWLEDGMENTS

This book began as a study of gifts and their meanings in early modern England. I had hoped to explore how changing understandings of community and of personal relationships were expressed through the objects people gave as gifts and the seasons of their giving. This is not that book. At the start, I found so much evidence related to the circulation of venison during the early seventeenth century, and to the keen pursuit of it, that I began to set aside the evidence for other forms of gift in order to make sense of this mania. I had little understanding of the statutes related to the hunt, much less the distinctive laws and offices of forests, in short the vast political economy and ritual that governed the killing of deer and the consumption of their flesh in early modern England. The various hunting reserves fostered an intense, but often elusive, poorly documented politics. The evidence of forest courts presents significant technical challenges. At times, this has felt more like drowning than being lost in the woods.

The result is a different book from the one I had intended to write. It is not a monograph. I have not tried to track down every early Stuart reference to the hunt or every scrap of surviving evidence for the local communities discussed in the book. But I have used some of the methods of micro-history, particularly its variety of scale, in what has become a brief account of hunting and popular politics, meaning generally the politics beyond court, council, and parliament, during the early seventeenth century. As the political economy of venison became its subject, the book's narratives increasingly converged on the crisis of late spring and summer 1642, and its familiar series of attacks on forests, chases, and parks across southern England. Unfortunately, many of the best accounts of the broad social experience of this political crisis lie in monographs that are difficult to adapt to the classroom. I have attempted to combine, in a short book, micro-history's focus on local communities and unfamiliar archives, its insistence that the superficially eccentric often conceals the deeper patterns of culture, with an account of early Stuart political culture that places forests and other hunting reserves in a larger context. If specialists are persuaded that forests were more than museums of law, if students are induced to explore further the wealth of recent historical work on political awareness in early modern England, this book will have served its purpose.

It is a pleasant task to record my debts to the staffs of archives and libraries where I have worked. Eric Novotny, the Head of History Collections at Pattee Library, Penn State University, has strengthened the library's now substantial resources in early modern history and deserves an honorary appointment in the History Department. I thank the staffs at the Huntington Library in San Marino, California, the Gloucestershire Record Office, and the Public Record Office in London for answering endless queries. David Chinn of the Public Record Office, in particular, handled an unwieldy microfilm order with extraordinary patience and skill. I thank Roy Ritchie and the research division of the Huntington Library for a Mayers Fellowship in summer 1997, and the opportunity it afforded to work on the Stowe papers. I have also received generous support from the College of Liberal Arts at Penn State for the preparation of microfilm. The formation of a Committee for Early Modern Studies at Penn State, involving colleagues from departments across the arts and humanities, has made the university an exciting place to study the early modern English past. In fall 2005, a fellowship from the Penn State Institute for the Arts and Humanities allowed me to finish the chapter on Windsor. I have presented early drafts of chapters at Princeton University, the University of Sheffield, the Institute for Historical Research at the University of London, and the Renaissance seminar in the English Department at Penn State. I thank my hosts for their generosity and the participants in these sessions for their criticism and encouragement.

I have benefited immeasurably from the advice and criticism of friends and colleagues. Keith Wrightson once again read and commented on the entire manuscript. His broad conception of social history and personal generosity have been sources of inspiration. The anonymous readers for Cambridge University Press offered helpful suggestions and expressed strong support for the project. I thank my father, Dan Beaver, Michael Adas, Miriam Bodian, Mike Braddick, Justin Champion, David Cressy, Barbara Donagan, Phil Jenkins, Newton Key, Laura Knoppers, Peter Lake, John Morrill, Nina Safran, Ethan Shagan, Bill Speck, Garrett Sullivan, Jim Sweeney, and John Walter for their comments on individual chapters. Of course, the errors that remain are my own responsibility.

I cannot properly acknowledge the numerous references I have received. I thank Mike Braddick, John Broad, Laura Knoppers, Sears McGee,

Garrett Sullivan, and John Walter for suggestions and texts that became part of the fabric of the book. Mike Braddick, Laura Knoppers, and Garrett Sullivan directed me to sources written in a poetic language that, needless to say, is not typical of forest court records. I thank Sabrina Alcorn-Baron, in particular, for her loan of a microfilm of the Sackville manuscripts. I have not consulted this collection at the Centre for Kentish Studies, although the bibliography and notes respectfully indicate this archive as the collection's home. I became aware of the importance of the Earl of Middlesex's correspondence for the history of Corse Lawn Chase while I was studying Gloucestershire parishes, and I used a handlist of the Gloucestershire documents in the Sackville collection prepared for the Gloucestershire Record Office to identify those relevant for a study of Corse Lawn. I was pleasantly surprised to find these letters included in the microfilm Sabrina had prepared for her research on the early Stuart Privy Council. Her generous, extended loan of this microfilm spared a good deal of time and resources for other parts of the book.

It is difficult to convey, much less properly acknowledge, the alchemy of influences among family, friends, colleagues, and ideas. Michael Adas has been a constant source of support and encouragement for many years. In the History Department at Penn State, Kumkum Chatterjee, Tony Kaye, Joan Landes, Oncho Ng, Bill Pencak, Matthew Restall, and Gregg Roeber have offered both friendship and critical perspectives from their own fields. As heads of department, Gregg Roeber and Sally McMurry have helped me through their office as well as their personal support. Greg Eghigian and I have been talking about violence for years. Most of our plans have come to nothing, but the graduate seminars we have taught together at Penn State on the history of violence in Europe have given me a chance to work through many of the ideas in this book. I have learned a great deal about early modern England, as well as the fortunes and misfortunes of Watford Football Club, from numerous conversations with Mike Braddick. Laura Knoppers and Garrett Sullivan have encouraged, and even promoted, my desecration of literary texts. I dedicate the book to my wife, Nina Safran, and my daughter, Anna, with thanks and love.

ABBREVIATIONS

CKS	Centre for Kentish Studies
CSPD	*Calendar of State Papers, Domestic Series*
CSP, V	Calendar of State Papers, Venetian
GDR	Gloucester Diocesan Records
GRO	Gloucestershire Record Office
HL	Huntington Library
HLRO	House of Lords Record Office
HMC	Historical Manuscripts Commission
HMSO	His/Her Majesty's Stationery Office
LJ	*(House of) Lords Journal*
PRO	Public Record Office
RO	Record Office
SCU	Seventeenth Century Undated
SP	State Papers
SR	*Statutes of the Realm*
STAC	Star Chamber
STLP	Stowe Temple Legal Papers
STMLP	Stowe Temple Miscellaneous Legal Papers
STMP	Stowe Temple Manorial Papers
STP	Stowe Temple Papers
VCH	*Victoria County History*

Dates are given in old style, with the year beginning on 1 January.

Introduction: Hunting, violence, and the origins of the English Revolution

> You go down new streets, you see houses you never saw before, pass
> places you never knew were there. Everything changes . . . Sometimes
> it changes even if you go the same way.
>
> Samuel R. Delany, *Dhalgren* (1974)

I

This book is about the series of attacks on parks, chases, and forests in
southern England during the late spring and summer of 1642. It is also about
the words used to define the meanings of the attacks and about how these
words were weighted with the histories of the places where the attacks
occurred. Many of those who killed deer or cut down woods during this
summer of violence justified their actions as a defense of high principles,
claiming the moral authority of law and commonwealth. Their words
evoked the long histories of communities embedded in the royal forests
or perched on the margins of forests, those great hunting preserves of the
English crown and nobility. As early as October 1641, neighbors on the
southeastern border of Windsor Forest had justified attacks on the king's
deer as a defense of their "ancient customs" and the status of their lands as
liberty of purlieu rather than forest, and these attacks continued in the
following year. In late April 1642, hunters in Waltham Forest cited the limits
of settled law as a defense for killing deer.[1] This book tells the political
histories that lay behind this choice of words and actions in 1642.

The histories merit the telling for their remarkable individuals and
revealing social dramas, but their larger interest lies in the significant
light they cast on the nature of the English Revolution, the often violent
process of political change that, in its most familiar form, resulted in the

---

[1] H[ouse of] L[ords] R[ecord] O[ffice]: Main Papers, 1509–1700: 27-10-1641; Main Papers, 1509–1700:
2-5-1642; [*House of] L[ords] J[ournal]*, vol. 4: 406–407, 434, 547.

transformation of a monarchy to a republic or "commonwealth" in 1649. Few would deny that this major transformation of the English regime depended on new forms of political belief, as well as new modes of political expression and action.[2] As John Walter has argued from the evidence of political violence in Colchester, however, this new politics of the 1640s emerged from the familiar political world of the early seventeenth century and retained many of its essential features.[3] The origins of the revolution explored in these pages concern the complex ways political ideas were expressed in speech and action in the forest communites of Stuart England during the decades before the Civil War.

Although the common culture of church and civil affairs marked these communities as it did all other corners of the realm, the unique law and institutions of forests fostered a distinctive political discourse. Moreover, this discourse inevitably touched on the symbolism of royal authority and honor. The law code of the Stuart forest regime upheld and protected the environmental demands of the hunt, standing among the highest ritual expressions of royalty and nobility. The regime's courts and officers negotiated the relationship between the needs of hunters and the rightful claims and "liberties" of the forest "commonwealth." As the conventional use of such terms suggests, the denizens of Waltham, Windsor, and other forests understood their rights and obligations as matters of principle long before 1642, though the politics of these principles had never involved a choice *between* crown and commonwealth claims in the forest.

The political crisis of the early 1640s affected all the domains of the Stuart regime. Indeed, the inability or unwillingness of its major figures to confine its impact to the relations between crown and parliament constituted a significant feature of the crisis.[4] Among forest communities, and especially in the important royal hunting preserves of Windsor and Waltham in southern England, the crisis brought to a head a process of law reform that made the traditional claims of crown and commons in the forest seem irreconcilable. Under these circumstances, defenders of the forest law in both court and parliament warned against the dangerous license of attacks on deer and woods and issued orders to uphold the new statute of August 1641, negotiated between crown and parliament to redress

[2] See the recent overview in Austin Woolrych, *Britain in Revolution, 1625–1660* (Oxford University Press, 2002), 189–233, 335–365.
[3] John Walter, *Understanding Popular Violence in the English Revolution: The Colchester Plunderers* (Cambridge University Press, 1999), 71–157.
[4] Woolrych, *Britain in Revolution*, 189–233; Mark Kishlansky, *A Monarchy Transformed: Britain, 1603–1714* (London: Penguin, 1996), 134–157.

the grievances of the forests.[5] But many others sought redress of grievances in a radical disafforestation that defied the statute, as local coalitions of gentry and commons killed thousands of deer and cut down hundreds of trees in Windsor, Waltham, Corse Lawn, and on the borders of many other forests, chases, and parks, showing a startling willingness to attack, and even to destroy, the traditional forest polity in defense of its commonwealth. If these divisions did not always make for easy choices between crown and parliament when it came to civil war, the polarization of forest politics remained an important feature of the political landscape on the eve of war and had an enduring impact on royalist and parliamentarian political ideologies.

In short, this book is about how these "special localities," to borrow the nineteenth-century historian Samuel Rawson Gardiner's term for the forests, fostered a distinctive ideological politics and about how this politics generated some quite radical challenges to the Stuart regime in the early 1640s.[6] It is a history of local speeches and actions that reveals as much about the longterm processes of political negotiation and change as about the revolution, and suggests that both were integral to the formation of an informed, activist political society in early modern England.

II

The politics of unmaking the forests of southern England in 1642 reveals aspects of the revolution that engage with three and a half centuries of historical writing about it. Since the seventeenth century, a great historiographic tradition has questioned the pace and timing of revolution in England, attempting to establish its boundaries in time. According to one major variation on this theme, the revolution, understood in terms of radical changes even if the word "revolution" is not used, was a total transformation of regime that followed and depended on the violence and disruption of civil war. In his *History of the Rebellion*, written in part during the war, the Earl of Clarendon began with the death of James I in 1625 and the "abrupt and ungracious breaking" of the first three parliaments of Charles I, but viewed the greater "perplexities and distractions" of the 1640s as a gradual process of compounded evils. Clarendon believed the "hand and judgment of god" had worked the "rebellion and civil wars" at

---

[5] 16 Car. I, c. 16, in *Statutes of the Realm*, 5: 119–120.
[6] Samuel R. Gardiner, *History of England from the Accession of James I to the Outbreak of the Civil War, 1603–1642*, 10 vols. (London: Longmans, 1894), 8: 281.

his own majestic pace, "making the weak to contribute to the designs of the wicked, and suffering even those by degrees, out of the conscience of their guilt, to grow more wicked than they intended to be." Only after the civil war, Clarendon observed, did "the violence of the stream" and "the wild fury of the [parliamentarian] army" force their way to the king's execution and the establishment of a commonwealth. A foul blasphemy, "introducing atheism and dissolving all the elements of christian religion," had led gradually to a corruption of the English political conscience. Clarendon lamented "the terror all men were under of the parliament, and the guilt they were conscious of themselves," following the war, such that "from one piece of knavery [they] were hardened and confirmed to undertake another, till at last they had no hope of preservation but by the destruction of [the king]." Clarendon alluded to the "tumults" of the early 1640s, before the war, as "the first declension of [the king's] power," suggesting an important crisis, especially significant in its impact on the practical uses of authority, but lacking the catastrophic moral, personal, and structural or institutional implications of later events.[7]

Clarendon's view of the pace and timing of radical change during the 1640s has been reiterated in Austin Woolrych's recent account of *Britain in Revolution*. Woolrych approaches the revolution as the culmination of processes set in motion by the great crises or "climacterics" of 1640 to 1642 and 1647 to 1649. He uses the term "climacteric" to remove the freight of modern meanings conveyed by "revolution" and to suggest the unscripted, unplanned qualities of major developments during these critical times. His approach makes descriptive sense but sidesteps the problem of how this first crisis, in particular, came to have such a profound impact on the regime's fortunes. On the whole, Woolrych seems to assume a dizzyingly rapid process of politicization in 1639 and 1640, punctuated by the expanding electorate's response to "national issues" in the elections to the Long Parliament. Partisan political information spread through "public readings of royal and parliamentary declarations by magistrates and parsons, many sermons, musters of the trained bands, a spate of pamphlets, and any amount of talk in taverns and alehouses." This process showed its effects quickly, culminating in such familiar moments of the general crisis as the display and defense of the parliament's "protestation" to justify political action in the demonstrations of January 1642, in London and in the many provincial petitions that followed. Crown and parliament engaged in the

---

[7] Edward Hyde, Earl of Clarendon, *History of the Rebellion and Civil Wars in England*, ed. W. D. Macray, 6 vols. (Oxford: Clarendon Press, 1888), 1: 1–2, 5, 6, 567; 4: 428, 453, 491.

"paper war" for political allegiance during spring and summer 1642, as both beneficiaries and victims of this newly broadened politics. It remains difficult to understand how new forms of political action could have come into being so quickly. Woolrych adduces the growing literacy and political awareness of the middling sort during the early seventeenth century to explain the rapidly alienated "hearts and minds" of English subjects, but this is difficult to reconcile with his view of the Civil War as the result of "a quarrel which until shortly before the fighting started involved few outside the governing class."[8] In fact, the problem here is that we know relatively little about the extent to which the English commons understood their concerns in political terms before the crisis of the early 1640s.

Within this tradition of historical writing, a quite different view of the revolution has drawn on the work of English republicans, who attempted to justify the new political order of the 1650s after the civil wars and regicide of the previous decade. Among this circle of writers, the English commonwealth could be justified as a practical choice made under the most dangerous circumstances: the bankruptcy and collapse of the Stuart monarchy had forced parliament and people to assume the responsibilities of governance between 1640 and 1642, and this revolution itself had caused the civil wars that led to the king's execution. In 1656, James Harrington famously concluded from his account of the English nobility's social and military decline that "the dissolution of this government caused the war, not the war the dissolution of this government." Between the late fifteenth and early seventeenth centuries, in Harrington's view, the displacement of the nobility as an effective military class had empowered the commons and destroyed the traditional social basis of English monarchy, a process that culminated in the political crisis after 1640 and the outbreak of civil war in 1642.[9]

Over three centuries later, Lawrence Stone accepted Harrington's observation as "a profound truth" and included it among the "presuppositions" of his analysis of the revolution. As Stone explained with characteristic assurance, "the outbreak of war itself is relatively easy to explain; what is hard is to puzzle out why most of the established institutions of state and church – crown, court, central administration, army, and episcopacy – collapsed so ignominiously two years before."[10] More recently, this

---

[8] Woolrych, *Britain in Revolution*, 14–15, 131, 138, 140, 157, 217–218, 227, 229–230.

[9] James Harrington, *The Commonwealth of Oceana* (Cambridge University Press, [1656] 1992), 54–56.

[10] Lawrence Stone, *The Causes of the English Revolution, 1529–1642* (London: Routledge, 1972, 1986), 48.

argument for the revolutionary significance of events during the early 1640s has shifted away from discredited allegations concerning the "collapse" of the Stuart regime and has focused instead on changes in forms of political communication and action or agency. It is worth recalling the precedent for this concern with agency in Thomas Hobbes's assertion that "the power of the mighty has no foundation but in the opinion and belief of the people" and his casting of the civil wars as the consequence of a battle to control such opinions and beliefs.[11] But the problem has found renewed currency in John Walter's innovative use of micro-history to study the Stour Valley riots, a common if imprecise term for the popular attacks on catholics and royalists in Essex and Suffolk from September to December 1642. Walter concludes that between 1641 and 1642 this region underwent a rapid transformation of its traditional forms of political action, involving their use in the service of more radical, parliamentarian political ends. A key feature of this process was the broad circulation of the "protestation," a formal bond of association drafted by parliament in May 1641, following Charles's failed attempt to seize the Tower, where his friend and councilor the Earl of Strafford awaited parliament's sentence for treason. In response to the catholic menace allegedly revealed by this attack, the protestation's subscribers took an oath to defend the crown, parliament, and church from all vile "popish" designs against the fundamental laws and religion of England. Although initially confined to the parliament, the broader administration of this charge in many parts of the country during the ensuing months changed the political meanings of such traditional forms of communication and action as swearing oaths, preaching sermons, and assembling for musters. Amidst fears of catholic plots and secret stockpiles of weapons, these traditional modes – and the swearing of oaths, in particular – were used in Essex parishes to "appropriate" the terms of the protestation in a powerful new "covenant" to defend the protestant religion from popish attacks. The most important feature of the "revolution" in 1642 becomes a new political activism, resulting in the mobilization of large but disciplined crowds for clearly articulated political ends. In Walter's view, this "interaction between events at the centre and the region promoted the belief that the people had a direct role to play" in political events, and became a major precondition of the mass demonstrations in support of parliament during the late summer and fall of 1642.[12]

[11] Thomas Hobbes, *Behemoth or the Long Parliament* (Chicago: University of Chicago Press, [1682] 1990), 2–4, 16, 49–59.
[12] Walter, *Understanding Popular Violence*, 291–296.

Walter approaches politics as a cultural art, a molding of language and action that constrains as it constructs identities, limiting as it confers power upon those who attempt it. The momentous changes of 1641 and 1642 remained a "political" rather than a "social" revolution, an activism directed against "popish" and "royalist" enemies rather than an attack on "gentlemen," because the language of antipopery and parliamentarianism imposed the constraints of "a dominant discourse of political, not social, conflict."[13] In this way, much of the recent work on the problem of agency during the revolution has explored the boundaries and possibilities of language, including the political importance of print after 1640. Accounts of a "media revolution" between 1640 and 1642 have brought renewed attention to such familiar landmarks as the statute abolishing Star Chamber and High Commission in July 1641, which drastically curtailed the regime's control over printers. Joad Raymond has argued that "this plague of pamphlets" implied "a dramatic transformation in both political consciousness and the distribution of information," while David Cressy has revived the notion of "an explosion of print" after 1640 and has identified this "revolution in communications" as a key aspect of the "intensified national conversation" that distinguished the crisis.[14] In this view, literacy seems to furnish the crucial political skills to build a new politics, and events often seem less important in themselves than in their representation in the media, especially in newsbooks. A new kind of political publication thus facilitated a new awareness of events and their implications, a new political consciousness, that served as a new framework for political action.

Both of these traditional views of the revolution's pace and timing have tended to approach conflict in the Caroline regime in terms of the high political dispute over the proper relationship between prerogative and law, whether in religious or in civil affairs. Moreover, the accounts that have looked for the broader social context of conflict have often merely stressed a more general awareness of these principles, rendered as fears of popery and arbitrary power, in English political culture.[15] The present book departs from this pattern in its use of a less familiar political narrative, involving the

---

[13] Ibid., 345.

[14] Joad Raymond (ed.), *Making the News: An Anthology of the Newsbooks of Revolutionary England, 1641–1660* (New York: St. Martin's Press, 1993), 6; David Cressy, *England on Edge: Crisis and Revolution, 1640–1642* (Oxford University Press, 2006), 281–376.

[15] See the references to a few among the many relevant contributions in Jonathan Scott, *England's Troubles: Seventeenth-Century English Political Instability in European Context* (Cambridge University Press, 2000), 56–57, 94–97.

history of forests and hunting preserves, to explore the significance of a politics of honor both in the making of the Caroline regime and in its crisis during the early 1640s. The dominance of a limited view of the crisis, defined in the high political terms of prerogative and law, has tended to overlook a politics of honor in forests that involved an intense and sometimes violent competition among gentry families, leading often enough to attacks on the king's deer. It is difficult to understand the significance of "law" and "commonwealth" principles in the forests apart from the honor, status, and reputation to be won in their defense. But forest politics also involved a negotiation between royal claims to the forest as a hunting preserve and the legitimate rights of the commons to fuel, pasture, and other forest resources. The forests, chases, and parks of Stuart England, often dismissed as little more than quirks of early modern power, thus constituted dynamic political arenas, defined by an ideologically charged interplay among the interests of crown, gentry, and commons. This poorly understood political domain served as a platform for some of the highest expressions of royal honor and power and for some of the most radical "commonwealth" aspirations in the popular politics of the early seventeenth century.

III

Historians have long been aware of the attacks on Windsor and Waltham forests in the months before the outbreak of the Civil War. Clarendon recalled that, following the dissolution of parliament in 1629, "projects of all kinds, many ridiculous, many scandalous, all very grievous, were set on foot." Among these projects, Clarendon included the revival of the forest laws and the "great fines" imposed, a burden "most upon persons of quality and honor" but also an element in the "tumults which might easily be brought to Windsor from Westminster" in early 1642.[16] Historians since Clarendon have ascribed many different meanings to the "tumults" in the hunting preserves of southern England, a fluidity of interpretation due in part to changing styles of historical interpretation and in part to uncertainties regarding the records of these episodes, touched in many ways by the first blasts of civil war. Gardiner classified the early Stuart forests among the "foremost" of "special localities," whose grievances lacked the national scale of ship money yet revealed in a unique setting the "encroachments upon the rights and liberties of subjects, made in the most insidious

---

[16] Clarendon, *History of the Rebellion*, 1: 85, 567.

form possible, under the cloak of the law and under the sanction of those who should have been its guardians."[17] More recent work has questioned the long history of attempts, including those of parliament in 1640 and 1641, to fit the forest laws "smoothly into a series" of grievances, including ship money, feudal incidents, and monopolies, "linked by the fiscal exploitation of anachronistic prerogatives of the crown."[18] To an earlier generation of historians, the forest eyres, or high courts, used to enforce the royal prerogatives of the forest during the 1630s had helped to drive this Caroline fiscal machine. There is a tendency now to explain the forest eyres in Windsor in 1632, Dean and Waltham in 1634, the New Forest in 1635, and Rockingham in 1637 as more or less discrete events, a mixture of reform and opportunism lacking a coherent national design. In the absence of such a design, the "tumults" of the early 1640s become little more than a species of local opportunism.

Indeed, historians have only recently begun to explore the way participants in these local episodes understood their own actions. The earliest ventures evoked a "popular politics" almost entirely separate from the matters of law, authority, liberties, and formal political concepts debated between crown and parliament. Rejecting the assumption that the crown and parliamentary classes defined all "politics" worthy of the name, Brian Manning viewed the forest violence in 1642 as a "peasant hostility against the king and the great landlords," directed against "the most hated symbol of the aristocrat," and "only loosely connected with the challenge of parliament to the king."[19] This notion of "social protest," enabled but not defined by the division of king and parliament, has been used to analyze the "village revolts" in the Forest of Dean and in the fenlands during the 1630s and 1640s, and local grievances continue to form a layer in an increasingly sophisticated understanding of popular politics.[20] But a substantial body of evidence, including much of the evidence of forest politics, resists explanation in the same Malthusian terms as local protests over food

[17] Gardiner, *History of England*, 7: 362–366; 8: 77, 86, 281–282; 9: 383, 415.

[18] George Hammersley, "The Revival of the Forest Laws Under Charles I," *History*, 45 (1960): 85–102; see also Philip A. J. Pettit, *The Royal Forests of Northamptonshire: A Study in Their Economy, 1558–1714* (Gateshead: Northumberland Press, 1968), 83–95; Kevin Sharpe, *The Personal Rule of Charles I* (New Haven: Yale University Press, 1992), 242–245.

[19] Brian Manning, *The English People and the English Revolution* (Harmondsworth: Penguin, 1976), 181, 207–212.

[20] Buchanan Sharp, *In Contempt of All Authority: Rural Artisans and Riot in the West of England, 1586–1660* (Berkeley: University of California Press, 1980), 263–266; Keith Lindley, *Fenland Riots and the English Revolution* (London: Heinemann, 1982), 253–254; Roger Manning, *Village Revolts: Social Protest and Popular Disturbances in England, 1509–1640* (Oxford: Clarendon Press, 1988), 2–3, 310–311.

prices and the enclosure of land. David Underdown has suggested concepts and language common to elite and popular politics, "a culture whose elements included assumptions about the permanent validity of ancient laws and customary rights, and about the existence of appropriate modes of government in church and state."[21] Although Underdown stresses the traditional qualities of this political culture, its principles indicate a capacity for political as well as social protest. During the early seventeenth century, a local knowledge of courts and the law, the result of broad experience in local office as well as religious conflict and other forms of dispute, began to inform a politics increasingly defined in terms of ideology or principle and capable of direct action in support of crown or parliament in 1642, an activism radical in practical implications even if justified by such conservative texts and oaths as the "protestation."[22] Depending on the quality of evidence available for its study, the term "popular politics" may refer to a wide range of behavior, from a person's presence at a local protest to active participation in episodes addressed to the political nation. The meanings and motives of political action often lie in the relationship between the formal statements made before such institutions as courts of law and the subtle calculations of a pervasive politics of honor and reputation. This inclusive notion of politics is particularly important in the "special locality" of the forest, because the system of forest law and its courts meant "social problems" or grievances in forest neighborhoods were often understood in the formal political terms of prosecution, court procedure, and law. In 1642, the political culture derived from this experience articulated powerful statements of both royal prerogative and commonwealth, the notion of a forest as many interests surmounted by the crown.

The attacks on forests, chases, and parks involved distinctive styles of violence, a contrast in styles related to the meaning of the attacks. The mass killings of deer in Windsor and elsewhere took their meaning from the closely observed rituals used to dispatch individual deer in the hunt. In its highest form, the royal hunt elevated this ritualized killing to a form of sacrifice, the blood and flesh of the slain deer offering a fertile medium for

---

[21] David Underdown, *Revel, Riot, and Rebellion: Popular Politics and Culture in England, 1603–1660* (Oxford: Clarendon Press, 1985), 119–130; David Underdown, *A Freeborn People: Politics and the Nation in Seventeenth Century England* (Oxford: Clarendon Press, 1996), 45–89.

[22] Ann Hughes, *The Causes of the English Civil War*, 2nd edn. (London: Macmillan, 1998), 64–72, 132–133; Daniel C. Beaver, *Parish Communities and Religious Conflict in the Vale of Gloucester, 1590–1690* (Cambridge, MA: Harvard University Press, 1998), 113–194, 384–406; Walter, *Understanding Popular Violence*, 71–157, 292–296; Andy Wood, *The Politics of Social Conflict: The Peak Country, 1520–1770* (Cambridge University Press, 1999), 164, 267–270.

symbols of honor, nobility, and authority. The forests furnished a landscape for this theater of honor, a political ecology created by the crown through a Chancery writ, thus conjuring the administrative order of a forest from a tangle of mere woodland. The lesser franchises of the hunt, such as chases and parks, required a royal license and ultimately derived from this royal prerogative of forest. In this context, it is hardly surprising to find the politics of forests often expressed through the symbols of the hunt, taken as the primary meaning of forests and the motive for their creation as political institutions. Because the hunt made the deer a symbol of gentility, and a powerful source of honor, a forest politics of local influence among powerful families and of land use in the forest focused on these symbols and the manner of their killing in culturally meaningful ways. As a result of this dynamic, the violent episodes in the forests and other hunting preserves in 1642 present an opportunity to rethink the nature of political violence in early modern England. As a political phenomenon, violence is commonly viewed in the familiar Weberian terms of the process whereby states have attempted to establish a monopoly of coercive force under the law.[23] Those claiming legitimate authority use such force as a weapon to defend the social order from either external or internal enemies. The ritual violence of the hunt, and the politics of the forest, enter this discussion as a mode of violence used to fashion the social order itself. A knowledge and expertise in the art of the hunt informed gentle status, a masculine quality essential to the successful exercise of office and especially the exercise of judicial power. Gentlemen perceived the hunt as a school of honor and gentility, a testing experience that prepared the heart and mind for magistracy; and a diverse print culture of courtly and domestic manuals endorsed this passage from the hunt to magisterial rank. Perhaps it is useful here to differentiate the constitutive violence of such rites as the hunt, embodied in politically significant symbols and ceremonies, from the instrumental violence of practical coercion. This approach to the hunt recalls Peter Stallybrass's description of carnivalesque violence "as a set of rhetorical practices within the social, a set which includes, but is by no means limited to, linguistic devices."[24]

---

[23] Max Weber, *Economy and Society: An Outline of Interpretive Sociology*, ed. Guenther Roth and Claus Wittich, 2 vols. (Berkeley: University of California Press, 1978), 1: 312–315; 2: 956; Julius R. Ruff, *Violence in Early Modern Europe, 1500–1800* (Cambridge University Press, 2001), 44–72, 248–253; Michael J. Braddick, *State Formation in Early Modern England* (Cambridge University Press, 2000), 16–20; Steve Hindle, "The Keeping of the Public Peace," in Paul Griffiths, Adam Fox, and Steve Hindle (eds.), *The Experience of Authority in Early Modern England* (New York: St. Martin's Press, 1996), 213–248.

[24] Peter Stallybrass, "'Drunk With the Cup of Liberty': Robin Hood, the Carnivalesque, and the Rhetoric of Violence in Early Modern England," *Semiotica*, 54 (1985), 114.

Despite the pervasive influence of antipopery in popular politics, forest
grievances tended to confirm John Morrill's distinct strands of conflict or
"modes of opposition," derived from both civil and religious grievances, in
the crisis of the early 1640s.[25] Perhaps because of the unique law, institutions, and traditions of forests as "special localities," their grievances were
not easily subsumed in the religious politics of the crisis, and in 1641, crown
and parliament acknowledged this political tradition in a new statute of the
forests. During the early seventeenth century, honor and custom motivated
the most important forms of conflict in forest politics. A competition for
the masculine honor acquired through expertise in hunting animated a
distinctive gentry or "great man" style of violence against the king's forests
as well as the parks and chases of neighbors. This politics, articulated in
some cases through debate over "rights and liberties" of purlieu, measured
the skill of such notable local families as the Temples and Dayrells in
Stowe; the Quarles, Carrows, and other families in Waltham Forest; the
Hanburys of Datchett in Windsor Forest; and the Comptons and Tracys in
Corse Lawn Chase. A second political arena in the forests involved the
efforts of communities to protect their customs, particularly against the
enclosure of forest land to create parks. This "country" style of politics was
often expressed in terms of a "commonwealth" interest against avarice, and
sometimes escalated into attacks on forest enclosures and officers. The
meanings and ideological significance of this politics are easily overlooked
in histories that view violence from the perspective of the state, contrasting
the legitimate violence of hunting with "social protest" or to the "criminal"
violence of poaching. On the contrary, long before the crisis of the 1640s,
conflict in the forests assumed political qualities because forests were
defined in political terms, as sites for fashioning the reverend symbols of
royal authority and honor in the hunt. The assumptions, beliefs, and
political practices in early modern English forests thus reveal both an
important domain of the dynastic state and a distinctive forest politics,
including ideologically coherent critiques of forest administration and a
practical political leadership recruited from gentry families and from
substantial farming households.

This forest politics forms an intriguing counterpoint to the politics of
religion, a vital means of mobilizing the antipopish crowds for parliament
in the months before the war. As parliament had settled the forest

---

[25] Walter, *Understanding Popular Violence*, 285–330; John Morrill, "The Religious Context of the
English Civil War," in John Morrill, *The Nature of the English Revolution* (London: Longman, 1993),
47–52.

grievances by statute in August 1641, it became impossible to harness the attacks on hunting preserves in the late spring and summer of 1642. To the diverse groups involved in this broad campaign of disafforestation, the statute's restoration of the Jacobean forest boundaries seemed to implicate the parliament itself in a forest despotism. As the local episodes in Windsor, Waltham, and Corse Lawn reveal, the violent campaign to restore the principle of "commonwealth" in the forests – a notion of multiple interests protected by forest law – confronted the statutory position of both crown and parliament in 1642 and was construed by both as a dangerous species of disorder. The forest attacks entered the familiar narrative of the crisis in the form of "tumults," and as figures in the index of disorder acknowledged by both sides as a deplorable result of the schism between crown and parliament. Historians have tended to see a series of protests rather than a popular political campaign. But the notion of "social protest" seems inadequate to explain such spectacular and enigmatic acts of violence as the killing of 600 deer in Corse Lawn, the Earl of Middlesex's chase in northern Gloucestershire. This manner of killing explicitly violated the rites of the hunt, destroying animals in the indiscriminate butchery of common farms. Similar attacks on the king's deer in Windsor and Waltham conflated "great man" and "country" political styles in a violent critique of the despotism and arbitrary power perceived in both the Caroline forest regime of the 1630s and the new statute of 1641. In this way, forest politics underscores the difficulties of a negotiated settlement after 1640 and confirms the capacity for radical action in this conservative political culture. The scale and manner of deer killing in the forests exemplify the uses of a traditional, conservative, carnivalesque style for the radical ends of disafforestation, as degradations of royal honor and the nobility of both crown and parliamentary officers – a legitimate punishment of despotism – defeated the statutory attempt to restore the bounds of the forests in 1641 and 1642.[26]

This brief analysis, like all histories, is based on a selection of evidence. Although the first chapter draws on a wide range of printed and manuscript sources to recover cultural aspects of the hunt, the four subsequent chapters focus on sites and episodes that have left sufficient records to sustain a detailed analysis. The building of Stowe Park and its problems are the subject of a variety of records in the Temple family papers. Apart from its

---

[26] Underdown, *Revel, Riot, and Rebellion*, 106–145; Walter, *Understanding Popular Violence*, 2–4; Peter Burke, *Popular Culture in Early Modern Europe* (London: Temple Smith, 1978), 198–201; Mikhail Bakhtin, *Rabelais and His World* (Cambridge, MA: MIT Press, 1968), 18–24.

importance in the attacks of 1642, Waltham Forest offers a substantial archive of swanimote court and Star Chamber records. Windsor Forest is unrivaled both as a symbol of royal honor and power in the forest and as the best documented of early modern English forests; its series of swanimote records in the Chancery archive unbroken from the middle of the sixteenth century to the early 1640s. The administration and politics of Corse Lawn Chase occupied a substantial correspondence between the Earl of Middlesex and his local servants in Tewkesbury that survives among his papers. The micro-histories of episodes at these four sites, comprising two forests, a park, and a chase, explore the many meanings of forest and hunt in local communities and attempt to recover their distinctive politics. This method affords the best means to understand the motivations behind local actions in 1642. In the style of micro-history, the focus remains tightly on particularly well-documented episodes. The qualities and many perspectives of the sources offer clues to the politics of these episodes. This particular history has been the goal of my study, at the expense perhaps of a broader survey of the attacks on forests, chases, and parks and their diverse motives, including the opportunism of looters. It was doubtless a powerful testament to the political atmosphere in 1642 that, when asked to explain their attacks on the king's deer, one group in Waltham Forest replied merely "that others do so in other places, and why should not they do so here."[27] Despite a certain loss of breadth, however, this micro-history of hunting and forest politics in early modern England may offer insight, first, into the unexplored subject of sacrificial violence in the making of social and political order. But the constitutive violence of the hunt made symbols that were contested as well as revered. If the blood shed and honor earned in hunting informed the social order, the ideologically charged conflicts of forest politics, often expressed through the carcasses of killed deer, just as clearly informed the political transformations of the early 1640s.

[27] HLRO: Main Papers, 1509–1700: 2-5-1642.

I

Blood, sacrifice, and order: meanings of the forest and hunt in culture, politics, and society

And some certain significance lurks in all things, else all things are
little worth, and the round world itself but an empty cipher . . .
                                        Herman Melville, *Moby Dick* (1851)

I

In 1618, Horatio Busino, a chaplain to the Venetian ambassador, famously
described the highest form or "very noble manner" of royal hunt in
England under James I, "when his majesty chooses to hunt without taking
any advantage" of the stag in firearms or in wounding before the chase.
After a prolonged pursuit, the king approaches the dead stag,

dismounts, cuts its throat, and opens it, sating the dogs with its blood as reward of
their exertions. With his own imbrued hands, moreover, he is wont to regale some
of his nobility by touching their faces. This blood it is unlawful to remove or wash
off, until it fall of its own accord, and the favored individual thus bedaubed is
considered to be dubbed a keen sportsman and chief of the hunt and to have a
certificate of his sovereign's cordial good will.[1]

In 1655, Margaret Cavendish observed the purifying powers ascribed to this
blood in "a usual custom for ladies and women of quality, after the hunting
a deer, to stand by until they are ripped up, that they might wash their
hands in the blood, supposing it will make them white."[2] These ritual uses
of deer blood both conveyed and expressed a quality of human blood.
Sir Thomas Chaloner's translation of Erasmus's hunting scene in *Praise of*

[1] See CSP, V, vol 15 (1617–1619): 260; Keith Thomas, *Man and the Natural World: Changing Attitudes
  in England, 1500–1800* (Oxford University Press, 1983), 29, 313; Manning, *Hunters and Poachers*, 27;
  Edward Berry, *Shakespeare and the Hunt: A Cultural and Social History* (Cambridge University Press,
  2001), 40.
[2] Margaret Cavendish, marquionesse of Newcastle, *Philosophical and Physical Opinions* (London,
  1655), 100–101.

Folly suggested this reciprocity of blood, noting among "ceremonies" of the hunt that

every poor man may cut out an ox or a sheep, whereas such venison may not be dismembered but of a gentleman, who bareheaded and set on knees, with a knife prepared properly to that use (for every kind of knife is not allowable), also with certain gestures, cuts a sunder certain parts of the wildbeast, in a certain order very circumstantly.[3]

In a potent language of religious ritual, Chaloner rendered the

standers by, not speaking a word, beholding it solemnly, as if it were some holy mystery, having seen the like yet more than a hundred times before: then whose hap it be to eat part of the flesh, he thinks verily to be made thereby half a gentleman.[4]

In 1575, George Gascoigne extolled the virtues of the hunt as "a sport for gentle bloods, ordained first for men of noble kind."[5]

These explicit references to the power of blood obtained by prescribed lethal force suggest many of the familiar beliefs and rituals of sacrifice. Although the term may seem too solemn for an activity often treated as a mere diversion of nobility, the circulation of blood in these actions and texts reveals a purifying and transformative power, even a sacred quality, that cannot be explained in terms of noble entertainment. The use of blood to signify the influence of favored courtiers, and the power of venison to convey gentility, attest to the political implications of ritualized killing in a culture that represented the social order as a part of natural order.[6] This sacrificial dimension is in some respects uncontroversial, as historians have long appreciated the importance of regenerative ritual forms, such as the Whitsuntide processions around parish borders, in the making of parish communities.[7] These Christian rites of renewal and expiation share much of the rationale, if not the technique, of Frazer's "agrarian sacrifice in which, in order to ally oneself to the god of the fields at the term of his

[3] Desiderius Erasmus, *Praise of Folly*, trans. Sir Thomas Chaloner (Oxford University Press, [1549] 1965), 54; Berry, *Shakespeare and the Hunt*, 40.

[4] Ibid.

[5] [George Gascoigne], *The Noble Arte of Venerie or Hunting* (London, 1575), A4r.

[6] The relationship between views of social order (particularly its patriarchal forms), natural hierarchies, and politics is explored in Glenn Burgess, *The Politics of the Ancient Constitution: An Introduction to English Political Thought, 1603–1642* (University Park, PA: Pennsylvania State University Press, 1993), 133–135; Michael J. Braddick, *State Formation in Early Modern England, c. 1550–1700* (Cambridge University Press, 2000), 35, 101–175.

[7] John Brand (ed.), *Observations on the Popular Antiquities of Great Britain*, 3 vols. (London: George Bell and Sons, 1877), 1: 197–212; Underdown, *Revel, Riot, and Rebellion*, 80–81, 90–91; Beaver, *Parish Communities and Religious Conflict in the Vale of Gloucester*, 32–35, 355.

annual life, he was killed and then eaten."[8] But the king's "imbrued hands" reach beyond the sacrificial metaphors of processions to express the power of blood as a natural symbol, its ritual circulation creating powerful social networks instrumental in the constitution of order. In this manner, the hunt joined social order and violence in a creative "shedding of blood."[9] During the rites of the hunt, carefully orchestrated violence became a means to constitute and encounter the transcendent values of gentility and honor. Because these qualities often defined candidates for magistracy and the exercise of power through office, the various arts of their acquisition possessed an aura of sanctity. The making of a gentleman in early modern England was often the making of a Christian magistrate. As a powerful ritual element in this process of manufacture, the evidence of early modern hunting suggests the useful notion of sacrifice as communication between sacred and profane.[10] As the object of sacrifice, the deer often seemed to serve as a means of communication between an abstract *honos* or source of honor and a particular aspirant to gentle status. To claim that in the Christian society of the late sixteenth and early seventeenth centuries the rites of the hunt constituted a religious sacrifice would be a travesty. But these hints of a sacrificial power in early modern hunting nevertheless raise important questions concerning the relationship between hunters and their prey, the meanings and politics of forests as both sacrificial sites and complex social and economic landscapes, and the significance of this ritual killing in the making of such authoritative elements of social order as gentility, honor, and magistracy.

II

A substantial literature on sacrifice has maintained a decisive contrast between sacrificial systems and judicial systems, asserting a functional equivalence of sacrifice and judicial trial based on the definitive limitation of social violence in both instances. Hubert and Mauss observed: "the similarity between the rites of punishment and sacrifice, the shedding of blood which took place in both, gave a punitory character to communions of piacular origin and transformed them into expiatory sacrifices."[11] René Girard has expanded this account in his theory that "the judicial system

---

[8] Henri Hubert and Marcel Mauss, *Sacrifice: Its Nature and Functions* (Chicago: University of Chicago Press, 1898, 1964), 5; James George Frazer, *The Golden Bough: A Study in Magic and Religion* (Oxford University Press, 1915, 1994), 288–292.
[9] Hubert and Mauss, *Sacrifice*, 4.   [10] Ibid., 11.   [11] Ibid., 4.

and the institution of sacrifice share the same function, but the judicial system is infinitely more effective."[12] This emphasis on the function of judicial systems to suppress violence implies the absence of sacrifice in modern societies characterized by "rule of law" ideologies and complex judicial forms. Sacrifice leaks through cracks in the modern state only in rare moments of crisis. Alain Corbin, attempting to explain a spectacularly violent incident in rural France in 1870, evokes the atmosphere of crisis and panic, "anxiety and rumor" rendering the state and its judicial institutions powerless in the face of perceived enemies.[13] As a result of this influential macro-historical narrative, historians have seldom looked for sacrifice in early modern polities and not surprisingly have not found it. Because its cultural context has remained unclear, the substantial evidence in moral justifications of the hunt, detailed practical manuals, meticulous printed codes for hunters, and pervasive metaphoric references to the hunt in sermons, poems, and plays has been largely ignored, or taken to reveal little more than the superficially arresting but politically irrelevant diversions of courtiers. The best recent attempt to make sense of the evidence reflects this methodological uncertainty, inadvertently adopting a utilitarian approach to early modern culture. Roger Manning interprets the similarities between the activities of hunters and those of soldiers as evidence that hunting became "a symbolic substitute for war" in English society during the long peace of the early seventeenth century.[14] Although this may have been the case for a few hunters, a broader cultural approach to the hunt might take a hint from ethnographic method, identifying elements of sacrifice in the phases of ritual; in much of the ethnographic record, this ritual violence expresses "the attempt to create the transcendental in religion and politics."[15] Girard's theory of the displacement of sacrificial rites by judicial forms also becomes a red herring in this context. The indirect influence of the hunt on the authority of law in early modern England resulted from the power of its ritualized killing to constitute gentility and honor, essential qualities of magistrates in the exercise of their offices.

---

[12] René Girard, *Violence and the Sacred* (Baltimore: Johns Hopkins University Press, 1972), 20–27.

[13] Alain Corbin, *Village of Cannibals: Rage and Murder in France, 1870* (Cambridge, MA: Harvard University Press, 1992), 61–86.

[14] Manning, *Hunters and Poachers*, 35–56. Although this hypothesis is intriguing, Manning furnishes no evidence that martial opportunities diminished participation in the hunt.

[15] Maurice Bloch, *Prey into Hunter: The Politics of Religious Experience* (Cambridge University Press, 1992), 4–7.

During the sixteenth and seventeenth centuries, forests were not wildernesses but ranked among the most cultivated and civil landscapes as high expressions of kingly prerogative and the authority of law. This notion of the forest as an elevated sphere of royal power and gentility fostered a general competition among gentlemen to acquire honor in the hunt, the noblest activity of the forest and indeed its essential meaning.[16] An analysis of sacrificial elements of the hunt thus clarifies its cultural importance in the differentiation of the noble class and also helps to explain its violent ethos. As both an externally afforded status and an internal sense of worth, honor in this setting expressed a distinctively English mythology.[17] A symbolism of deer and the hunt lay close to cherished histories of English culture, as the nobility of the hunt reflected both its antiquity and its descent from mythic heroes of the distant past.[18] In 1575, Gascoigne attributed the introduction of the hunt and hounds in Britain to Brutus, the descendant of Aeneas and eponymous founder of civilization in the British Isles.[19] William Harrison attributed the introduction of deer in England to the Romans.[20] Across the centuries, scions of the British royal line and their noble courtiers had elevated the hunt to an art form. In 1591, Sir Thomas Cockayne described "Sir Tristram, one of the knights of King Arthur" as the codifier of "the honorable and delightful sport of hunting" in its "first principles" and inventor of "the terms in hunting, hawking, and measures of blowing," the specialized language and music of the hunt.[21] The activities and the animals of the hunt symbolized a glorious royal past as well as a noble present, and could be used to evoke a mythical charter of the English polity. The ceremony of the hunt derived this mythic charter of gentility from the blood of a noble animal, a potent natural symbol.[22]

As a form of sacrifice or ritualized killing, the most important cultural processes of the hunt involved the identification of hunter and hunted in a

---

[16] This interpretation of the hunt builds on the discussion in Dan Beaver, "The Great Deer Massacre: Animals, Honor, and Communication in Early Modern England," *Journal of British Studies*, 38 (1999): 189–196.

[17] See Frank Henderson Stewart, *Honor* (Chicago: University of Chicago Press, 1994), 12, 21, 24–26, for internal and external forms of honor.

[18] A fine survey of early Stuart prescriptive literature on the hunt is Manning, *Hunters and Poachers*, 5–17.

[19] Gascoigne, *Noble Arte of Venerie*, 1–4. This manual was reprinted in 1611, the only substantial alterations being the images of James superimposed on the images of Elizabeth in the illustrations of the royal hunt.

[20] Harrison, *Description of England*, 254.

[21] Sir Thomas Cockayne, *A Short Treatise of Hunting* (London, 1591), A3r; Gascoigne, *Noble Art of Venerie*, 39, 96, 235; Gervase Markham, *Country Contentments* (London, 1615), 28.

[22] See Mary Douglas, *Natural Symbols: Explorations in Cosmology* (New York: Pantheon, 1982), xix–xxvii; Laura Rival (ed.), *The Social Life of Trees: Anthropological Perspectives on Tree Symbolism* (Oxford: Berg, 1998), 1–3, for the qualities of natural symbols.

common nobility and the practical separation of the individual animal from the general population as the object of the hunt. Much of the prescriptive literature stressed the noble qualities displayed by beasts of the chase, as the animal at bay became a model of courage and resistance to the death, or a reminder of the subtle calculations of policy. This metaphoric play effectively united hunter and hunted in the pursuit and possession of the highly esteemed qualities of honor. George Gascoigne marveled, in his poetic prelude to "the noble art of venery,"

> How fighting out at bay, of hart, buck, goat or boar,
> Declares the valiant Roman's death when might may do no more.
> And how the nimble hare, by turning in her course,
> Does plainly prove that policy, sometimes surpasses force.[23]

An anonymous poet of the Ashridge hunt praised "the stateliest beast the forest yields, excelling all brutes belonging to the fields, the royalest game for king and lords, this noble sort of deer a park adorns."[24] Through the blood of this ennobled animal, a hunter encountered an abstract and ancient *honos*, or source of honor, and demonstrated a rightful claim to gentility by the technical proficiency of his pursuit. As the Ashridge poet sang in the 1660s,

> His flesh it makes the noblest dish of meat
> For heroes brave their ladies for to treat.
> That Grecian brave Achilles, stout and strong,
> Was fed with marrow which to harts belong.[25]

Robert Burton feared this powerful component of the hunt, expressing concern that hunters of less noble blood might lose their humanity in the chase and degenerate into beasts.[26] Burton's fears for the boundaries between human and animal recalled the regimen of Katherine, Lady Berkeley, who in the mid-sixteenth century had "kept commonly a cast or two of merlins, which sometimes she mewed in her own chamber, which falconry cost her husband each year one or two gowns and kirtles spoiled by their mutings."[27] As hunter and hunted were joined in the chase, a successful hunter knew how to separate an individual animal from the group and how to track and pursue this unique quarry. Sir Thomas Cockayne observed that the skilled hunter knew the individual deer hunted

---

[23] Gascoigne, *Noble Arte of Venerie*, A4r.
[24] HL, Ellesmere Manuscripts, EL 8362: Anonymous, "A Keeper Poem in Applause of a Stag," c. 1660, ll. 5–7, 17.
[25] Ibid., ll. 21–24.   [26] Robert Burton, *Anatomy of Melancholy* (London, 1621), 157–161.
[27] John Smyth of Nibley, *The Berkeley Manuscripts*, 3 vols. (Gloucester, 1885), 2: 285.

by the shape of its head, "for diverse bucks have sundry slots in their palms, some have slots on both sides, other some are plain palmed without any advancers with long spillers out behind, the most bucks have some kenspeck mark to know them by upon their heads."[28] This identification of sacrifier and victim and the separation of victim from general population were essential to the sacrificial meaning of the hunt, as communication between a hunter and the source of honor itself.

The ceremony of the hunt unfolded as a dramatic self-sacrifice, a display of the gentility of the sacrifier and an initiation into the circle of nobility. During this ceremony, the deer became a surrogate for the sacrifier and its blood expressed both *honos* as an abstract principle and the ethos of the nobility as a service class. Cockayne acknowledged this initiation in the dedication of his treatise to Gilbert Talbot, Earl of Shrewsbury, the grandson of the lord responsible for Cockayne's first experiences of the hunt. As the art of the hunt had initiated Cockayne, the commoner, into the ranks of gentility, so Cockayne returned this gift in the form of a pamphlet dedicated to the "increase of all honorable virtues" in Shrewsbury's person and lineage.[29] Among initiates, the hunt expressed an exclusive discourse of privileged knowledge and experience, virtue and honor. In 1587, William Harrison asserted that "venison in England is neither bought nor sold as in other countries but maintained only for the pleasure of the owner and his friends." According to Harrison, gentlemen who trafficked in the trophies of the hunt "belong not to men of honor but to farmers and graziers" and "degenerate from true nobility and take themselves to husbandry."[30]

According to the prescriptive literature, the hunt furnished a school for character and built noble virtues. Gascoigne described "venerie" as a "profitable and godly" art for "the pleasure of all noblemen and gentlemen."[31] The dedication of Cockayne's pamphlet, a work "compiled for the delight of noblemen and gentlemen," expressed an assumption of aristocratic leadership in this school of honor, as the art of the hunt flowed from

---

[28] Cockayne, *Short Treatise*, D1r. A gentleman hunter had to master this specialized language or jargon. According to the *Oxford English Dictionary*, a "palm" is "the flat expanded part of the horn in some deer, from which finger-like points project." A "spiller" is "a branchlet on a deer's horn," and an "advancer" is the second branch of a buck's horn. A "kenspeck mark" is any conspicuous or distinctive mark.

[29] Cockayne, *Short Treatise*, A2r–v. Cockayne was styled a "gentleman" of Ashbourne in Derbyshire.

[30] Harrison, *Description of England*, 255. Harrison cited Roman precedents for concern over this degeneration of nobility in a commonwealth.

[31] Gascoigne, *Noble Arte of Venerie*, A2v. This manual placed the study of the hunt second only to the study of divinity as "commendable and necessary" for noblemen and gentlemen.

aristocrat to commoner.[32] The "honorable virtues" of the hunt enriched both the person and the body politic. Gascoigne deemed the hunt an antidote to idleness and sinful pride, a stimulant to bodily health and "honest meditations."[33] The poetic prelude of his *Noble Art of Venerie* suggested that the chase presented scenes to improve the moral nature of the hunter, as the animal at bay became a model of noble resistance to the death, or a reminder of subtle calculations of policy. A mind formed in contemplation of this noble display in nature could avoid idle entertainments, the "common shows of interludes, of tumbler's tricks, of antics, mocks, and mowes."[34]

This cultivation of the personal virtues produced conscientious servants in the body politic. Although the descent from ancient royalty joined the hunt to the sovereign virtues, manuals boasted additional practical benefits. According to Cockayne, the hunt instructed and physically hardened gentlemen through "continual travail, painful labor, often watching and enduring of hunger, of heat, and of cold," and thus served as a school "to the service of their prince and country in the wars."[35] The hunter's contemplation of the dens built by foxes and badgers could readily turn to thoughts of military fortifications and the tactical problems of war.[36] The hunt also contributed to the ends of civil government in its clearance of beasts of prey, particularly wolves, from forests near human settlements.[37] "In Ireland," Gascoigne observed, "there are great store of [wolves], and because many noblemen and gentlemen have a desire to bring that country to be inhabited and civilly governed, and would God there were more of the same mind, therefore I have thought good to set down the nature and manner of hunting at the wolf."[38] The royal hunt offered the clearest interrelationship of the chase and civic virtue, because the royal hunt offered a microcosm of the polity, a hierarchy of nobles and commoners defined by a clear division of labor and rank among courtiers, butlers, cooks, and huntsmen, yet held all strictly subordinate to the tastes and needs of the monarch.[39]

The hunt expressed an exclusive discourse of knowledge and experience. Both the animals and the honor of the hunt were intended to circulate

---

[32] Cockayne, *Short Treatise*, A2r–v. [33] Gascoigne, *Noble Arte of Venerie*, A3r–v. [34] Ibid., A4r.
[35] Cockayne, *Short Treatise*, A3r–v. Cockayne offered George Clifford, Earl of Cumberland, and Ambrose Dudley, Earl of Warwick, as models of the relationship between the hunt and military service.
[36] Gascoigne, *Noble Art of Venerie*, A4r. [37] Cockayne, *Short Treatise*, A3v.
[38] Gascoigne, *Noble Art of Venerie*, 205. Much of the prescriptive literature stressed the civic usefulness of the hunt in a balanced education. See Markham, *Country Contentments*, 3.
[39] Gascoigne, *Noble Art of Venerie*, 90–97, 132–135.

among aristocracy and gentry. In the 1630s, Sir Peter Temple presented Christmas gifts of venison to Edmund Dayrell, hoping such noble gifts might persuade Dayrell to sell or exchange the woodlands that Temple wanted to add to Stowe park.[40] Charles I regularly presented bucks from his forests and parks as gifts to "ambassadors and agents of princes," and similar gifts of venison flowed annually to the tables of the Lord Mayor and aldermen of London.[41] Another common form of noble currency was the hound offered as a favor between gentlemen. Cockayne enjoined prospective hunters to "borrow one couple of old hounds of some gentleman or yeoman" in order properly to introduce younger hounds to the hunt.[42] In 1637, Sir Richard Tracy, master of game in Corse Lawn, the Earl of Middlesex's chase in northern Gloucestershire, complained to Middlesex of "great distress in [the chase] for [want of] hounds" and assumed Middlesex had only to ask his noble friends Edward Denny, Earl of Norwich, or James Hay, Earl of Carlisle, to secure the favor of a "good couple of hounds, such as may delight you to see them hunt."[43] A statutory barrier formally restricted access to such honorable delights, excluding "the vulgar sort and men of small worth" and enhancing the prestige of venison, dogs, and all tokens of the hunt as gifts.[44] In 1603 and 1606, the sale or purchase of animals or birds killed contrary to law became subject to stiff fines, and guns, bows, crossbows, nets, ferrets, and dogs were permitted only to the proprietors of £40 in freehold land or £200 in moveable property.[45] These statutes gave sharper teeth to the traditional laws of the forest, asserting a stricter control over access to deer, pheasants, partridges, and hares – animals and birds perceived as a currency of rank and honor. A symbolism of gentility and honor, derived from its sacrificial rites, thus imparted meaning and power to the circulation of the products of the hunt.

---

[40] HL: STP, 565: Edmund Dayrell to Sir Peter Temple, undated. In a cagey response, Dayrell acknowledged himself "beholding" to Temple for the gift, "being ready and willing to show you any kindness I can, excepting that which concerns my estate."

[41] Between 1638 and 1640, Charles distributed forty-two bucks annually as political gifts. See PRO: SP 16/384, Orders and Warrants Concerning Forests, ff. 10r–11r, 30r–v, 47r.

[42] Cockayne, *Short Treatise*, B1v, B3v, C1r.

[43] CKS: U 269 Sackville Mss/4/2/1 (Correspondence of Lionel Cranfield, Earl of Middlesex): Sir Richard Tracy to Middlesex, 15 June 1637.

[44] 1 Jac. I, c. 27, in *SR*, 4: 1055. An excellent discussion of the differences between the game laws of the seventeenth and eighteenth centuries, particularly as regards the status of deer under the law, is P. B. Munsche, *Gentlemen and Poachers: The English Game Laws, 1671–1831* (Cambridge University Press, 1981), 1–27.

[45] The new fines were 40s for each deer, 20s for each pheasant, 10s for each partridge, and 10s for each hare either sold or purchased. See 1 Jac. I, c. 27, in *SR*, 4: 1056; 3 Jac. I, c. 13, in *SR*, 4: 1089; Manning, *Hunters and Poachers*, 6, 25–26, 59–61.

This culture of the hunt furnishes an excellent example of the forms of knowledge, speech, and ritual action common to gentlemen in the sixteenth and seventeenth centuries. A gentleman, even if not an active hunter, would have been expected to know how the forms and beasts of the hunt divided the seasons and the calendar.[46] According to the prescriptive literature, a gentleman could hunt the roe from Easter to Michaelmas, the hart and buck from Midsummer to Holyrood Day, the boar from Christmas to Whitsuntide, and the hare from Michaelmas to Midsummer.[47] The manuals of the hunt offered a complex lexicon of standardized terms for the various parts and products of the animals, for the tactics of the chase, and even for the diverse cries of the hunt, and attempted to regulate "how a young huntsman should speak before masters of the game."[48] A successful hunter, then, displayed many forms of specialized knowledge, such as the ability to focus the power of the chase on a particular animal rather than a general type, identifying the hunted deer by the shape of its head and other distinctive marks.[49] A hunt consisted of a series of prescribed actions, the form sufficiently important to describe as ritual, and resulted in a spectacle of interrelated scenes set to human and animal music: formulaic blasts of the horn announced the assembly of the hunt, its phases and fortunes, as well as the final battle against the exhausted prey; in the deer hunt, "the best man" or "chief hunter" then performed the assay or ritual dissection of the deer; more blasts of the huntsman's horn announced the kill and the assay, followed by the "double rechate" of the entire company, blown in the ancient manner of Sir Tristram, and the music of the hounds.[50] As a performance, a hunt demanded specific forms of knowledge, comportment, and ritual action.

---

[46] Harrison distinguished between beasts of the chase or beasts domesticated in parks – the buck or fallow deer, the roe, the fox, and the marten – and beasts of venery or wild beasts properly of the forest – the hart or red deer, the hare, the boar, the wolf, and, in eastern Europe, the bear. See Harrison, *Description of England*, 259–260. This pattern of classification varied, and gentility might require moderate study. Manwood differentiated the wild beasts of the forest – the hart, the hind, the hare, the boar, and the wolf – from the beasts of the chase – the buck, the doe, the fox, the marten, and the roe – and the beasts and fowls of warren – the hare, the cony, the pheasant, and the partridge. See Manwood, *Laws of the Forest*, ff. 19r–20v.

[47] Gascoigne, *Noble Art of Venerie*, 238. Cockayne, *Short Treatise*, C1v, C2v, provides an incomplete sketch of the calendar. Both manuals stress moderate participation in the seasons of the hunt as an "honest recreation" and a refreshment from hard labor, not to interfere with "the service of god, her Majesty, or your country." Gascoigne, *Noble Art of Venerie*, A3r; Cockayne, *Short Treatise*, A4r.

[48] Gascoigne, *Noble Art of Venerie*, 97–100.   [49] Cockayne, *Short Treatise*, D1r.

[50] Gascoigne, *Noble Art of Venerie*, 124–135; Cockayne, *Short Treatise*, C2r, C3r, D3v–4v. Manning refers to the ceremonial closure of the hunt as a restoration of order, but the hunt itself reproduced the hierarchic structure of the English polity, and it is not clear whether contemporaries viewed the hunt as a liminal moment. See Manning, *Hunters and Poachers*, 39–40.

A gentleman's world consisted of many such disciplines and performances, described in terms of courtliness, sociability, or martial valor, and in each context a successful performance redounded to the gentleman's credit in the potent form of honor.[51]

III

The ritualized killing of the hunt occurred first and foremost in the royal forests, and these forests possessed many of the conventional meanings of sacrificial places during the late sixteenth and early seventeenth centuries.[52] The iconography and activities of forests offer powerful evidence of the interrelationship of royalty and gentility in early modern England. A forest was consecrated to royal pleasure and separated from everyday landscapes. As only the words and institutions of the crown could transform mere woodland into forest, a forest expressed the unique nature and power of royalty.[53] In 1615, the work of John Manwood, erstwhile keeper in Waltham Forest, law officer in the New Forest, and barrister of Lincoln's Inn, expressed the profoundly political nature of forests and their unique royal attributes.[54] According to Manwood,

a forest is a certain territory of woody grounds and fruitful pastures, privileged for wild beasts and fowls of forest, chase, and warren to rest and abide in the safe protection of the king for his princely delight and pleasure, which territory of ground, so privileged, is meered and bounded with unremoveable marks, meers,

---

[51] The best introductions to forms of honor in early modern England are Mervyn James, "English Politics and the Concept of Honour, 1485–1642," in Mervyn James, *Society, Politics, and Culture: Studies in Early Modern England* (Cambridge University Press, 1986), 308–415; Anthony Fletcher, "Honour, Reputation, and Local Officeholding in Elizabethan and Stuart England," in Anthony Fletcher and John Stevenson (eds.), *Order and Disorder in Early Modern England* (Cambridge University Press, 1985), 92–94; Felicity Heal and Clive Holmes, *The Gentry in England and Wales, 1500–1700* (Stanford University Press, 1994), 276–318.

[52] Frazer, *Golden Bough*, 82–97; Hubert and Mauss, *Sacrifice*, 25–28. My discussion of sacrifice here draws on the recent work of Valerio Valeri, *Kingship and Sacrifice: Ritual and Society in Ancient Hawaii* (Chicago: University of Chicago Press, 1985), 37–83, and his *Forest of Taboos: Morality, Hunting, and Identity among Huaulu of the Moluccas* (Madison: University of Wisconsin Press, 2000), 302–324.

[53] The most ambitious statement of the forest as an expression of the royal sensibility and prerogative is John Manwood, *A Treatise of the Laws of the Forest* (London, 1598, 1615), ff. ivr–v, 18r–v, 20r–v, 33v–34r. This forest discourse often exercised greater influence as a part of the discourse of honor than as a technical discourse of forest law. See *Laws of the Forest*, ff. *ir–v, 69v–70v, for his view of forest law's marginality relative to other forms of law in the 1590s and early 1600s.

[54] Manwood died in 1610. An enlarged edition of his influential treatise on forest laws, published in 1615, contained substantial additions to an earlier collection, printed at Manwood's expense and "dispersed among his learned friends" in 1592, and to the published editions in 1598 and 1599. See "John Manwood," in *Dictionary of National Biography*, 990; Manwood, *Laws of the Forest*, f. iiir.

and boundaries, either known by matter of record or else by prescription; and replenished with wild beasts of venery or chase, and with great coverts of vert, for the succor of the said wild beasts, to have their abode in; for the preservation and continuance of which place, together with the vert and venison, there are certain particular laws, privileges, and officers belonging to the same, meet for that purpose, that are only proper to a forest and not to any other place.[55]

A forest consisted of beasts of venery and chase, the covert and pasture necessary to their survival, the laws and officers required to protect the animals and their subsistence, and the pleasure of the king, "the principal head and governor of this commonweale," in the hunt. As "the fountain of peace," the king provided "peace and safety ... privilege and protection" both to "the wild beasts and fowls" of forest, chase, and warren, and to his "liege people and good subjects."[56] As "the head of the body of the commonweale," the king maintained "a watchful eye for the preservation of peace and quietness at home among his own subjects but also to preserve them in peace and quietness from any foreign invasion."[57] In return, the law afforded the king, in addition to many other privileges, the prerogative to reserve the pleasure of "wild beasts" and to create forests for their protection, as a reward "in respect of his continual care and labor for the preservation of the whole realm, being the residue of the body."[58] By a kind of similitude, the "excellency" of the king's function as head entitled him to a monopoly of the "most excellent" pleasures and delights of forests and the hunt.[59]

According to Manwood, the exercise of this royal monopoly in the late sixteenth and early seventeenth centuries expressed a benign process of environmental and political change. A slow growth of population in the centuries before the arrival of the Saxons had destroyed vast woods and had driven "wild beasts" into the remaining tracts of woodland. Saxon kings then decimated wolves and foxes, discovering afterwards that the surviving species were "beasts of great pleasure for the king and for noble men to hunt and chase, and also dainty meat for the king and the best sort of men in the realm."[60] These kings made "forests" to protect their pleasures, but over the centuries the harsh Saxon forest system, imposing severe penalties for killing "wild beasts" under any circumstances, had been moderated by the cumulative wisdom and clemency of the English crown.[61] By the early

---

[55] Ibid., f. 18r–v.   [56] Ibid., ff. 20r, 25r–26v.   [57] Ibid., f. 25r–v.   [58] Ibid., f. 25v.

[59] Ibid. According to Manwood, the same law of similitude underlay the royal claim to control deposits of gold and silver discovered on the property of subjects.

[60] Ibid., f. 29v.

[61] Ibid., ff. 29r–30r. Manwood's notes indicate a substantial debt to Raphael Holinshed in this historical view of English forests.

1600s, forest laws applied only in clearly delimited forest territories, and the creation of new forests reflected a "benign" royal desire to protect subjects from involuntary trespass. Only a slow and deliberate extension of royal power could create a new forest. A commission under the great seal, issued from the court of Chancery and sometimes directed to sheriffs, ordered a perambulation or circuit of the boundaries of the new forest, and the return of certificates to Chancery created the "territory" of the forest. A writ from Chancery to the appropriate sheriffs then described this forest territory, directed the sheriffs to proclaim the forest in the boroughs, fairs, and markets of their counties, and transformed the territory into a chase. A proper "forest" emerged only after this chase acquired a political structure through the appointment of officers, such as verderers, foresters or keepers, regarders, agisters, and woodwards, and following the establishment of forest courts: the woodmote, the swanimote, and the court of the Lord Justice of the Forests. Such forest hierarchies might vary in detail. A forest required agisters, for instance, only if it contained royal woods requiring agistment, meaning the seasonal determination of claims to common pasture, usually for swine, by other inhabitants of the forest.[62]

Gentlemen could share this royal dignity of the forest and hunt for a price: thus Sir Thomas Temple purchased a patent of free warren in Stowe manor from James I in 1617, prior to the building of a park in the 1620s.[63] According to law, a free warren applied only to beasts and fowls of warren, a flexible category in the sixteenth and seventeenth centuries that nevertheless tended to exclude beasts of forest and chase or park, such as most species of deer, except perhaps the roe. In practice or custom, it is not clear that holders of free warren would have required an additional franchise before building a park, and the term "warren" was sometimes used to describe a general liberty of the hunt.[64] Such markers of gentle status thus signified dependence on the crown, as chases and parks required a royal franchise, and unlawful enclosures were subject to *quo warranto* proceedings.[65] In most cases, the transition from royalty to gentility also withdrew the forest law and its special courts – expressions of royal prerogative – and

---

[62] This process of making a forest is described in ibid., ff. 26v–30r. Manwood also notes the king's use of parliament in place of Chancery to create the forest at Hampton Court in 1540.

[63] William Page (ed.), VCH *Buckingham*, 4 vols. (London: Dawsons, 1927, 1969), 4: 232–233; HL: STMP, Box 3, file 12: Petition to Bishop of Lincoln from Westbury, 10 May 1625.

[64] In the 1510s, Robert Fabyan defined a royal grant of warren to the citizens of London "to mean that the citizens have free liberty of hunting certain circuit about London." See Sir William Blackstone, *Commentaries on the Laws of England*, 4 vols. (Oxford, 1765–1769), 2: 38–39; Robert Fabyan, *Chronicle*, 4th edn. (London, 1559), 7: 43.

[65] Manwood, *Laws of the Forest*, f. 26r–v.

introduced the common law proper to chases and parks.[66] These distinctive yet interrelated properties of forest and chase, as symbols of royalty and gentility, embodied a diffusion of power and a statement of hierarchy central to the early modern English polity. William Harrison observed in the 1580s that "forests and frank chases have always been had and religiously preserved in this island for the solace of the prince *and* recreation of his nobility."[67] The forest discourse expressed the honor and authority of royalty and gentility in a common pursuit of venison, yet the distinction between royal forests and chases or parks clearly marked the transcendent nature of royal power and subordinated the places and activities of gentility to this superior power.

A forest expressed the power of a king, but a park enclosed that power, by virtue of a royal grant, as the absolute property of a gentleman. This distinction between forests and parks joined forest discourse to broader debates over the moral uses of personal property in a commonwealth. According to Manwood, forests might contain small enclosures but by definition "lie open and not enclosed, having only meers and boundaries to know the ring and uttermost skirts."[68] In the 1580s, Harrison observed that forests and frank chases had never been "enclosed more than at this present or otherwise fenced than by usual notes of limitation ... from time to time."[69] These new parks, exemplified by the enclosures of the Temples in Stowe, used a royal franchise to enhance the honor of gentle property, and the franchise then extended the protective aura of crown authority to newly empaled properties.[70] Some doubted the nobility of this enterprise. Gentlemen needed grants for their parks precisely because emparking represented the trespass of a corrupt or selfish interest against the proper royal nature of the forest. According to Harrison,

in times past many wealthy occupiers were dwelling within the compass of some one park, and thereby great plenty of corn and cattle among them ... whereby the realm was always better furnished with able men to serve the prince in his affairs; [but] now there is almost nothing kept but a sort of wild and savage beasts,

---

[66] A subject could possess a forest in the full political sense of the term. A royal grant of a forest *cum pertinentiis* preserved the law, officers, and courts of the forest, reserving the justice in eyre for the crown. A grant of *iura regalia* gave the grantee the additional power to appoint a justice in eyre to hear major cases of trespass and appeals from the forest courts. See ibid., ff. 24r, 35v–38r.

[67] Harrison, *Description of England*, 260 (my emphasis).

[68] Manwood also stressed that a forest was enclosed in its meers and bounds by the "eye and consideration" of the law "as if there went a stone wall in the place to enclose the same." *Laws of the Forest*, ff. 19r, 20v.

[69] Harrison, *Description of England*, 260.   [70] Ibid., 259.

cherished for pleasure and delight; and yet some owners, still desirous to enlarge those grounds ... do not let daily to take in more.[71]

Although forests were

far greater in circuit than many parks and warrens, yet are they in this our time less devourers of the people than these latter, since beside much tillage many towns are found in each of them, whereas in parks and warrens we have nothing else than either the keeper's and warrener's lodge or at least the manor place of the chief lord and owner of the soil.[72]

Harrison did not share Manwood's sanguine view of forest history, instead tracing the destructive and selfish proliferation of pales and parks to the Norman subjugation of England. Despite the efforts of such populist rulers as John to disempark the north in the early 1200s, a conspiracy of avaricious prelates and lords had protected this vast system of parks for centuries.[73] In the forest discourse parks were ambiguous in their meaning, capable of signifying an honorable devolution of royal privileges in the forest or a selfish appropriation of territory to the detriment of crown and commonweal.

This forest regime – its ceremonies and symbols; officers, courts, and laws – proclaimed and enforced an absolute boundary between nobility and commons; but the prescriptive codes and laws of the forest also concealed an intense local competition for honor and a negotiation of gentility. As a distinctive form of society, the forests paradoxically embodied both the vast power of royal prerogative and the often violent, everyday negotiations of gentle status. Amidst evidence of local conflict in Waltham Forest, John Browne and his friends offered a hint of this competition in their claim of "no law settled" as a justification for their assaults on the deer of Waltham in 1642. John Rands of Stowe and his companions vowed to "lose their lives" rather than suffer the dishonor of surrendering a slain deer to their enemies. These impassioned claims implicitly recognized the *conventional* power of forest law and statute to exclude from the hunt, to distribute venison among a narrowly defined elite of favorites. As the political crisis deepened in the early 1640s, these laws became less persuasive as a frame for the negotiation of gentle status. Political crisis became social crisis in forest societies because forest and statute law had traditionally defined orderly relations between local nobility and commons. The process of negotiation, and a few clues regarding the manner and meaning

---

[71] Ibid., 256. Harrison, a critic of this "curse" of emparking among the nobility, estimated in the 1580s that "the twentieth part of the realm is given over to deer and conies."
[72] Ibid., 260.   [73] Ibid., 258–259, 261–262.

of its suspension in 1642, emerge more fully from the evidence of local conflicts in Stowe, Waltham, Windsor, and Corse during the early seventeenth century.

IV

The restoration of the hunt's sacrificial aspect and its relationship to notions of honor and the making of gentility opens a new perspective on early modern forest politics. Historians have long appreciated the political volatility of the forests as arenas of conflict over land use. Buchanan Sharp observed of the Forest of Dean during the early 1630s that "many cottagers who were economically dependent on the forest in varying degrees came into conflict with the crown's fiscal needs and its consequent revivification of legal rights that threatened their livelihood," although this conflict remained "one episode in a long struggle between the crown and some segments of the forest population."[74] Because forests, chases, and parks were sites for the ritualized killing of the hunt as well as complex economies, the violent negotiations of gentle status integral to the culture of the hunt easily became entangled in disputes over land use. As the micro-histories in succeeding chapters reveal, local conflicts over honor and status among gentry families, great and small, often incorporating extensive social networks, could alter the terms of land disputes and thus introduce a new ideological dimension in forest politics. These conflicts, and especially the cases prosecuted in Star Chamber, evoked concepts of loyalty and sedition, justice and oppression, as well as notions of "ancient rights and liberties," and disputed the styles of politics appropriate in a healthy commonwealth. As such cases became more common during the late 1610s and 1620s, the involvement of friends and neighbors in the prosecutions made the concepts and language of an ideologically slanted politics increasingly familiar.

This view of the forests as distinctive, ideologically charged political arenas has important implications for analyses of popular politics before the Civil War. The attacks on parks and forests across southern England in late spring and summer 1642 comprise familiar episodes in narratives of disorder on the eve of civil war. Most historians have found the context for

---

[74] Hammersley, "The Revival of the Forest Laws Under Charles I," 85; Buchanan Sharp, *In Contempt of All Authority: Rural Artisans and Riot in the West of England, 1586–1660* (Berkeley: University of California Press, 1980), 175–200.

these conflicts in disputes over land use.[75] We have already encountered Brian Manning's eloquent account of the way "peasant hostility towards the king and great landlords broke out in 1642 in attacks on the most hated symbol of the aristocrat, his deer park." As Manning explains, "In the face of the pressure of an increased population on the land and of the poorer people for smallholdings, the reservation of vast acreages merely for game and the sport of the rich, was an even more cynical affront and an even more bitter grievance."[76] To the extent that he approached deer parks as symbols, Manning's work invited further study of their meaning, extending beyond disputes over the use of land. This invitation has led to the more recent emphasis on the importance of ideological conflict, recovering interrelationships among the nature of woodland property as a hunting preserve, conflicts over land use, and broader notions of legitimate authority and commonwealth.[77] The following micro-histories of Stowe, Waltham, Windsor, and Corse Lawn attempt to join this distinctive forest politics to recent work on the creative intermingling of locality, economics, religion, and general attitudes to the use of power in popular politics.[78]

---

[75] Manning, *The English People and the English Revolution*, 207–212, 258–259; Sharp, *In Contempt of All Authority*, 223–225; Victor Skipp, *Crisis and Development: An Ecological Case Study of the Forest of Arden, 1570–1674* (Cambridge University Press, 1978), 101–107.

[76] Manning, *The English People and the English Revolution*, 207.

[77] I have attempted to make this case using evidence from Gloucestershire and Buckinghamshire in Beaver, "The Great Deer Massacre," 187–216; and in "'Bragging and Daring Words': Honor, Property, and the Symbolism of the Hunt in Stowe, 1590–1642," in Michael J. Braddick and John Walter (eds.), *Negotiating Power in Early Modern Society: Order, Hierarchy, and Subordination in Britain and Ireland* (Cambridge University Press, 2001), 149–165, 278–286.

[78] See, for example, Walter, *Understanding Popular Violence in the English Revolution.*

2

Honor, property, and the symbolism of the hunt in Stowe, 1590–1642

> Some of them being armed with guns, some of them with swords, and some with clubs or pikestaves, were a hunting upon Sir Peter Temple's ground in the parish of Stowe, and killed a deer upon Sir Peter's ground, and gave out many bragging and daring words, some of them swearing that the deer was theirs and that they would carry him away or else they would lose their lives in the place.
>
> John Symons, June 1642[1]

I

On 7 June 1642, John Symons, a servant of Sir Peter Temple, uttered this challenge, attempted to seize the deer, and received a painful blow to the head from John Rands, a servant of Peter Dayrell, his master's enemy. This violent wrangling over a dead animal in an obscure corner of northwestern Buckinghamshire may seem like a dubious place to begin a discussion of the common notions of order and hierarchy expressed in hunting. Most forms of violence, personal and collective, are taken as expressions of disorder, as evils usually banished from prescriptive notions of a rightly ordered world. John Symons himself held this view of the matter. According to Symons, the trespass on Sir Peter Temple's "ground" in Stowe, a disorderly and perhaps criminal action, caused the violent affray that culminated in the assault on his person. But even discounting Symons's obvious interest in redress for a sore head, violence is seldom construed as a part of the way order is made.[2] This chapter explores the

[1] HL: STMP, Box 5, SCU (A), files 1, 2, 4: Deposition of John Symons, servant to Sir Peter Temple, 22 June 1642.

[2] See James, "English Politics and the Concept of Honour," 308–415, for the uses of violence in the sixteenth century; Roger B. Manning, *Hunters and Poachers: A Social and Cultural History of Unlawful Hunting in England, 1485–1640* (Oxford: Clarendon Press, 1993), 36–56, offers a suggestive discussion of the martial and theatrical aspects of the hunt.

angry words and blows between Symons and Rands, and the martial conflict between the Dayrell and Temple families in Stowe that motivated them, to uncover the violent contests inherent in the culture of gentility, an essential element in early modern English views of order. In Stowe, a competition for honor and status between powerful families and factions came to focus on the building of a deer park. This competition often demanded the participation of servants and tenants, such as Symons and Rands, for the hunt's theatre of honor required a generous cast to play the script's many supporting parts. Indeed, Rands managed to turn a minor role into a major speaking part and momentarily took over the stage in the impassioned brawl of June 1642. Yet the increasingly violent scenes of the chase in Stowe would disclose a precarious order, fashioned from the symbols of status, honor, and possession or property.[3]

Much recent work on the social contexts of politics has noted the limited formal powers of the early modern English state and the importance of local variations in the exercise and experience of authority.[4] A similar approach to the practice of gentility, as distinct from its prescriptive code, reveals the diverse means used to acquire honor, a quality inseparable from the power and prestige of royalty and joined to distinctive places, such as forests, and uniquely honorable activities, such as the hunt. To display great symbols of masculine gentility, such as a chase or a deer park, was to acknowledge a subordination to the crown in the acquisition of its license. Yet this hierarchic diffusion of honor conceals its competitive nature as a scarce commodity among noble lineages. This chapter examines the micro-politics of this competition in conflicts over property claims, assertions of honor, and hunting privileges in Stowe, on the border of Whittlewood Forest in northwestern Buckinghamshire. During the 1630s, the Temple family's decision to build a deer park threatened and angered other families of gentle status, particularly the Dayrells of Lamport, and led to disputes

---

[3] This emphasis on the broad significance of honor departs from a tradition of work on forest law and hunting that has overstressed their power to *differentiate* gentry and commoners and to enforce elite views of land use and work discipline in the seventeenth century, an interpretation better suited to the eighteenth-century evidence. See Manning, *The English People and the English Revolution*, 207–212, 258–259; Sharp, *In Contempt of All Authority*, 4–5, 82–125; Douglas Hay, "Poaching and the Game Laws in Cannock Chase," in Douglas Hay, Peter Linebaugh, John G. Rule, E. P. Thompson, and Cal Winslow (eds.), *Albion's Fatal Tree: Crime and Society in Eighteenth-Century England* (New York: Pantheon, 1975), 189–253; E. P. Thompson, *Whigs and Hunters: The Origin of the Black Act* (New York: Pantheon, 1975), 27–54.

[4] See the essays and references in Paul Griffiths, Adam Fox, and Steve Hindle (eds.), *The Experience of Authority in Early Modern England* (New York: St. Martin's Press, 1996); and Michael Braddick, "State Formation and Social Change in Early Modern England: A Problem Stated and Approaches Suggested," *Social History*, 16 (1991): 1–17.

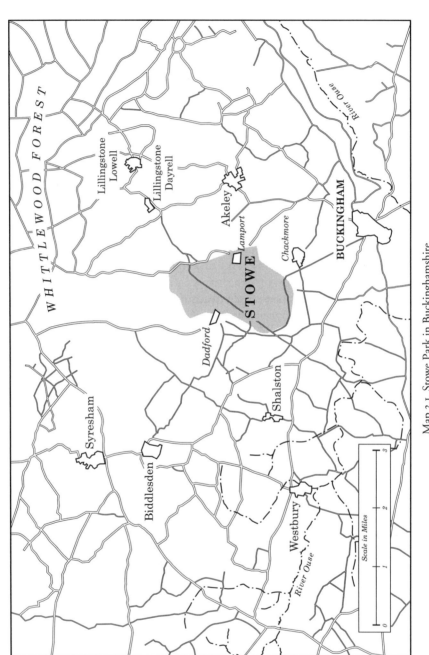

Map 2.1. Stowe Park in Buckinghamshire

over the ownership of lands enclosed in the park and over liberties of the hunt. As the competition between the Dayrells and Temples became more intense and virulent, the networks of friends, servants, and tenants drawn into the dispute expressed their interests in terms of honor; and the Dayrells and other local gentlemen led the resistance to "oppression" in hunting raids on the park and deer claimed by the Temples as an exclusive preserve.[5]

This small-scale war to control Stowe park and its symbolism of honor tends to confirm the recent skepticism about any mere deference to the authority of law in the seventeenth century, raising important questions about the political implications of these attacks.[6] Justice and the "right" seemed to demand action. The combatants had a flair for both invoking the law and taking decisive action against perceived injustices. In 1640, the crown became involved in the contest, as nocturnal clashes in the park were compounded by forms of judicial combat. Sir Peter Temple and his faction initiated a lawsuit in Chancery, and in the early months of 1642, Abel Dayrell and his supporters presented a petition to parliament, as both families attempted to use the authority and procedural weapons of the courts for local ends. Yet the courts proved ineffective in this contest over "ancient lands" and claims to purlieu, perhaps because neither family held a decisive advantage in terms of financial means, knowledge of their options under the law, or determination to vindicate the honor of lineage from abuse. As judicial maneuvers resulted in stalemate, Stowe Park became the site of a violent theater of honor in the summer of 1642, its cast recruited from the gentry families of northwestern Buckinghamshire, their friends, and their servants. In the composition of the dispute, judicial officers of the crown had to accommodate the micro-politics of honor, and contained but could not suppress local violence.[7] At least one justice of the

---

[5] This pattern of participation significantly complicates the conventional distinction between elite and commons in collective action, as the culture of gentility legitimated both the authority of law and the necessity of resistance to oppression. The rationale for the Dayrells' raids on Stowe Park – a duty to resist avarice in the interest of the commonweal – did not differ fundamentally from the rationale for other forms of crowd action. See E. P. Thompson, "The Moral Economy of the English Crowd in the Eighteenth Century," *Past and Present*, 50 (1971): 76–136; and James C. Scott, *Domination and the Arts of Resistance: Hidden Transcripts* (New Haven: Yale University Press, 1990), 45–69, 108–135, for the "public transcripts" of domination and the "hidden transcripts" of dissident subcultures.

[6] Manning, *Hunters and Poachers*, 232–233. See also Anthony Fletcher, *Reform in the Provinces: The Government of Stuart England* (New Haven: Yale University Press, 1986), 39–83, on the authority of law and expansion of the dynastic state in the seventeenth century.

[7] This accommodation of local violence in early modern England provides a useful contrast to the "simplification" of local societies recently observed in the formation of modern bureaucratic states. See James C. Scott, *Seeing Like a State: How Certain Schemes to Improve the Human Condition Have Failed* (New Haven: Yale University Press, 1998), 1–8.

peace entrusted to negotiate the settlement was himself a veteran of this battle of Stowe park.

II

At the heart of the violent darkness in Stowe lay a complex discourse of forests, forest properties of different types, and distinctive activities that expressed the unique qualities of forests in early modern England.[8] As settlements on the southern border of Whittlewood Forest, Stowe and its hamlets had escaped the formal law and institutional hierarchy of the forest.[9] Yet the building of a deer park conventionally signified the honorable devolution of royal powers in the forest, "a franchise of such noble and princely pleasure," to a favored commoner.[10] Moreover, symbols of service in the forest had become badges of honor among the families of gentle status in Stowe. A tradition of service in forest offices and privileged participation in the hunt may explain the figure of a buck's antlers included in the elaborate table tomb built for Paul Dayrell of Lillingstone Dayrell in the early 1570s.[11] Dayrell was the father of Francis Dayrell, a younger son who moved to Stowe parish in the middle of the sixteenth century and settled on the family estate in Lamport, a little over a mile southwest of the ancestral seat in Lillingstone Dayrell.[12]

The discourse of forest and hunt made the decision to build a park into a crucial event in the calculus of honor. A park expressed a distinctive relationship to royal power, asserted claims to privileges of the forest and hunt, and enhanced the builder's stock of honor and gentility relative to

---

[8] As a discourse of honor, this forest discourse had a greater influence on the Temples and Dayrells than did technical matters of forest law. See Manwood, *Laws of the Forest*, ff. *1r–v, 69v–70v, for the variable significance of forest law in the 1590s and early 1600s.

[9] Several parishes on the borders of Stowe contained woodlands included in Whittlewood: Akeley on the eastern border, Biddlesden on the northwestern border, and Lillingstone Dayrell on the northern and northeastern border. Stowe faced the forest on three sides. Page, *VCH Buckingham*, 4: 145, 154, 188, 192. After afforestation in the late twelfth century, the woodlands of Lillingstone Lovell, three miles northeast of Stowe, were not included in the perambulation of Whittlewood Forest in 1300.

[10] See Harrison, *Description of England*, 253–254, 259; and Manwood, *Laws of the Forest*, ff. ivr, 24r–v, 26r, 36v–38r, for the connotations of a park, which is "next in degree to a frank chase" in a venerable hierarchy of properties related to forests. A park differed from a chase only in being enclosed; both lacked in theory the forms of law, the hierarchy of courts, and the officers characteristic of a forest.

[11] George Lipscomb, *The History and Antiquities of the County of Buckingham*, 3 vols. (London: Robins, 1847), 3: 37. In Lillingstone Dayrell, the Dayrells held hunting privileges and served as rangers in the tracts of Whittlewood Forest that extended into the parish. In the 1880s, the family owned a horn known as the "purlieu horn," dated 1692. See Page, *VCH Buckingham*, 4: 188.

[12] Ibid., 234–235; W. Harry Rylands (ed.), *The Visitation of the County of Buckingham, 1634* (London: Harleian Society, 1909), 36–37.

other local families. This competitive dimension of gentility became particularly marked in Stowe, where the Temples empaled Dayrell lands in Stowe park and thus enhanced their own honor at the expense of neighbors. In 1640, Abel Dayrell complained bitterly in Chancery that Temple had "enclosed in his park a great part of the soil and grounds belonging to [Dayrell's] own inheritance" and had then "stored his park with 700 or 800 deer, some of them being stags and red deer and others being fallow deer."[13] In response, Dayrell and his sons, servants, and friends "caused the pales set upon [Dayrell] ground by Sir Peter Temple to be pulled down" and in effect declared war against the Temples in the late 1630s, assaulting the park in armed bands.[14] Although the Dayrells justified their actions in terms of justice and law, Temple rejected these violent local assertions of family honor and estate as a disorderly inversion of the stately legal procedures used to adjudicate the issues in Chancery and in the common law courts. In early 1642, he invoked royal authority in defense of his franchise, initiating a series of lawsuits against the Dayrells and their accomplices "for breach of charter in hunting and disturbing his deer in his park."[15] Yet the recourse to law could not inhibit the use of terror and violence in Stowe, a dramatic expression of the competitive violence endemic in the culture of gentility.

III

The fragmentary manorial evidence from Stowe and Lamport suggests how honor worked as a kind of currency in a distinctive political economy. This economy was not entirely separate from the conventional agrarian economy of northwestern Buckinghamshire, but matters of "estate" extended beyond simple monetary calculations for such families as the Temples and Dayrells. An awareness of the sources of honor, difficult to reduce to monetary terms, gave subtle inflections to discussions of "estate" and "ancient lands," inflections that registered gradations of gentility and

---

[13] HL: STLP, Case 142, Sir Peter Temple v. Abel Dayrell: Answer of Abel Dayrell, gentleman, to Sir Peter Temple's Bill of Complaint in Chancery, 16 February 1640.

[14] Ibid.

[15] HL: STMLP, Box 5, SCU (A), files 1, 2, 4: Notes on Lawsuits against the Dayrells, 1641–1642. The first note lists possible actions in law against the Dayrells after their assault on the park in August 1641, and was probably the work of John Nicholls, Sir Peter Temple's law clerk. The second note lists actions under way following a second attack on the park in December and may have been the work of Temple himself.

honor relative to other families of comparable status.[16] These subtle calculations help to explain costly disputes between affluent families over relatively small economic stakes. Contests over the power to keep or recover economically marginal slivers of land reveal the extent to which honor represented an end in itself in the political economy of gentility, an end more significant than other more conventional expressions of prosperity. The act of possession certainly became more potent than the material income of the land in disputes between the Temples and Dayrells in Stowe, and few acts of possession registered more powerfully in the culture of gentility than the construction of a deer park. These competitive displays of possession were inseparable from notions of order, for families of "estate" and "ancient lands" served as the natural leaders of local societies; but the contests to display honorable possession held significant potential for conflict.

During the early seventeenth century, the economy of Stowe parish reflected the mixed arable, pasture, and woodland husbandries of northwestern Buckinghamshire, its lands being distributed among the three manors of Stowe, Dadford, and Lamport.[17] John Temple had acquired most of the land in the manors of Stowe and Dadford in the 1580s and 1590s.[18] Dayrells possessed the moiety of a lordship known as Lamport, joined to their ancestral estates in Lillingstone Dayrell, northeast of Stowe, until Francis Dayrell made the lordship a separate estate in the late sixteenth century.[19] A series of rentals and surveys from the 1620s and 1630s reveals the familiar contours of an economy increasingly dominated by the households of these major families. In 1623, Sir Thomas Temple reserved to his son Peter the income from "all the timber trees growing in coppices in Stowe and in all its wastes, pastures, and meadows."[20] Stowe

---

[16] The myriad meanings of "estate" and "ancient lands" are suggested in HL: STT 564, Edmund Dayrell to Sir Peter Temple, c. 1630; STLP, Case 248, Sir Richard Temple v. Abel Dayrell and Edmund Dayrell: Answer of Abel and Edmund Dayrell to Bill of Complaint in Chancery, c. 1653–1655.

[17] Boycott manor, west of Stowe, was included in Oxfordshire until the nineteenth century, and participation of its inhabitants in the ceremonial life of Stowe parish became a subject of a major local controversy in the 1630s. The manor seems gradually to have become part of Stowe Park in the eighteenth century. See HL: STMP, Box 3, Buckinghamshire, 1630–1640: Notes on Status of Boycott Manor in Stowe Parish; Page, *VCH Buckingham*, 4: 229, 232–236.

[18] Stowe and Dadford had been ecclesiastical estates prior to the Dissolution of the Monasteries. Temple acquired Dadford in 1587 and Stowe in 1590, shortly after their inclusion in crown grants. In addition, Temple held a manor known as Lamport, unrelated to the Dayrells' lordship, that had become part of Stowe after the Dissolution. To avoid confusion, this land is treated here as part and parcel of Stowe manor. See Page, *VCH Buckingham*, 4: 232–234; HL: STMP, Box 3, file 25: Survey of Stowe and Lamport, 1591, 1631; Rylands, *Visitation of the County of Buckingham*, 211–212.

[19] Page, *VCH Buckingham*, 4: 234–235; Rylands, *Visitation of the County of Buckingham*, 36–37.

[20] HL: STMP, Box 3, file 8: A Note of Timber in Stowe, 1623. Trees and furze in "the old park at Stowe" and in the closes belonging to the tenements were excluded from this arrangement.

timber produced a steady income of £130 to £200 annually in the early 1620s.[21] Tenancies were flexible in Dadford and Stowe. In 1620, Dadford manor consisted of four leaseholds, two copyholds, and seventeen tenancies at the will of the lord.[22] Stowe manor supported seven copyholders in 1620, but ten leaseholders and eighteen tenants at will farmed most of the estate.[23] A survey in 1631 described 70 per cent of the land in Stowe manor, around 600 acres, as demesne, as tenancies in possession only, or as tenancies at the will of the lord.[24] Moreover, the total population of tenants in Stowe manor declined from thirty-seven in 1620 to twenty-eight in 1634.[25] The tenants at will and leaseholders were closely linked to the Temple household. Of nineteen male servants to the Temples in 1620, six were leaseholders or tenants at will.[26] Sir Thomas Temple's enclosure of land for a deer park in the early 1620s and his son's decision to expand the park must be understood in this context of local centralisation and gradual depopulation in Stowe.[27]

A tract of land the size of the Dayrell estate in Lamport presented a significant obstacle to the building of a compact lordship in Stowe manor and posed tactical problems for the expansion of Sir Thomas Temple's park. In the 1620s, Edmund Dayrell possessed a substantial house and enclosure of thirty acres in Lamport, but the remainder of his estate was dispersed across the fields of Stowe and Lamport, including lands in Windmill field "shooting up to the park," lands in Stowe furze "shooting up to the park gate and within the park," and land in Lamport furze "shooting up to the park pale."[28] As early as 1590, the first year of their cohabitation in Stowe, John Temple and Francis Dayrell had clashed over

---

[21] Timber sales to the town of Buckingham, in particular, increased from £48 in 1620 to £71 in 1621. HL: STMP, Box 3, file 2: Robert Hickman's Wood Accounts, 12 December 1620, 24 February 1622.

[22] HL: STMP, Box 3, file 2: Stowe and Dadford Rental, 1620.

[23] Ibid. In the 1620s, Stowe copyholds varied considerably in size: one contained 1.5 yardlands at roughly sixteen acres to the yardland, one contained 1.25 yardlands, three contained a full yardland, two contained a half yardland, and two contained a quarter yardland. I include the two copyholds, seven leaseholds, and seven tenancies at will recorded on Temple lands in the manor of Lamport absorbed in Stowe.

[24] HL: STMP, Box 3, file 25: Survey of Stowe and Lamport, 1591, 1631.

[25] HL: STMP, Box 3, file 2: Stowe and Dadford Rental, 1620; Michaelmas Rent Roll, 1634.

[26] HL: STMP, Box 3, file 2: Stowe and Dadford Rental, 1620–1622. This observation is based on a comparison of the rent roll and a list of servants and wages in the same source. The six servants were John Buckbye, John Davie, Ralph Hands, Robert Hickman, Edward Robins, and Thomas Tyler. Their duties ranged from Hickman's service as overseer of accounts, netting an additional annual income of £1, to Davie's work as a mole catcher, earning him 10s to 12s per year.

[27] As early as 1625, the expansion of the Temples' park surfaced as a grievance in local records. See HL: STMP, Box 3, file 12: Petition to Bishop of Lincoln from Westbury, 1625.

[28] Despite the expansion of Stowe Park, the Dayrell estate in Lamport remained relatively constant in size between the 1620s and the 1640s. An informal "paper" assessed the estate at 146 acres in 1625. A survey

their intermingled possessions, dueling in Chancery over a sliver of meadow in Middle Field, a mere "one rod and eight perches" (*sic*) that Temple claimed as part of his demesne. Dayrell apparently hoped that, because his servant had once mistakenly mowed this meadow, it might be wrested from the new lord of Stowe.[29] This early competition for estate later became a more conventional neighborliness. By 1597, Francis Dayrell could write to John Temple about a piece of pasture in Oxfordshire, "as fine and good as most about Winchendon manor," and offer to approach the owner if Temple was interested in a purchase.[30]

Sir Peter Temple's desire to expand the deer park in Stowe had implications for the entire neighborhood of northwestern Buckinghamshire. In 1625, Edmund Perwiche of Shalston, west of Stowe, sent a petition to John Williams, Bishop of Lincoln and Lord Keeper of the Great Seal, on behalf of Shalston and Westbury. Perwiche complained that Temple had injured both parishes "by causing a parcel of Westbury ground to be empaled to his park, wherein Westbury vicar and the parson of Shalston, with other commoners, have right of commoning." According to Perwiche, a general hardship had been the price of Temple's gratification, for

his park has in it ground belonging to six towns, in which towns are a thousand living souls or very near; and in one of these towns are decayed eleven ploughs already; and in one of the other towns was decayed so much ground as made a park, out of which park was driven seven score deer and odd with other cattle, as it was reported, and so is disparked and set on a racked rent. Of these [towns], 1,800 may go beg if [Temple's] plot may take effect.[31]

Perwiche "humbly craved" that Williams might declare this "miserable cause" in parliament, but the petition failed.[32] Edmund Dayrell, son of Francis and lord of Lamport in the late 1620s, did not share the concern of his neighbors. Dayrell had already enclosed portions of his own estate and

---

in 1631 described it as 146 acres of "freehold." Another survey in 1646 fixed the estate at 157 acres. See HL: STMP, Box 3, file 14: Paper on the Dayrell Lands, c. 1625; file 25: Survey of Stowe and Lamport, 1591, 1631; Box 4, Buckinghamshire, 1640–1650: Survey of Dayrell Lands in Lamport, 1646.

[29] HL: STLP, Case 137, John Temple v. Francis Dayrell, 1590: Interrogatories; Depositions. In his testimony for Temple, Paul Hillesdon of Syresham in Northamptonshire, sixty years old in 1590, recalled that in the 1550s, long before Temples had come to Stowe, he had been accustomed to tether his master's horses on this sidelong, and "that on one Whitsun even, he had been at roll for barley, and before appointed for one of Robin Hood's men, and having overmatched himself laid himself to sleep on that sidelong."

[30] HL: STT 566: Francis Dayrell to John Temple, esquire, 7 May 1597.

[31] HL: STMP, Box 3, file 12: Petition to Bishop of Lincoln from Westbury, 1625. The "decayed" park presumably refers to land previously enclosed as Temple's park, transformed in 1625 into a leasehold within the newly expanded bounds of the park.

[32] Ibid. As if the petition's inclusion among the Temple family papers is not sufficient testimony of its failure, the endorsement reads, "no good to be done with this."

merely hoped to reach a fair settlement in any exchange of lands or enclosure relating to the park. In 1630, Dayrell received letters and a Christmas gift of venison from his "very good friend," Sir Peter Temple, as part of negotiations for a mutually beneficial exchange.[33] Dayrell did not strive to make the best profit from this exchange but rather refused unfair bargains in frank terms. "I know if you had my land and my right of common there," Dayrell explained,

you would quickly make it worth £40 or £50 a year to you at the least, and, to be plain with you, I will not part with any land and common but I will have better land for it that shall be of some worth to me, although nothing near to that which my land will be to you. As I have said, so I say again, if your desire of enclosing may be as well for my good as for yours, I shall be content with it.[34]

Dayrell thus skirted an unseemly interest in profit and stressed a fairness of exchange and mutual advantage. "If these offers be not to your liking," Dayrell concluded, "yet I desire your love and goodwill, that we may use the fields as we have done in peace and quietness, as the servants of god and good neighbors."[35]

Edmund Dayrell died in 1633, and this irenic attitude to the problem of Stowe Park did not survive him.[36] His son Abel had complained of Temple's new enclosures even before his father's death. On his deathbed, Edmund had "charged his son Abel that he should not molest or trouble Sir Peter Temple concerning his park" and reportedly received Abel's promise to keep the peace.[37] Abel apparently honored this promise for four years after his father's death. In 1637, however, Temple's unilateral enclosure of the "wood commons," empaling in his park Dayrell lands that had been denied to him in 1630, led to Abel Dayrell's impulsive

---

[33] HL: STT 564: Edmund Dayrell to Sir Peter Temple, c. 1630; STT 565: Edmund Dayrell to Sir Peter Temple, c. 1630. Temple offered land in Bycell and Lyncroft Corner, south of Lamport, in exchange for Dayrell's woodland and common in northeastern Stowe. Dayrell wanted to keep his estate compact, refused "to part with land lying at our gate for land lying three quarters of a mile from us," and insisted on land in Hawkwell or Stockhold fields, adjacent to his own possessions in Windmill field.

[34] HL: STT 564: Edmund Dayrell to Sir Peter Temple, c. 1630. Under pressure from his son Abel, Dayrell later informed Temple that enclosers in Northamptonshire commonly offered freeholders "three acres for two in exchange for their goodwill." HL: STT 565: Edmund Dayrell to Sir Peter Temple, c. 1630.

[35] Ibid.

[36] Edmund Dayrell's burial on 1 June, 1633, is noted in HL: STLP, Case 33, Miscellaneous Papers from Case 142, Sir Peter Temple v. Abel Dayrell: A Note on the Stint of Stowe and Lamport Commons, 1641.

[37] Although the evidence for this scene comes from Temple's papers, John Dayrell of Shalstone and Paul Dayrell of Thornton, Abel's brothers, were prepared to support Temple's account. See HL: STLP, Case 142, Sir Peter Temple v. Abel Dayrell: Interrogatories for Temple, 1641; STMP, Box 3, Buckinghamshire, 1630–1640: Notes on Sir Peter Temple's Complaint against Abel Dayrell, c. 1640.

violation of the customary stint of the commons in Stowe and Lamport.[38] According to Temple, Dayrell "takes away the waste from the field and says that he will keep as many [cattle] as he please there because I keep deer."[39] After several verbal warnings, three of Temple's tenants, serving as "tellers of the fields," impounded Dayrell's cattle in 1639.[40] Abel claimed that Temple had violated the stint first, by his decision to stock deer, and had enclosed parts of Dayrell's "ancient lands" and "inheritance" in his park. In February, 1640, Abel "caused the pales set upon his ground to be pulled down and then handed the cattle into the park to use his common."[41]

After the confiscation of Dayrell's cattle and this retaliatory assault on the park, the personal dispute between the Temples and Dayrells in Stowe became joined to broader issues. In 1640, Sir Peter Temple initiated a lawsuit in Chancery against Abel Dayrell. The court documents construe the conflict in terms of two major themes: the destructive impact of personal interest on the commonweal and neighborhood; and the duty of power to protect the commonweal in the interest of the poor and vulnerable. Temple accused Dayrell of a corrupt violation of the stint in Stowe and Lamport commons.[42] This stint limited the commoners to four "cows or cow cattle" for every yardland, and the Dayrells were allowed six horses in the wood commons in recognition of their four yardlands in Lamport. Prior to the introduction of this stint in 1590, the commons had been "overcharged," and families of Stowe and Lamport "were utterly disappointed of milk, butter, and cheese, which is their whole subsistence they live by, their wives and children, their

---

[38] In 1632, a year before his father's death, Abel had been upset over the setting of Temple's "park pale" in Stowe Hewings, a tract of waste land used as pasture in northeastern Stowe, near Lamport. See HL: STT 565: Edmund Dayrell to Sir Peter Temple, c. 1630; STLP, Case 142, Sir Peter Temple v. Abel Dayrell: Draft of Temple's Bill in Chancery, 1640; STMP, Box 3, Buckinghamshire, 1630–1640: Notes on Sir Peter Temple's Complaint against Abel Dayrell, c. 1640.

[39] Ibid.

[40] These tenants were Henry Davy of Dadford, a tenant at will; Thomas Jeffs, either the seventy-two year-old copyholder or his son, Thomas, a tenant at will; and Thomas Sayer, a leaseholder. See HL: STLP, Case 142, Sir Peter Temple v. Abel Dayrell: Draft of Temple's Bill in Chancery, 1640; STMP, Box 3, file 2: Stowe and Dadford Rental, 1621; file 25: Survey of Stowe and Lamport, 1591, 1631; Michaelmas Rent Roll, 1634.

[41] HL: STLP, Case 142, Sir Peter Temple v. Abel Dayrell: Dayrell's Answer to Temple's Bill in Chancery, 16 February 1640.

[42] In his personal papers, Temple invoked his royal franchise against the Dayrells "for breach of charter in hunting and disturbing his deer in his park." Temple's decision to stress the stint of commons and to address the issue in a Chancery suit acquires significance in the political circumstances of 1640. See HL: STMLP, Box 5, SCU (A), files 1, 2, 4: Notes on Lawsuits against the Dayrells, 1641–1642.

livings being but small."[43] After the stint, the annual value of "a cow's common" in Stowe Hewings had increased dramatically from twelve pence to three or four shillings.[44] According to Temple's complaint, Abel Dayrell and his sons, "being rich and having great stocks of cattle," had violated the stint for their "private profit and advantage, to oppress the commoners and to spoil their cattle on the commons by rotting and tainting them with multitude of cattle together."[45] In his answer, Dayrell maintained that Temple's "oppressive and injurious" enclosures for his "great park" had violated the "ancient lands" of the Dayrell family, had divested poor neighbors of their commons, and had poisoned the commonweal, and referred himself "to the grand judgment of this court whether he was likely to oppress Sir Peter Temple and his tenants or was plainly oppressed by him."[46] The accusations in this lawsuit transformed the dispute between Dayrells and Temples into a contest to represent the commonweal in Stowe. Defined in this way, Chancery could not adjudicate the matter. In early 1642, the court's slow process produced only stalemate. Arthur East and Peter Harris, Temple's servants, secured a *supplicavit*, a binding over to keep the peace, in order to curb violence in Stowe Park, but Dayrell used indictments against Temple's servants to obtain a *supersedeas*, effectively blocking the *supplicavit*.[47] Both Temple and Dayrell mobilized their tenants to support their views of the spoiled commonweal, and each accused his opponent of coercion against the weak in this practice.[48]

---

[43] In addition, many animals had died, and local harvests suffered "for want of their sheep to foal upon their fallow fields." The new stint reduced the number of cattle allowed on the commons from six to four beasts for every yardland. See HL: STLP, Case 142, Sir Peter Temple v. Abel Dayrell: Draft of Temple's Bill in Chancery, June 1639; Draft of Temple's Bill in Chancery, 1640.

[44] HL: STLP, Case 142, Sir Peter Temple v. Abel Dayrell: Draft of Temple's Bill in Chancery, 1640.

[45] Ibid.   [46] Ibid., Dayrell's Answer to Temple's Bill in Chancery, 16 February 1640.

[47] HL: STLP, Case 33, Miscellaneous Papers from Case 142, Sir Peter Temple v. Abel Dayrell: Indictment of John Pollard and Thomas Pollard of Leckhamstead, Edward Abbot, Tristram Busby, John Charter, Richard Charter, Richard Cleedon, Arthur East, George Hillier, Ralph Middleton, Thomas Turpin, and Edward Wolcott of Stowe, Peter Harris of Westbury, and Stephen Smith of Lillingstone Dayrell [Sir Peter Temple's tenants and servants] for Riot and Assault, 14 December 1641; Order of *Supplicavit*, 7 February 1642; Order of *Supersedeas*, 25 April 1642.

[48] According to Dayrell, Temple had "stirred up" many tenants "to compose his own designs." Thomas Jeffs the elder, Thomas Sayer, and Thomas Tyler of Lamport, and William Stephens of Stowe, were Temple's leaseholders. Anne Channel, Henry Davy, Thomas Jeffs the younger, Edward Robins before his death in 1641, Thomas Spatcher, and William Turpin were tenants at will. Although Temple was "at the sole charge of the suit," these tenants were listed as complainants. On the other side, Temple suggested that Dayrell received support from his tenants Richard May, Robert Wills, and Goodwife Fayrie of Shalston. See HL: STLP, Case 142, Sir Peter Temple v. Abel Dayrell: STMP, Box 3, Buckinghamshire, 1630–1640: Notes on Sir Peter Temple's Complaint against Abel Dayrell, c. 1640; Dayrell's Answer to Temple's Bill in Chancery, 16 February 1640; Interrogatories for Temple, 1641.

In early 1642, a petition to parliament by the Dayrells and their supporters expressed these moral issues more explicitly in terms of honor and
the discourse of the forest.[49] Abel Dayrell and Peter Dayrell of Lillingstone
Dayrell used the petition to denounce Sir Peter Temple's park as a personal
affront, a selfish despoliation of the commonweal, and a violation of the
purlieu of other gentlemen.[50] According to the petition, the hamlets of
Stowe, Dadford, and Lamport contained "ancient purlieu grounds, where
the freeholders had liberty to hunt and chase." Over the previous sixteen
years, Sir Peter Temple, member of the house for Buckingham, had
"depopulated ten or twelve ancient farms in Stowe, where the farmers
had formerly lived very well, maintaining tillage, [before Temple] had
turned them out with diverse other poor people, to the heavy burden of the
neighborhood." After this clearance, Temple had "emparked a great part of
these farms and their common fields in his own lands, [including] forty
acres of Mr. Abel Dayrell, gentleman, being his demesne lands and lord of
the manor [of Lamport], and made a very large park, storing the same with
red and fallow deer." Because the animals had "increased to so great a
multitude" and parts of the park lay open, deer had "overrun the country,
destroying corn and barking and spoiling [Temple's] own woods, the
woods [in Akeley] belonging to New College, Oxford, and Sir Thomas
Dayrell's woods." As a result, the wood commons no longer furnished
adequate firewood, and landholders were likely to be ruined, having
already suffered damages in "corn, grass, and goods" valued at £500.

To make matters worse, Temple had denied his neighbors any defense
against this plague of deer. According to the Dayrells, Temple protected
any deer killed beyond the pale of the park as "his majesty's game" and
forced the hunters to appear before Henry Rich, Earl of Holland, chief
justice in eyre of the forests south of the Trent, "to their great vexation and

---

[49] HL: STMP, Oversize Box 2, file 38: Petition of Inhabitants of Stowe to Parliament, 1642. The
petitioners were Peter Dayrell, Abel Dayrell, Paul Dayrell, Rowland Norman, William Stokes, John
Rands, John Frankyshe, Paul Frankyshe, Richard Webb, Nicholas Hickman, and Thomas Pattsall.
This draft petition is undated, but an internal reference to an attack on the Dayrells and their friends
by Sir Peter Temple's servants in Stowe Park on 29 January, and the indictment of Temple's servants
for riot and assault on Peter Dayrell the younger in Lamport on 14 December 1641, appear to place
the petition in the early months of 1642. HL: STLP, Case 33, Miscellaneous Papers from Case 142,
Sir Peter Temple v. Abel Dayrell: Indictment for Riot and Assault, 14 December 1641.

[50] In purlieu, or disafforested land on the boundaries of a forest, freeholders possessed liberties of the
hunt and use of woods denied in the forest proper. See Manwood, *Laws of the Forest*, ff. 146r–187r.
Although bits of the Dayrell estate in Lillingstone Dayrell and tracts of woodland in Akeley formed
part of the purlieu of Whittlewood Forest, I have found nothing to support the purlieu status of
Stowe. See Page, *VCH Buckingham*, 4: 145, 154, 188, 192; Lipscomb, *History and Antiquities of
Buckingham*, 3: 37.

expenses."[51] Only Temple had liberty to hunt in Stowe, and his servants defended this monopoly by force of arms. On 29 January, some freeholders of Stowe had "hunted purlieu in New College woods and in other purlieu grounds, as is lawful for them to do." Arthur East, Temple's keeper, had not only interrupted this hunt, but had "bent his bow and put in a forked arrow, threatening to shoot one of them." Later on the same day, "diverse of Sir Peter Temple's tenants and servants assaulted and struck [the hunters] and their servants in the purlieu, as some of them hunted in the woods twelve or fourteen red deer besides great store of fallow deer, the keeper at that time having made gaps and passages through the park pales." In conclusion, the petitioners begged "that the lands so enclosed be laid open again," that Sir Peter Temple "keep up his pale, according to his license to empark, if he has license," that the freeholders "be restored to their ancient liberty of purlieu," and that Temple make satisfaction for damages. Despite its distortions, the petition expressed Abel Dayrell's view of Sir Peter Temple's enclosure of his land as a form of humiliation. Dayrell's account of conditions in Stowe joined an indictment of depopulation and avarice to a lament for violated "demesne lands" and diminished honor, embodied in lost liberties of purlieu and the hunt. In 1641 and 1642, the symbols and indignities evoked in this petition were used to justify a violent defense of the Dayrell patrimony in a battle for Stowe Park.[52]

IV

The political economy of the manor or manors of Stowe and Lamport became inseparable from the calculus of local honor in the late 1630s, as the Dayrell estate in Lamport became a smaller and smaller island in the rising sea of Stowe Park and the honor of the Temple family. After Sir Peter Temple initiated the lawsuit over the commons in Stowe, the Dayrells retaliated against the park and its keepers. In 1640, Abel Dayrell of Lamport defended his actions as the only honorable response to avarice. Temple had "plainly oppressed" the Dayrells and others in the neighborhood. These neighbors now depended on the resistance of the Dayrells,

---

[51] Sir Peter Temple's notes on his options in law do not support this accusation. HL: STMLP, Box 5, SCU (A), files 1, 2, 4: Notes on Lawsuits against the Dayrells, 1641–1642.

[52] Moreover, the Dayrells may have intended their appeal to "liberty of purlieu" to exploit parliamentary hostility to the expansion of royal forests. In 1641, this expansion had been described as "a great grievance and vexation" and as a symptom of "arbitrary and tyrannical government," words taken from the impeachment of John Finch, Lord Keeper of the Great Seal, and from a statute designed to halt the expansion of the royal forests. See John Rushworth (ed.), *Historical Collections*, 8 vols. (London, 1721), 4: 136–39; 16 Car. I, c. 16, in *SR*, 5: 119–20.

"for if [Dayrell] was excluded [from his lands and commons in Stowe], the [neighbors] would quickly be excluded also, since Sir Peter Temple already excluded them by paling in the park, until [Dayrell] had caused the same to be thrown open again."[53] Because a deer park expressed both honor and interest or exclusive property, the Dayrells found ample justification for their behavior in the culture of gentility. Since the late fifteenth century, a gentleman might find honor in defense of the commonweal from the depredations of the powerful, including the building of deer parks, the "curse of the Lord, to have our country converted from the furniture of mankind to the walks and shrouds of wild beasts."[54] After the initial destruction of the pale in Stowe, resistance assumed the form of a series of armed raids on the park and dramatic gestures by the Dayrells and their servants and friends. Many families formerly subordinate to the Temples and Dayrells as servants and tenants in Stowe and Lamport received active and sometimes quite vocal parts in this violent theater of honor evoked by the divisions among the local gentlemen.

On 25 August, 1641, Richard Charters, a keeper of the park in Dadford, witnessed one of the expeditions of the Dayrell family "within the pale of the park" during a late evening walk in his tract of the chase.[55] As Charters watched, Edmund and Paul Dayrell, sons of Abel Dayrell of Lamport, and Gideon Fisher the younger, a friend of the Dayrells from Carlton in Bedfordshire, entered the park around midnight, carrying a crossbow and swords or rapiers. A second account, the statement of keeper Arthur East, expanded this expedition to include Richard Scott, a servant of Abel Dayrell, and limited its arsenal to "swords and bucklers and long pike-staves, about five yards long," more gentlemanly arms for a hunt than a crossbow.[56] In any event, Charters understandably disliked the look of the

---

[53] HL: STLP, Case 142, Sir Peter Temple v. Abel Dayrell: Dayrell's Answer to Temple's Bill in Chancery, 16 February 1640. According to Dayrell, some of Temple's tenants had informed him that Temple alone carried the charges of the lawsuit in Chancery and had included his tenants only to "compose his design."

[54] Harrison, *Description of England*, 256. See James, "English Politics and the Concept of Honour," 343, for the interrelationship of honor and resistance to oppression.

[55] HL: STMLP, Box 5, SCU (A), files 1, 2, 4: Deposition of Richard Charters, 13 May 1642.

[56] By the time John Nicholls, Sir Peter Temple's law clerk, had made notes of potential lawsuits against the Dayrells in the autumn of 1641, unspecified "others" had been added to this group of four, and the use of visors or masks had been alleged. Yet the keepers' easy identification of the Dayrells, as well as the group's fear of recognition, make the use of disguises seem unlikely, an aggravating circumstance in law added to the charges against the Dayrells after the event. See HL: STMLP, Box 5, SCU (A), files 1, 2, 4: Deposition of Arthur East, in Articles of Good Behaviour Exhibited in Chancery, 25 January 1642; Notes [of John Nicholls, clerk] on Lawsuits against the Dayrells, undated [August–December, 1641]; draft deposition of Arthur East, 24 May 1642.

props in this play and elected not to challenge the intruders, claiming that he "presently lost sight" of the group. An hour later, Charters heard "somebody hallowing, shouting, or crying out" and made for the sound of the disturbance. He emerged from the forest to discover Arthur East, lying "sore wounded, cut, beat, and bruised" on the lawn of the park, unable to walk unassisted.[57] East had apparently surprised the Dayrells and their companions in the midst of their nocturnal sport, and the gang had beaten and knocked him down, had "almost cut off one of his arms with a sword, so that he [was] lamed, and [had] thrust him in two several parts of his body with one of the pikestaves." According to East, one of his assailants wanted to "kill him outright," claiming that East knew his attackers and would ensure Sir Peter Temple's revenge, and had charged East with a sword, "wherewith he had nailed [him] to the ground as he lay if the thrust had not been prevented."[58] Before Charters arrived on the scene, the Dayrells and their friends had fled, but East quickly identified the Dayrells as two of his assailants. Leaning heavily on Charters for support, East staggered back to his lodge and then pressed his colleague to take his bloodhound in pursuit of the intruders. Charters took the hound back to the site of the attack and picked up a trail that led across the park, into the disputed territory of Stowe furze, "where he found a deer warm and newly killed." Ultimately, the hound followed the scent to the door of the Dayrell house in Lamport, "and as [Charters] was going into the yard he met a hound coming out with a shoulder of venison or the greatest part in his mouth."[59] Apparently, Charters had no warrant to pursue the matter beyond the closed door.

The violent assaults on the park became more frequent in the autumn and winter of 1641, as Temple's Chancery lawsuit against the Dayrells entered the commission phase.[60] Abel Dayrell now began to receive armed support from extended kin, as his powerful cousin, Peter Dayrell, lord of Lillingstone Dayrell, entered the field.[61] On 8 November and 1 December, Paul Dayrell, Abel's son, entered "the old park" at Stowe in search of "small

---

[57] Ibid., Deposition of Richard Charters, 13 May 1642.
[58] Ibid., Deposition of Arthur East, in Articles of Good Behaviour Exhibited in Chancery, 25 January, 1642.
[59] The clerk subsequently deleted Charter's account of the hound carrying the shoulder of venison. HL: STMLP, Box 5, SCU (A), files 1, 2, 4: Deposition of Richard Charters, 13 May 1642.
[60] HL: STLP, Case 33, Sir Peter Temple v. Abel Dayrell: Expenses of Commission, 11 October 1641; Case 142, Brief of Interrogatories for Commission on Behalf of Sir Peter Temple, 12 October 1641. Most of the papers in this file seem to be miscellaneous documents related to the Chancery case.
[61] Page, *VCH Buckingham*, 4: 189; Rylands, *Visitation of Buckingham*, 36–37.

birds" and "shot a handgun, charged with powder and hailshot."[62] These minor disturbances of the peace culminated in full-scale raids later in the month. On 14 December, Paul again walked into the park looking for trouble, pointed his gun at Arthur East, cocked it, and reportedly said "if he had [East] out of the park, he would shoot him."[63] Two days later, a raiding party composed of Edmund and Paul Dayrell of Lamport, their cousins Peter Dayrell of Lillingstone Dayrell and his son Peter, their servants John Salisbury and John Rands, and "diverse others to the number of about twenty persons," descended on the park "in warlike manner, armed with targets, swords, guns, pikes, crossbows, and bills."[64] "After many braving and boasting words," the Dayrells and their companions began to fire into the park, killing a favorite hound, a gift to Sir Peter Temple from Thomas, Viscount Savile. According to Arthur East, Peter Dayrell the younger "wished that the dog's master were there."[65] In January 1642, Peter Harris, a servant of the Temples, confirmed East's account of this Dayrell *comitatus*, their "riotous assemblies" and "threatening speeches," as the common enterprise of the Dayrells in Lamport and Lillingstone Dayrell.[66] Harris feared to perform his duties in Stowe Park because this gang was routinely "armed in terrible manner with guns, swords, targets, and pikestaves" and had threatened "to shoot him or otherwise kill him; so he is afraid for his life and dare not stir."[67]

During the spring of 1642, Temple's Chancery lawsuit over the stint of the commons became inseparable from the prosecutions that stemmed

---

[62] HL: STLP, Case 142, Sir Peter Temple v. Abel Dayrell: Indictments of Paul Dayrell and Peter Dayrell the younger, at Assizes, 1642. These four separate indictments all related to the violence of November and December, 1641.

[63] The events of 14 and 16 December 1641 are sometimes conflated in the law documents. See HL: STMLP, Box 5, SCU (A), files 1, 2, 4: Articles of Good Behaviour to be Exhibited in Chancery by Arthur East and Peter Harris, 25 January 1642; STLP, Case 142, Sir Peter Temple v. Abel Dayrell: Indictments of Paul Dayrell and Peter Dayrell the younger at Assizes, 1642.

[64] HL: STMLP, Box 5, SCU (A), files 1, 2, 4: Articles of Good Behaviour to be Exhibited in Chancery by Arthur East and Peter Harris, 25 January 1642. As Temple's servants were disposed to magnify disturbances of the peace, these breathless descriptions of the weapons on display cannot be accepted at face value. On the other hand, the Dayrells and their supporters tended to justify their violence, rather than to deny it.

[65] Ibid.

[66] Ibid. Harris cited threats from Abel, Edmund, and Paul Dayrell, and Richard Scott of Lamport; Peter Dayrell the elder, Peter Dayrell the younger, Thomas Madkins, Rowland Norman, John Rands, and John Salisbury of Lillingstone Dayrell; and Gideon Fisher the younger, the Dayrells' friend from Bedfordshire. See John Wilson (ed.), *Buckinghamshire Contributions for Ireland* (Buckinghamshire Record Society, 1983), 21: 102; HL: STMLP, Box 5, SCU (A), files 1, 2, 4: Deposition of Edward Abbot and John Symons, 7 June 1642.

[67] Ibid., Articles of Good Behaviour to be Exhibited in Chancery by Arthur East and Peter Harris, 25 January 1642.

from assaults on the park, but the local war only became more fierce, as the Dayrells enlisted the Tyrells of nearby Thornton, an influential gentry family, for their next and most ambitious campaign against Stowe Park.[68] On 13 May, Arthur East had appeared before Robert Heath, chief justice of king's bench, to untangle the "businesses" concerning the *supplicavit* against the Dayrell *comitatus*, secured in Chancery after the December raids. Five days later, the Dayrells and Tyrells attacked the contested northeastern corner of the park around Stowe furze.[69] A hunting party of perhaps one hundred friends and servants was recruited from Chackmore, south of Stowe, and from Nash and Wicken, several miles further east, closer to the seat of the Tyrells in Thornton. Sir Edward Tyrell commanded the expedition, consisting of his sons Toby and Francis "with diverse of their servants and shepherds, whereof William Wrighton, John Ethersay, and Timothy Scott had guns, and [Michael] Kent, Sir Edward's servant, held a brace of his master's greyhounds." Peter Dayrell, the elder, of Lillingstone Dayrell, and his sons Thomas and Peter, led the assault alongside the Tyrells, but the servants were as heavily armed as their masters in a party reportedly carrying "above forty guns, swords, and pikestaves" into the park. According to Temple's servants, this group "rode and hunted up and down in Sir Peter Temple's ground, beat in the furze, and hunted a deer in Stowe furze and over Sir Peter's ground in Stowe field, hunting him into College woods in Akeley, where he was killed by Richard Symons of Wicken with a gun." As later raids on the park would confirm, the supporting players in these dramas were often the most forward in verbal threats and boasts. James Kiplyn of Nash, for example, a "pricker" or mounted attendant "in Sir Edward Tyrell's company, threatened to beat Edward Abbot, a servant of Sir Peter Temple," and boasted "that he would be the death of forty of Temple's deer."[70]

The male heads of elite households and their sons invariably assumed the lead in these affairs of honor. As the battle of Stowe Park reached its peak in the last week of May and first week of June 1642, Temples and Dayrells contended for honor in carefully choreographed scenes of violence. On 2 June, Sir Peter Temple, in the company of three of his servants, confronted and disarmed Paul Dayrell of Lamport, after Paul and his brother Edmund, their cousin Peter Farren of Northampton, and their usual confederate, Richard Scott, described as their father's servant, had spent morning and

---

[68] A genealogy of the Tyrells of Thornton is provided in Rylands, *Visitation of Buckingham*, 117–119.
[69] HL: STMLP, Box 5, SCU (A), files 1, 2, 4: Note Concerning Mr. Dayrell's Hunting, c. 2 June 1642.
[70] Ibid. According to a marginal note, Kiplyn had charge of "a harbouring hound" during the hunt.

afternoon coursing Stowe furze with greyhounds. Temple seized Dayrell's gun and challenged him to charge a felony.[71] Five days later, Peter Dayrell, the younger, under the approving eyes of his father and Abel Dayrell, stood over a freshly killed deer in Stowe Park and, in front of Temple's servants, "having drawn his sword, said whoever should try to take away the deer, he would run through."[72] Dayrell was sufficiently convincing to deter Robert Collison from taking the deer on Temple's behalf, although Peter's younger brother Thomas cut a less menacing figure. After Thomas "saw his brother's sword drawn," he tried eight times to draw his own, failed for unspecified reasons, and finally received help from a friend, then "shook his drawn sword in his hand, and gave many daring and boasting words."[73] Despite his technical difficulties, Dayrell's "daring" words apparently inspired Francis Tyrell's "struggle and scuffle" to prevent Edward Abbot from hauling away the deer for Temple's use.[74]

These confrontations had their limits, defined in terms of both honor and law. The raids and defense of Stowe Park made controlled use of force to intimidate and produced no fatalities in more than a year of armed conflict. A confrontation between Peter Dayrell, the elder, and Arthur East, a keeper in Stowe, illustrates an awareness of the constraints of honor and law. On 24 May 1642, Dayrell led a hunting party in the vicinity of Stowe Park, consisting of his sons, his cousin Abel of Lamport, Abel's sons, Abel's cousin Peter Farren of Northampton, and several servants of the households in Lillingstone Dayrell and Lamport.[75] As the group approached Rueworth lane, near the pale of Stowe Park, Peter, the elder, became enraged at the sight of East making his rounds "and broke through the mound or fence to come into the lane." Dayrell "catched hold of East and shook him, and, holding his staff over his head, called him rogue, rascal, thief, and perjured knave, and otherwise threatened to beat him

---

[71] Ibid.

[72] HL: STMLP, Box 5, SCU (A), files 1, 2, 4: Draft Depositions, 24 March 1642, 7 June 1642, 7 August 1642.

[73] The finished deposition mentions only that Thomas drew his sword and spoke threatening words. Ibid., Notes for Depositions, June 1642; Draft Depositions, 24 March 1642, 7 June 1642, 7 August 1642; Depositions of Robert Collison and John Symons, 22 June 1642. On the same day, 7 June, Peter Dayrell the younger allegedly chased Temple's servant, Peter Harris, at full gallop for "almost a mile," shaking his drawn sword, and shouting, "Now, sirrah, I have that in my hand which will serve thy turn."

[74] Ibid., Notes for Depositions, June 1642; Draft Depositions, 24 March 1642, 7 June 1642, 7 August 1642.

[75] Ibid., Note Concerning Mr. Dayrell's Hunting, c. 2 June 1642; Draft Depositions, 24 March 1642, 7 June 1642, 7 August 1642. The servants included Edward Grimley, James Hobbs, John Lamley, Richard Scott, and William Warr.

sore."[76] Dayrell's anger and weapon were such that Peter Farren, "fearing some harm might ensue," dismounted, "took Dayrell in his arms and held him." "Cousin, let the keeper go," Farren advised, "You shall not beat him, for he gives you no bad words." After a few moments, Dayrell calmed himself sufficiently to reply, "Though you will not let me strike him, yet I will hold and shake him."[77] East then left the scene scared but unharmed. Farren carefully prevented the escalation of anger to murder and saved his cousin from a dishonorable assault on a servant who had offered no "bad words" or provocation.

This theatre of honor, enacted on a shifting border between intimidation, riot, and murder, offered numerous scenes of personal confrontation, designed to display an individual mastery of force. Yet the competition to hold the most honor required many hands, and the conflict endemic in the culture of gentility thus produced a diffusion of power and status among the supporting cast. Although masters generally controlled the script and the weapons, the theatre of honor held many opportunities to secure this power, and servants were among the most vocal participants in the raids on Stowe Park. The broader impact of "honor plays" on the societies clustered around noble households is best illustrated by the events surrounding Peter Dayrell the younger's impassioned defense of the killing of the deer on 7 June 1642. As Dayrell stood over the deer with his drawn sword, the "servants and company" declared their support with "many bragging and daring words, some of them swearing that the deer was theirs and that they would carry him away or else they would lose their lives in the place."[78] When John Symons attempted to take the deer in the name of Sir Peter Temple, John Rands, a servant of Peter Dayrell the elder, attacked Symons and "ran him into the forehead with the pike of an halberd or bill."[79] Local reputations might be built in the competitive boasts that followed such affrays. On the "morrow" after this "great hunting," William Channel, a servant of Peter Dayrell the elder, bragged to Arthur East and Thomas Dancer of Syresham, northwest of Stowe,

---

[76] Ibid., Note Concerning Mr. Dayrell's Hunting, c. 2 June 1642; Draft Depositions, 24 March 1642, 7 June 1642, 7 August 1642. The charge "perjured knave" was dropped from the final draft of East's deposition, suggesting that either East or Sir Peter Temple's law clerk may have wanted to avoid attracting undue attention to East's earlier depositions.

[77] Ibid., Note Concerning Mr. Dayrell's Hunting, c. 2 June 1642. In the final version of the deposition, Dayrell did not regain his composure but continued to threaten beatings.

[78] Ibid., Deposition of John Symons, 22 June 1642.

[79] Ibid., Draft Depositions, 24 March 1642, 7 June 1642, 7 August 1642; Deposition of John Symons, 22 June 1642.

that if any blows had been struck when the deer, killed the day before by his master, was in taking away, that they on his master's side would have shot their guns as fast as they could at the men on Sir Peter's side, for he knew that his master's men had twelve guns and better staffs than Sir Peter's men; and further said that if blows had been struck there would a great deal of blood have been shed, and that he himself would have shot his gun on his master's behalf as long as he could have stood.[80]

The violent scenes in Stowe Park furnished the means for servants and other supporting players, such as William Channel, John Rands, and James Kiplyn of Nash, to build their own local reputations for courage, for martial prowess, and for the noble skills of the hunt.

Although the battle of Stowe Park reveals the small-scale dynamics of power in a hierarchic society, the most important evidence from this sordid affair for present purposes concerns the meanings of violence and the significance of hunting in the culture of gentility. This notion of gentility is inseparable from early modern understandings of the proper exercise of law and order. Yet the imbroglio of the Temples and Dayrells evokes the violent competition for honor at the heart of orderliness and power in the seventeenth century. The ripples from this local competition reached the centres of royal power in Temple's Chancery lawsuit of the late 1630s and in Dayrell's petition to parliament early in 1642, calling for the restoration of the commonweal and the destruction of "oppressive" enclosures in Stowe. Yet the actions in law and the petition did not replace or suppress violent activism in any meaningful sense. The extensive local use of intimidation and terror, the active pursuit of justice and defense of honor, moved *parallel* to civil actions in the courts and in parliament. In this context, the dynastic state had domesticated the violence of gentility only to the extent that martial assembly was justified in terms of law and the honorable defense of the commonweal and that local intimidation tended to stop short of murder.

V

The violent theater in Stowe reveals the complex interrelationship between a politics of honor, status, and reputation – key elements in the political world of gentlemen – and the authority of law as expressed in such formal texts as John Manwood's *Treatise*, in the neighborhood of Whittlewood Forest during the early seventeenth century. In this micro-politics of gentility, both factions invoked the authority of law but used that authority to justify

---

[80] Ibid., Notes for Depositions, June 1642; Draft Depositions, 24 March 1642, 7 June 1642, 7 August 1642; Deposition of Arthur East, 22 June 1642.

direct action against perceived injustices, irrespective of judicial decisions. Moreover, officers of the crown showed little inclination to intervene directly in the battle, maneuvering to accommodate and contain the violence of the local competition for honor. In September 1642, the assize court in Aylesbury appointed Sir Edward Tyrell, a friend of the Dayrells and sometime companion on their raids, and Sir Alexander Denton, a cousin of Sir Peter Temple, justices of the peace for Buckinghamshire, to investigate "the business" concerning Edmund Dayrell, Paul Dayrell, and "other delinquents" and allowed the justices broad discretion to bind the disorderly to keep the peace.[81] These relatives and combatants were entrusted to compose the delicate balance of honor, gentility, and subordination to the crown and its law. Ultimately, the contests for the commonweal and the hunting raids in Stowe became a local prelude to civil war, as Sir Peter Temple supported parliament after October 1642, and Peter Dayrell, the elder, of Lillingstone Dayrell defended the crown.[82]

Perhaps this account has not done justice to the courage and ambition of John Symons and John Rands. The forms and uses of power and authority, their making and unmaking, their myriad exchanges, remain elusive if the words and deeds of such as Symons and Rands appear only in lists of examples, as empty postures separated from the places, relationships, and principles that were their substance. Perhaps the angry opening scene of Symons and Rands wrestling over the remains of a deer now seems to have disappeared from view, but the broader evidence for the battle of Stowe Park – the violent passions and activism aroused by matters of honor – may begin to restore some colors to the scene, the meanings and motives of their fight. Because Symons and Rands stood at the intersection of a dynamic political economy, a conflict between two powerful households, and a vigorous martial culture of the forest and hunt, their confrontation over the deer acquires layers of significance and resists reduction to the comfortable dichotomies of elite and common interest, the economic priorities of the propertied and propertyless, or the distinct visions of order imposed by

---

[81] Ibid., An Order from the Assizes Concerning the Dayrells, 5 September 1642; Rylands, *Visitation of Buckingham*, 38. The evidence of judicial manipulation and violence in Stowe illustrates some of the contradictions in the forms of pacification described in Steve Hindle, "The Keeping of the Public Peace," in Griffiths, Fox, and Hindle, *The Experience of Authority*, 213–248.

[82] In 1645, Temple was noted as a "parliament man" and assessed at £200. Peter Dayrell the elder was present at the surrender of Oxford in June 1646, and was fined £788 for "adhering to the king." Sir Thomas Dayrell, Peter's son, also compounded for his delinquency. See M. Green (ed.), *Calendar of the Proceedings of the Committee for Advance of Money, 1642–1656*, 3 vols. (London: HMSO, 1888) 1: 554; M. Green (ed.), *Calendar of the Proceedings of the Committee for Compounding, 1643–1660*, 5 vols. (London: HMSO, 1889), 1: 67, 2: 1212, 1519.

governors on the merely governed. The drama of the hunting raid reveals a complex discourse of honor common to all the participants, both gentlemen and commoners. This discourse furnished a justification for active resistance to the Temples as powerful as the dynastic impulse to construct the deer park in Stowe. The daring words of two common soldiers in the battle of Stowe Park thus begin to challenge familiar distinctions among culture, politics, economy, and society, suggesting the pervasive significance of cultural forms such as the hunt, often treated as the exclusive concern of an elite class.

3

Ancient liberties and the politics of the commonweal in Waltham Forest, 1608–1642

> John Browne and others in April last assembled in riotous manner in Waltham forest and killed many of the king's deer, saying they came for venison and venison they would have, for there was no law settled at this time . . .
> John Peacocke, 1642

I

The clash of forces in Stowe Park joined a series of local battles fought over the forests, chases, and parks of southern England during late spring and summer, 1642. Among many reports of riot from Windsor Forest and elsewhere, on 2 May the House of Lords received a distressing affidavit from the officers of Waltham Forest in western Essex. John Peacocke, an underkeeper of Newlodge Walk in Waltham Holy Cross, and his assistant Richard Stocke reported that a "riotous assembly" had taken place on 25 April under the leadership of John Browne, a veteran offender against the forest laws.[1] Browne and at least eighteen companions used "guns, bills, pitchforks, and clubs" as well as "a mastiff dog" to "kill diverse of the king's deer" in the forest. When Peacocke demanded an explanation, several muttered defiantly that "they came for venison, and venison they would have," but Browne "made answer" more cogently that "there was no law settled at this time." Peacocke then presented a general warrant from James Hay, Earl of Carlisle, chief keeper of Newlodge Walk and lord of the manor of Waltham, for the arrest of "such as did spoils in the forest."

---

[1] HLRO: Main Papers, 1509–1700: 2 May 1642. A synopsis of the affidavit is included in HMC, *Fifth Report of the Royal Commission on Historical Manuscripts, Part I: Report and Appendix* (London: Her Majesty's Stationery Office, 1876), 20. On 2 May, the Lords issued an arrest order based on the affidavit (*LJ*, vol. 5: 37). John Browne of Waltham had been presented in the swanimote court in 1630 and fined 3s for keeping an unexpedited mongrel (PRO C99/144, Perambulations of Waltham Forest: Roll of Presentments in Swanimote Court, 14 September 1630: list of hunting dogs at end of roll).

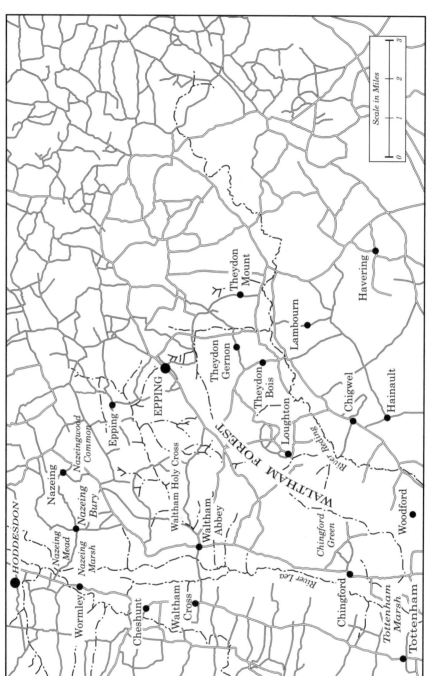

Map 3.1. Waltham Forest in Essex

John Dell, Browne's neighbor in Waltham and another veteran delinquent of the forest courts, examined the warrant and expressed doubts whether it was in Carlisle's handwriting, and Browne then declared that "whoever made that warrant was ashamed to set his hand to it and that nowadays justices of peace could not write."[2] In the absence of settled law, Browne implied in this sneering charge against the corruption so common "nowadays," only the most benighted, shameful justice would issue a general warrant to arrest hunters. Browne's friends took his defiance as a signal to continue "in their riotous courses," attacking deer and chiding the underkeepers that "if they complained of offenders, to complain of good store of them, that if they went to prison they might be merry together."

Peacocke and Stocke complained of "several companies" killing deer in Waltham, day and night, during the three weeks following Easter. Browne's friend Isacke Bellamy, who brought his "mastiff dog" along on Browne's hunting parties, threatened to lead "his company" further east against the fine "herd of bucks" maintained by Philip Herbert, Earl of Pembroke, chief keeper of Loughton Walk. On 3 May, a second affidavit from Peacocke included accusations against John Russell, the minister of Chingford, and his several companions for "daily assemblies" to kill deer in Waltham.[3] Russell's conformity to the Laudian church after his appointment in 1634 clearly failed to inculcate deference to the authority of the forest law.[4] Among others, Russell had recruited John Cordell of Chingford Green and John Grimston of Chingford, both linked in the 1630s to the raising of illegal hunting dogs in the southwestern reaches of the forest.[5] Although the forest officers were accustomed to enforcing the social boundaries of the hunt against the depredations of their neighbors,

[2] In 1630, John Dell of Waltham had been prosecuted alongside Browne in the swanimote court and was likewise fined 3s for an unexpeditated mongrel. PRO: C99/144, Perambulations of Waltham Forest: Roll of Presentments in Swanimote Court, 14 September 1630: list of hunting dogs at end of roll.

[3] HLRO: Main Papers, 1509–1700: 3 May 1642. On 12 May, after a vote on the matter passed the House of Commons, the Lords issued an order against the killing of the king's deer in Windsor and Waltham (*LJ*, vol. 5: 38, 61; HMC, *Fifth Report*, 22). John Russell was the rector of All Saints in Chingford. See W. R. Powell (ed.), *VCH Essex*, 10 vols. (London: Oxford University Press, 1966, 1973), 5: 111.

[4] In 1645, Russell was presented to the Essex county committee for "swearing, gaming, conformity to the church, and loyalty to the king," and was sequestered from his living in 1647. He had been assessed at £80 by the Committee for Advance of Money in 1644 and ultimately paid £30 for a discharge in 1646. See A. G. Matthews (ed.), *Walker Revised* (Oxford: Clarendon Press, 1948), 162.

[5] In 1630, John Cordell had been presented for Chingford and fined 5s in the same sweep of illegal hunting dogs that had netted Browne and Dell in Waltham. John Grimston was not implicated at this time, but his relations Thomas and Robert Grimston were prosecuted and fined 3s each. PRO: C99/144, Perambulations of Waltham Forest: Roll of Presentments in Swanimote Court, 14 September 1630: list of hunting dogs at end of roll.

these disturbances in 1642 present intriguing differences from such common offences against the forest law: first, in their explicit assertion of "no
law settled" as an ideological justification for killing deer and taking
venison; second, in their festive dismissal of the penal consequences as
little more than an opportunity for merrymaking. Implicit in the claims of
Browne and his friends was the conviction that the customary hierarchy of
the forest had dissolved in corruption and the coveted trophies of the hunt
had been released to the neighborhood.

This direct, violent challenge to the forest regime in Waltham raises
questions similar to those addressed in John Walter's recent work on the
massive crowd violence in the neighborhood of Colchester later in the same
summer.[6] As a series of critical events, the forest battles of 1642 point both
forward, to the meanings of political crisis and war between crown and
parliament, and backward, to social context and political consciousness in
the forest during the early seventeenth century. This chapter explores the
question of whether and in what ways the customary culture and political
economy of the forest regime in Waltham and elsewhere influenced the
attacks in 1642. The clues offered by the claim of "no law settled," and the
festive mockery of forest officers, suggest an approach to political
relations in the forest as negotiated settlements. Although the laws of forest
and hunt – prerogative and statute – prescribed absolute boundaries
between nobility and commoners, the political crisis of the early 1640s,
including a parliamentary attack on the decision to expand the royal forests
during the 1630s, clearly disturbed settled power relations in the forest and
offered opportunities for hunters customarily excluded from the chase. In
1642, claims of "no law settled" indicate a political consciousness of the just
bases of forest law and the circumstances of its legitimate suspension.

Many aspects of culture and political economy in forests served to
stimulate this political consciousness. As a distinctive regime derived
from royal prerogative and designed to promote the royal hunt, the
administration of forest law and the orderly discharge of forest offices
formed a powerful recurrent statement of the claims that just kingship
might legitimately make on its subjects. Because royal pleasure was a
primary justification for a forest, disputes over forest matters tended to
move quickly to the most intimate circles of power. Waltham Forest was
particularly significant during the early seventeenth century, since it served
as the bucolic retreat of a king wont to conduct state business from the

---

[6] Walter, *Understanding Popular Violence*, 1–9.

saddle.[7] In 1624, James I became intimately involved in a dispute between John Knight, an underkeeper of Chingford Walk in the southern tract of Waltham, and the keeper, Robert Leigh of Chingford.[8] Although the affair amounted to little more than a personal squabble, James demanded "a whole relation of the business ... his majesty conceiving it to be a hard thing if [Knight] had been an honest and faithful keeper of the deer and the woods of the forest, [that] he should be put out for particular displeasures."[9] The intimate involvement of the crown in matters related to the forest was reflected in Sir Thomas Edmondes's special charge, as the treasurer of the royal household and lieutenant of Waltham Forest, to investigate the dispute between Knight and Leigh and to prepare a detailed report for James himself.[10] The high politics of the conflict were not lost on the denizens of the forest. Edmondes's report commented on the neighbors' interest in the dispute, describing local knowledge of Knight's boast "that he is assured of friends who will hold him in his place notwithstanding anything that his master [Leigh] can do against him, which makes the world conceive that [Knight] could not prevail to put so great a shame upon his master unless [Leigh] were obnoxious for the committing of some foul offence."[11] By early December 1624, the affair had brought James's personal influence to bear on such momentous controversies of the realm as whether the dogs kept by Thomas Boothby and his servants, ostensibly to guard his oat fields, presented too great a danger to the deer of Chingford Walk.[12] Although banal in itself, this dispute illustrates both the unique structure of the forest regime in Waltham, intimately linked to the royal household, and its capacity to draw the authority of the crown into petty local squabbles.

Yet the significance of Waltham Forest for the royal state was not limited to James's personal interest in the preservation of the deer and protection of experienced keepers. Among the routine operations of the state in the early

---

[7] This royal fondness and care for Waltham was a rhetorical refrain of the Star Chamber bills relating to the forest in the early seventeenth century. See conventional statements to this effect in PRO: STAC 8/10/9: Sir Henry Hobart, attorney general v. Robert Quarles and Edward Carrowe, esquires, 1608; STAC 8/211/21: John Manwood v. Richard Humble, Augustine Simpson, and others, 1610.

[8] PRO: SP 14/175/37, Sir Edward Conway, Secretary of the Privy Council, to Sir Thomas Edmondes, 22 November 1624.

[9] Ibid.   [10] Ibid.

[11] PRO: SP 14/176, ff. 46–47, Sir Thomas Edmondes to Sir Edward Conway, Secretary of the Privy Council, 9 December, 1624.

[12] PRO: SP 14/176, ff. 49–52, Robert Leigh's Articles against John Knight, 9 December 1624. In 1610, Thomas Boothby, a freeman of the Merchant Tailors' company in London, purchased the manor of Chingford Comitis and its mansion house at Friday Hill. See Philip Morant, *History and Antiquities of the County of Essex*, 2 vols. (London, 1768), 1: 55–56.

seventeenth century was the annual distribution of "such number of deer of this season as we are pleased to bestow on ambassadors and agents of diverse princes residing with us" and "on the lord mayor, aldermen, and recorder of our city of London."[13] This political use of venison was a major component of the political economy of the southern forests in particular, and Waltham Forest accounted for 21 per cent of venison distributed for such purposes in the late 1630s.[14] Venison ranked among the noblest of gifts and, in this context, signified royal favor. Although the forest regime performed many functions, the offices of the forest existed first and foremost to facilitate the distribution of this gift and to restrict access to the hunt in the interests of royal prerogative, a royal monopoly of the noble dividends produced by forests. Perhaps, then, a clue to the broader significance of the satiric demand of John Browne, John Dell, and their friends for venison in April 1642 lies in the meanings of forest in early modern political culture. These meanings are difficult to recover now, but in the early seventeenth century the court of Star Chamber recorded numerous cases from Waltham Forest and elsewhere that turned on conflicts over the uses of forest land. In this substantial archive, the cultural significance of forests emerges from patterns of local conflict and their broader political significance.

II

The artful fictions in Star Chamber records make them notoriously tricky for historians to handle.[15] Much of the discussion of "sedition" and "oppression" in bills and answers reflects the judicial politics of presentation in the court, and the records thus conceal as much as reveal the dynamics and meanings of conflict. Yet a critical comparison of texts establishes the boundaries of such fictions in local decisions, actions, and events included in both accounts, though interpreted in each text in a manner calculated to justify a distinctive view and discredit the other side. Judicial tactics and their fictions served broader strategies in the politics of Waltham Forest, and the problem then becomes how to reconstruct this politics in local context, how to recover the world of village politicians and the meanings of their actions. The problem of local context touches on the

---

[13] PRO: SP 16/384, Orders and Warrants Concerning Forests, ff. 9v–11r. In 1638, the officers of London received as many as 23 deer from assorted forests, parks, and chases across the southeast.

[14] *Ibid.* Data of this kind are not available for the 1620s.

[15] Hindle, *State and Social Change*, 66–71, 78–87, describes and amplifies this problem in the literature of Star Chamber.

nature of the court records as evidence of politics. Much recent work has approached records of centrally located courts, Arches and Star Chamber, as evidence of the interrelationship of local communities and royal authority, the nature of authority in local communities, or the processes of state formation.[16] Although this approach finds coherent patterns in the varied strands of early modern social and political history, it subsumes conflict in a bland "process" of forming the state. An equally important aspect of this political system was its capacity to sustain and promote a range of views concerning the nature of authority and order. In this context, even judicial tactics reveal a political discourse that transcended the arena of the court. Although a variety of techniques would have served to discredit a rival, the meanings of conflict, as reflected in Star Chamber accounts, often turned on such key political concepts as loyalty, sedition, oppression or despotism, and political justice in the broadest sense. As these concepts were made relevant to disputes in Waltham, the court began to record evidence of opposed understandings of place, the conventions for their expression, and the practical politics required to sustain these views of community and interest. The term "political tradition" becomes helpful here as long as "tradition" is understood as flexible and adaptive to local circumstances.

Star Chamber cases from Waltham reveal two meanings of "forest" distinct from that of the royal hunt. Both of these definitions reflected views of social order in the forest and advocates of both were sufficiently versed in the terms of the forest law to describe their relationship to it as a form of negotiation. The first evoked the neighborliness of purlieu hunters in order to broaden local access to the social and political dividends of hunting. Many aspirants to gentle status in Waltham tried to manipulate claims to purlieu or a restricted liberty to hunt on their freehold land in disafforested territories.[17] They regarded the forest in the conventional terms of the hunt, but sought to negotiate a broader participation in this essential activity of the forest and in the status it conveyed. A second view of forest defined the preservation of commons as a primary responsibility of forest law and implicitly questioned the conventional emphasis on the hunt, especially the royal hunt in Waltham. Star Chamber cases from Waltham Forest record this negotiation to possess the social and political

---

[16] Dan Beaver, "Conscience and Context: the Popish Plot and the Politics of Ritual, 1678–1682," *Historical Journal*, 34 (1991): 297–327; Michael J. Braddick, "Administrative Performance: the Representation of Political Authority in Early Modern England," in Braddick and Walter, *Negotiating Power in Early Modern Society*, 166, 180, 186; Hindle, *State and Social Change*, 66–71, 78–93, 204–238.

[17] See Manning, *Hunters and Poachers*, 83–108, for a discussion of the politics and law of purlieu status.

dividends of the hunt as well as the judicial defence of this sacrificial order against contrary views of the forest.

The language of forest politics acquired its greatest ideological charge in the Star Chamber cases involving claims of purlieu.[18] In January 1608, Robert Quarles, Edward Carrowe, and a group of their neighbors from Romford were accused of a riotous hunt in Waltham Forest.[19] Quarles, Carrowe, and several other local gentlemen had chased and killed deer in Low Wood, on the eastern edge of the forest. According to the indictment, this uproarious affair had occurred despite full knowledge among partic005ipants of the king's desire to preserve Waltham's deer for his own "princely recreation and delight of hunting and chasing."[20] Quarles and Carrowe used claims of purlieu status in defence of their actions, asserting that the liberty of Havering had been "certain hundred years" earlier disafforested and freeholders given liberty to hunt on their own freeholds. These gentlemen of Romford had hunted only to "preserve their ancient liberties and inheritances" as forty-shilling freeholders in the purlieus of Waltham. At the same time, their words evoked the purlieu as a distinct form of neighborhood, for "time out of mind, purlieu men dwelling near together have used neighborly to meet and to hunt and course together, and to share amongst them such venison as they happened to kill with their greyhounds."[21] In response to the Star Chamber charge of ignoring "sundry speeches from your majesty's own royal mouth" aimed to preserve the "pleasures and delights" of Waltham for "any vacancy from the great and weighty affairs of the state," Sir William Smith of Theydon Mount, near Loughton Walk, asserted the purlieu liberties of his estate "to course the deer in his grounds homewards to the forest and to take the deer so killed for his own use, which by the laws of the forest he might lawfully do."[22] In 1609, this politics of the forest defeated John Manwood himself during his tenure as steward of Waltham. Manwood presented a bill against Richard Humble, a Southwark vintner and alderman of London, for "unlawful assemblies and uproars, most undutifully and unlawfully presuming to spoil and destroy your majesty's deer in the forest," but lost the case to

---

[18] A useful introduction to the history of purlieu is William Fisher, *The Forest of Essex* (London: Butterworths, 1887), 159–170.
[19] PRO: STAC 8/10/9, Sir Henry Hobart, Attorney General v. Robert Quarles and Edward Carrowe, esquires, 1608. This case does not include depositions, but the bill and answer at least offer a view from both sides of the affair.
[20] Ibid.
[21] Ibid. A neighborly association of purlieu hunters was also implied in PRO: STAC 8/211/21, John Manwood, steward of Waltham v. Richard Humble and Augustine Simpson, 1609, bill and answer.
[22] Ibid., 8/29/14, Sir Thomas Coventry, Attorney General v. Sir William Smith, 1622, bill and answer.

Humble's vigorous claims of purlieu status for his manor of Goseyes in the liberty of Havering.[23]

As we have seen, the royal demands on the forest reflected the political uses of the hunt as a masculine display of martial skill, but the forest accounts also reveal networks of influence crafted in part from a continuous and predictable circulation of venison. These venison networks were vital expressions of royal favor, constructed from the tokens of honor derived from the hunt. Yet the status of local gentlemen, such as Robert Quarles and Edward Carrowe, was equally dependent on participation in the cult of gentility expressed in the hunt. Both families ranked among the parish gentry in the vicinity of Romford. In 1607, Quarles possessed his own deer park and served as coroner of the liberty of Havering; Carrowe had formerly held the offices of coroner and chief constable of the liberty.[24] Other participants in the hunt, such as Nicholas Fookes and William Latham, were described as gentlemen; Latham's family had held the office of coroner during the late sixteenth century.[25] Peter Humble of Goseyes in Havering, prosecuted by John Manwood in 1609, served as the manorial bailiff in 1613.[26] Status and influence in these local networks could ascend to the court itself. William Smith, prosecuted alongside his father Sir William in 1622 and 1623, accompanied Prince Charles to Madrid in 1623 and subsequently received a knighthood.[27]

The informal hunts of influential local families were occasionally described in their written answers to Star Chamber charges. Robert Quarles, Edward Carrowe, Edmund Wallinger, and John Evans had met to hunt in Low Wood on 31 October 1607, killing and sharing three fallow deer: a pricket or two-year-old buck, a fawn, and a barren doe. In August 1607, Carrowe, Evans, and Robert Lyman had hunted in the wood with their greyhounds, killing a sorel or three-year-old buck. Lyman had joined a hunt in progress near his house at Noke, several miles southwest of Romford, the following October, only "coming in" for the killing of a pricket not far from his house. Richard Hilles and John Rucke allegedly joined this hunt in the same way, Rucke "being not far from his house, and

---

[23] Ibid., 8/211/21, Manwood v. Humble and Simpson, 1609; Morant, *History of Essex*, 1: 62–63.

[24] The local influence of the Quarles family figures prominently in Marjorie McIntosh, *A Community Transformed: The Manor and Liberty of Havering, 1500–1620* (Cambridge University Press, 1991), 376, 391–392.

[25] PRO: STAC 8/10/9, Hobart v. Quarles and Carrowe; McIntosh, *Community Transformed*, 425.

[26] PRO: STAC 8/211/21, Manwood v. Humble and Simpson, 1609; McIntosh, *Community Transformed*, 370, 423. In 1617, Humble held an impressive estate of 764 acres in the liberty of Havering.

[27] Ibid., 8/147/2, Elizabeth Finch v. William Smith, 1623, bill and (3) answers: answer of Sir William Smith the younger.

seeing two dogs running after a pricket, followed and found the pricket pulled down in Richard Hilles's ditch."[28] Sir William Smith of Theydon Mount and his sons, William and Thomas, customarily hunted in a group comprised of servants, such as their household cook Edward Norrington, and neighbors dwelling near the family seat at Hill Hall and in Theydon Garnon.[29] Smith, Quarles, and their companions used a claim of purlieu status to augment their claims to gentle status, based in part on their accustomed participation in the hunt. These local circles of hunters were quite common on the margins of forest societies and were inseparable from the codes of honor and gentility that defined local status and, not infrequently, the exercise of magistracy.

Although not defined in terms of "ancient liberties," the politics of copyholds and commons in the forest transcended local concerns once plaintiffs and defendants translated their disputes into the formal charges of Star Chamber bills and answers. This tendency to describe local conflict in terms of a broader polity marked the litigation between Sir Bernard Whetstone and his tenants in Woodford, eight miles northeast of London.[30] In 1622, Whetstone tried to use his judicial power as verderer of Waltham in the court of attachments or woodmote to override copyholders' claims to woodlands in Woodford. After his woodmote judged the trees in Rowden's Grove prejudicial to the covert for deer, Whetstone issued a court order in April asserting his possession and right to clear the grove as lord of the manor. On 28 April, Whetstone's workers felled fifty trees, the bark from the trees alone amounting to twelve cartloads worth £20. This enterprise resulted two weeks later in a violent affray between a gang led by Whetstone's son Bernard and, on the other side, the friends and relatives of Robert Hillary, who claimed Rowden's Grove as part of his copyhold. As local conflict became litigation, both the bill and answer in Star Chamber conceded the violence of this midnight confrontation on 13 May, but the dispute over its causes revealed strikingly different views of the forest, expressed in ideological terms. Whetstone in this case honored the primacy of the hunt in his stewardship of the forest, using the woodmote's recognition of his lordship in the manor of Woodford to strengthen his claims to property in its woodlands under the forest law. He sent his son to protect

[28] Ibid., 8/10/9, Hobart v. Quarles and Carrowe.
[29] Ibid., 8/29/14, Sir Thomas Coventry, Attorney General v. Sir William Smith, 1622, bill and answer; STAC 8/147/2, Elizabeth Finch v. William Smith, 1623, bill and (3) answers; Morant, *History of Essex*, I: 155–163; Manning, *Hunters and Poachers*, 74, 173.
[30] PRO: STAC 8/298/21, Sir Bernard Whetstone, verderer of Waltham v. Robert Hillary, gentleman, 1622, bill and (3) answers.

this property from the depredations of Hillary's rioters. Robert Hillary sent his nephew William to collect the harvest of his woodland. Although his copyhold did not convey the authority to take down trees, Hillary claimed the bark from the harvested timber as a customary dividend of his holding. Both groups described their own behavior in terms of a concern to protect "god's and his majesty's peace" and ascribed to the other a "warlike and riotous manner," inducing "terror" among the people, "contrary to the laws and statutes of the realm."[31] The complexity of this politics of forest uses – and especially its ideological dimensions – are more fully revealed in the detailed evidence of a dispute over Nazeing wood in 1622.

III

In June 1622 it was alleged, and perhaps even believed, in a small village in northwestern Essex that women were becoming masculine, men were becoming feminine, the commoners of the manor were hatching dreadful conspiracies against the king's peace, and the lord's officers were tainted by the most hideous moral corruption and disease. As crown and parliament debated the need for a war against the dark ranks of popery, local hatreds were expressed in terms of a general moral crisis. The local consequences of this crisis were ultimately brought before the court of Star Chamber for remedy, and the record of what was said in the court reveals a political world more often encountered on the eve of civil war, a generation later, than in the "stable consensual system" of the 1620s.[32] Although most would accept in some fashion that "resistance to Stuart innovations prompted the growth of national political consciousness," this consciousness is usually approached as a development of the Caroline regime.[33] Viewed from the perspective of civil war, it becomes a product of the political short term. To the extent that "political consciousness" is understood as a branch of parliamentary politics, its study has focused on the spread of newsbooks after 1626, on the custom of instructions to members of parliament, and especially on the many local petitions of the

---

[31] Ibid.

[32] Burgess, *Politics of the Ancient Constitution*, 115. A connection between the war debates of the early 1620s and a campaign for the reformation of manners, especially concern to protect conventional masculinity, is explored in Michael B. Young, *King James and the History of Homosexuality* (New York: New York University Press, 2000), 85–101.

[33] Anthony Fletcher, *The Outbreak of the English Civil War* (New York: New York University Press, 1981), xxv.

early 1640s.[34] Broader accounts of "popular politics" have stressed the influence of conflicts over forests, ship money, and religious innovation during the 1630s on local interpretations of the political crisis of the early 1640s.[35]

Although John Walter has uncovered libels that circulated among the godly in Colchester during the early 1620s, and Thomas Cogswell has stressed the importance of "an underground news network" in a broadly based opposition to the Spanish match, little is known of the processes and practices whereby a popular "political consciousness" was sustained before the late 1620s and 1630s, particularly in rural communities.[36] Discussion of these problems may benefit from work that has begun to map a common political culture in early modern England. A substantial literature has established the importance of protestantism and antipopery in understandings of the proper and improper uses of political authority; writing and print served to spread this view of politics and to promote its authority.[37] Glenn Burgess has suggested, if not explored, a diffuse interest in political knowledge based on the meaning of such concepts as "sedition."[38] Although many aspects of this political culture have become familiar, much less is known of practical politics. The evidence only rarely reveals how everyday disputes came to be expressed in general terms and symbols, and just as rarely discloses the occasions, institutions, and techniques used in the pursuit of power.[39] Difficult questions remain concerning the nature and scope of political memory, justifications of resistance to authority, and the institutions used to organize and direct political action. Judicial sources, and particularly cases that involved allegations of sedition, afford the best opportunities to study this practical politics because an account of actions in terms of their premeditation and organization was central to the

---

[34] Ibid., xxv–xxvi, 222–223; Richard Cust, "Politics and the Electorate in the 1620s," in Richard Cust and Ann Hughes (eds.), *Conflict in Early Stuart England: Studies in Religion and Politics, 1603–1642* (London: Longman, 1989), 134–167.

[35] Manning, *The English People and the English Revolution*, 13–58; Walter, *Understanding Popular Violence*, 18, 21–25, 81–84, 161–200; Beaver, "The Great Deer Massacre," *Journal of British Studies*, 38 (1999): 187–216.

[36] Walter, *Understanding Popular Violence*, 168–170; Thomas Cogswell, "England and the Spanish Match," in Cust and Hughes, *Conflict in Early Stuart England*, 110, 119–126.

[37] Tessa Watt, *Cheap Print and Popular Piety, 1550–1640* (Cambridge University Press, 1991), 88–90, 150–159, 178–179, 319; Peter Lake with Michael Questier, *The Antichrist's Lewd Hat: Protestants, Papists, and Players in Post-Reformation England* (New Haven: Yale University Press, 2002), xxvii, xxix–xxx, 713–715; Steven Justice, *Writing and Rebellion: England in 1381* (Berkeley: University of California Press, 1994), 17–22; Walter, *Understanding Popular Violence*, 18, 21–25.

[38] Burgess, *Politics of the Ancient Constitution*, 9.

[39] Justice, *Writing and Rebellion*, 156–168, and others have suggested the importance of customary church festivals as a structure used to express "the idiom of rural politics."

case for their seditious nature. A complete case, including the answers of defendants, offers some protection from the vested interest of plaintiffs in a judgment of sedition. Moreover, such records reflect the political significance of the courts, as their detailed rehearsals of events and speeches helped to sustain the memory of political action.

In this context, an analysis of participation, order, and meaning in particular local incidents is required to uncover political forms and dynamics. This section explores the nature of politics in the village of Nazeing in northwestern Essex during the 1620s, using the Star Chamber records of conflict between Edward Denny, lord of the manor of Nazeing, and a large group of copyholders. Although much of the political significance of this case lies in its conflicting accounts of events, many of those involved found its meaning in a commonly reported incident. On 14 June 1622, several copyholders struck William Gardiner, Denny's servant, at the village pound southeast of Nazeing. Denny had ordered Gardiner and several other servants and officers in Nazeing to drive the six-hundred-acre wood common that dominated the local landscape and economy, impounding the commoners' sheep and other cattle. The drive would precede the introduction of a stint or limit on the number of animals pastured on the common. Some of the copyholders perceived this stint as a violation of both custom and law, and their appearance at the pound to reclaim their animals resulted in a tense confrontation, a volatile milling of bodies in close space. According to Bennett Turner, when she asked Gardiner, who was keeping track of reclaimed animals by cutting marks on a stick with his knife, "how they should maintain themselves if he spoiled their cattle," Gardiner replied that "they should have maintenance in the house of correction."[40] Turner then picked up an axe near the pound and angrily struck its poles, Gardiner striding forward to stop her. Because of the knife and stick in his hand, Turner's friends feared Gardiner might hurt her. Sarah Grave used a pitchfork found beside the pound to restrain Gardiner, and others raised herding staves against him. In the ensuing struggle, Gardiner was roughed up, being hit several times on the head and shoulders. Although the women then released their sheep and cattle into the wood, the subsequent investigation and prosecutions focused on the nature and extent of Gardiner's injuries. According to John Leverton, Denny's servant, Gardiner "complained on his deathbed that the blows he had received [at the pound] would be the occasion of his death."[41] Denny described Gardiner in court as the victim of a conspiracy against lawful authority in Nazeing, a conspiracy hatched in "several assemblies," and he attributed the women's attack on Gardiner to incitement by their husbands and other male copyholders "clothed and disguised in woman's apparel."[42] When Gardiner died later in the year, Denny, as justice of the peace, ordered a coroner's inquest to establish the cause of death. A jury impaneled in Waltham, south of Nazeing, heard testimony from Gardiner's family, friends, and neighbors, found no "wound, bruise, scar, or blow" on the body, and concluded that Gardiner died of natural causes. After a conference with Denny, however, the coroner refused to record the jury's verdict, and the women of Nazeing were bound over to the assizes.[43] Surely the higher court would find the evidence of Denny's righteous cause on the body of his dead servant.

William Gardiner's ordeal began long before this beating at the hands of his neighbors. A more intimate violence, steeped in general beliefs regarding dishonor and sin, preceded and helps to explain the assault at the village pound. Gardiner's gonorrhea and its impact on his household had made the rounds for months in local rumor.[44] One of the defendants in Star Chamber, John Tay, insisted this disease had caused Gardiner's death, and some of Gardiner's "friends, kindred, and alliance" agreed in 1623 that Gardiner had been "long weak and full of diseases."[45] According to Tay, John Grave, another defendant, had carried a sample of Gardiner's urine to a London doctor, who refused to take the case because Gardiner "was rotten within and he could not get any credit by administering physic to him." Grave further disclosed that Gardiner had "run away from his wife" and was "so full of corruption that his laundress did loathe to wash his linen and could not endure the sight nor scent of his clothes." In his desperation, Gardiner had consulted a local healer, "one Scattergood's wife, who professes the curing of those that be burned." This term "burned" or "burning" conventionally referred to gonorrhea and thus carried among its meanings the ignominy of the biblical city destroyed for its corruption. Tay "heard it generally reported" that Denny had dismissed Gardiner from

[41] Ibid., Denny v. Tay, f. 72v; deposition of John Leverton of Waltham Cross, yeoman, 9 May 1623.
[42] Ibid., f. 75; Interrogatories of Plaintiff, 18 July 1622.
[43] Ibid., ff. 1r, 4r–5r, 8r–v, 11r; depositions of Jeremy Adam, carpenter, 10 May 1623, Robert Keyes, yeoman, 9 June 1623, Robert Graves, yeoman, 11 June 1623, and Thomas Becke, yeoman, 12 June 1623.
[44] Ibid., Edward Denny, Lord Denny of Waltham v. John Tay, gentleman, and others, 1622, ff. 4r–v, 51r, 56v; depositions of Robert Keyes, yeoman, 9 June 1623, John Campe, husbandman, 30 September 1622, and John Tay, gentleman, 4 October 1622.
[45] Ibid., Denny v. Tay, f. 4r–v; deposition of Robert Keyes, yeoman, 9 June 1623.

his service over the matter and that Gardiner "lay in an alehouse burned." Tay observed, "if the speeches were true which he heard of Gardiner, he would, if he were the women, meaning the defendants, tell his lordship that Gardiner might well say he was hurt by women but not by any so honest as they were."[46] These statements raised questions beyond the inquest's concern over cause of death, making Gardiner's sickness a general matter of integrity and honor, attributes essential to the exercise of authority and office. Moreover, during the judicial maneuvers of 1622 and 1623, debate over Gardiner's physical condition came to express distinct, conflicting views of community in Waltham Forest. Because the nature of forest communities and forest law was a matter of the royal prerogative, these debates and conflicts easily transcended narrowly local matters of political order. Both sides in this dispute used the investigation of bodily health and disease to justify their views of the forest and to render "natural" judgments regarding the morality of particular practices. By fighting their forest battles in the common symbolism of the body politic, Denny and his local opponents demonstrate how the meanings of such symbols and terms could become ideologically charged, expressing differences and even hatreds as fluently as common loyalties and mutual dependence.

The judicial politics of William Gardiner's condition overlay an equally contentious forest politics. This layer of conflict resulted from Nazeing's anomalous position in the vast forest of Waltham. Nazeing parish was included in the forest, enjoying the customary rights of pasture on the forest wastes and accepting the strictures of forest law as administered by its forest reeve and his assistants. Yet the six hundred acres of Nazeing wood common had been disafforested in 1285 as the culmination of a series of royal favors to its owners, the monks of Waltham Abbey. This "liberty" within the forest became the exclusive common pasture of the lord and tenants of Nazeing manor, leased from the crown by Anthony Denny, Edward's grandfather, after the dissolution of the monastery.[47] As a result of division of the wood common from the forest, farming in Nazeing acquired a distinctive political quality, based on local knowledge of the status of particular grounds under the forest law. Among lands excepted from this law, like the wood common, the 260 acres of Nazeing mead were held in severalty and mowed from Candlemas to Lammas, then opened to other commoners until All Saints; Nazeing marsh, on the western border of

---

[46] Ibid., f. 56v; deposition of John Tay, gentleman, 4 October 1622; see *Oxford English Dictionary* under "burning" and "gonorrhea" for meanings and references.

[47] Fisher, *The Forest of Essex*, 271–273; *VCH Essex*, 5: 142, 144–145.

the parish, contained more than 650 "cowleazes," conveying to their owners rights of pasture beyond those of the other commoners. Otherwise, the majority of the common lands in the parish, arable and pasture, came under the jurisdiction of forest law, in particular the "fence month" or "forbidden month." During these fifteen days on either side of the nativity of St. John or midsummer, on 24 June, forest law suspended rights of common pasture and many routine human activities in the forest to protect the fawning deer from disturbance.[48] Although generally the forest law protected rights of common pasture, during the fence month the law required its officers to drive the wastes and pastures of the forest, usually once before and once after midsummer, to remove the cattle that might harass the deer and damage the forest as a hunting preserve.

The forest politics on both sides of this dispute are readily apparent because the bill and the answer have survived in the case file. Both positions rested on a detailed knowledge of law and local circumstances. Denny clearly wanted to return Nazeing wood common to the jurisdiction of Waltham Forest. His decision to drive the common in June 1622 followed the order of forest law for the fence month, and his bill of complaint defined the wood common as "an ancient park for the preservation of deer and other cattle of the lords and owners."[49] Denny's politics reflected his dual status as lord of Nazeing manor and chief forester or master keeper of Newlodge Walk, just south of Nazeing in Waltham.[50] As long as the wood remained a common, Denny needed the consent of the other commoners to harvest timber for any purpose other than his own use. If the wood came under forest jurisdiction, however, he could begin to exploit the commercial market for timber.[51] Denny's influence in the parish would remain powerful as a result of his forest offices, despite the subjection of his park to the restrictions of forest law. The interest of the copyholders had no such protections. As forest pasture, Denny's park would be opened to cattle from other forest parishes, and the commoners of Nazeing manor would lose the exclusive control of the wood expressed in their franchise.[52] Denny could reasonably hope to profit even from failure. If Nazeing wood was not declared part of the forest, the cost of judicial battle would pressure the

[48] Fisher, *Forest of Essex*, 182, 272–273, 277–280; Powell, *VCH Essex*, 5: 145.

[49] PRO: STAC 8/125/16, Denny v. Tay, bill of information, 9 July 1622.

[50] PRO: SP 14/176, ff. 46–47, Edmondes to Conway, 9 December 1624.

[51] See PRO: STAC 8/125/16, Denny v. Tay, f. 56v; deposition of John Tay, gentleman, 4 October 1622, for this view of Denny's interest in the forest boundaries. Although the forest law restricted some commercial uses, Denny would have had more options if the liberty had been dissolved.

[52] See Fisher, *Forest of Essex*, 265–311, for transhumance on the common pastures of the forest.

commoners finally to accept Denny's proposed stint of the commons. Denny had complained of "the surcharge of the common by [the copy-holders and by] new erected cottagers and others, no tenants of the manor, nor having any right of common at all."[53] Although the tenants asserted their right of commons "without being stinted to any number or kind of cattle," Denny surely hoped the memory of their prosecution in Star Chamber would increase the prospects for success of future negotiations over a stint to restrict both commoners and cattle.[54] Prosecution served to intimidate tenants; an enforced stint of the commons would increase Denny's portion as lord of the manor. Moreover, a failure to incorporate the wood in the forest would leave Denny no less than owner of a rich franchise in the common. Lord Denny would have his political dividend regardless of how the Nazeing affair was resolved.

John Tay and the copyholders of Nazeing rejected Denny's view of Waltham Forest in their answer to the complaint, based on local knowledge of the law and the patchwork of forest land in Nazeing parish.[55] According to the copyholders, their wood common was neither part of Waltham Forest nor an "ancient park" in the forest, forest land by prescription, as Denny had claimed. These copyholds conveyed common pasture in the wood "at all times in the year at [their] several wills and pleasures, as belonging to their lands and tenements, without any stint of the cattle." Denny had driven the wood common, "without any lawful right," only "to molest, vex, and weary" his tenants, "hoping to draw [them] to some composition rate touching the common, to stint it, and to divide and enclose it, conceiving, as it is true, that these defendants, being poor for the most part, should thereby be compelled to relinquish their several rights, whose livelihoods much depend on the common." According to this view, Denny had no desire to preserve the wood as a park for deer, a project likely to appeal to James himself as central to the forest law, but rather planned to enclose the wood and to depopulate the village of Nazeing, "in execution whereof [Denny] had already cut and sold unlawfully the principal oaks and diverse hawthornes by which, in the acorns and otherwise, [his tenants] of the manor had much relief." In this "great and universal oppression," Denny subjected his tenants to "diverse suits at law" as well as "unfitting and threatening speeches to dispark the wood, lay it into Waltham forest,

---

[53] PRO: STAC 8/125/16, Denny v. Tay, bill of information, 9 July 1622.

[54] See ibid., ff. 2r–v, 6r–v, 9r–v; depositions of Robert Keyes, yeoman, 9 June 1623; Robert Graves, yeoman, 11 June 1623; Thomas Becke, yeoman, 12 June 1623, for the absence of any customary stint for the commoners in Nazeing wood.

[55] The following is based on PRO: STAC 8/125/16, Denny v. Tay, answer of defendants, 15 July 1622.

and convert it into a warren." A legitimate drift was a manorial concern and required a "competent number of the ancient tenants," who policed the common themselves. This system "pained every tenant and commoner that does not set his own mark on every particular of his cattle commoning in the wood and has besides provided a town mark, whereby his lordship may easily discern the tenants' cattle from waifs and estrays and impound them in his lawful pound, not in the pen in the wood, which is no lawful pound."[56] If a surcharge had occurred, Denny was responsible, having allowed his friends, his bailiff Thomas Beck, keepers of his deer, and his tenants in Nazeingbury, southwest of the village proper, "though not tenants of the manor to usurp the common of the wood." Denny had oppressed and intimidated his tenants; his scheme to include the wood common in the forest would damage the local economy and community and, ultimately, Waltham Forest itself.

This forest politics helps to explain the differing interpretations of events during the drifts, especially the violence done to William Gardiner. Denny viewed local opposition to his plans for the wood common, the resistance to the drifts, and the attack on Gardiner as movements in a local faction's pursuit of its own selfish interests. "Seditious persons to the number of fifty or more" had premeditated a series of abuses and insubordinations, ending in the attack on his servant.[57] On 7 June, this "extraordinary multitude," mostly "strangers or dwellers in new erected cottages and diverse other seditious persons," had "assembled in unlawful manner and plotted together to resist, by force of arms and strong hand, the driving or survey-ing the park or any course for reforming of abuses." A conventional arsenal of "long staves, forest bills, swords, guns, and such like weapons, as well invasive as defensive," made this crowd into a militia, and the militia then "marched to Nazeing wood and lay in ambush, according to their con-federacy." After attacking Denny's officers to halt the drift, this militia had menaced a constable, and "for diverse days, these riotous and disordered persons marched up and down Nazeing, arrayed in this most insolent manner, vaunting and bragging of their exploit, threatening to kill all that should come near, either to proceed in the drift or question their misdemeanor," and generally striking "a great terror and amazement." On 14 June, Denny's attempt to restore order and to complete the drift had resulted in a second battle of Nazeing wood. During the fight, his servant

---

[56] The forest officers also required these "town marks" to identify cattle properly pastured on the forest wastes. See Fisher, *Forest of Essex*, 273, 299–301.

[57] PRO: STAC 8/125/16, Denny v. Tay, bill of information, 9 July 1622.

William Gardiner "was struck down in a swoon" and, though "unable to resist, was dragged in such cruel and barbarous manner that he lies dangerously sick and in peril never to recover his former strength." According to Denny, these "tumults" reflected a concerted plan of "sedition and rebellion" against an authority perceived as the enemy of a factious design to ruin the commons. The copyholders' actions had broad *implications* for the king's peace but were *motivated* by selfish local interests. Although Denny's account stressed the copyholders' power to plan and execute action on a significant scale, politics conceived in this way could speak only indirectly on matters of principle. Denny, on the other hand, had acted to defend the principles of order and commonwealth.

In their answer, the copyholders denied allegations of sedition and stressed the spontaneity of their actions in the wood.[58] The violence had resulted, at least in part, from confusion and fear. Because Denny's actions had departed from custom, his tenants in Nazeing could not understand their authority. According to custom, the lord of Nazeing manor was permitted to keep only deer in the wood common. Sheep and other cattle were not his concern, and the copyholders policed the common themselves alongside other complicated intercommoning arrangements in the parish.[59] Moreover, Denny's servants made the drifts at short notice at "unseasonable times in the year" and never consulted "the ancient tenants of the manor." The drifts had avoided authority's accustomed places, animals being confined in "a pen in the wood" rather than in the village pound. According to the answer, diverse of the tenants' sheep had been "lamed and killed" as a result of this questionable "chasing" of cattle from the common. A justifiable fear of further injury to their cattle from "heat" had led the wives of some of the copyholders, "their husbands being from home," to recover their animals from the pen after the second drift on 14 June. These women had walked to the pen in as

lawful, peaceable, and quiet manner as they could, some of them with small walking staves or sticks, and some of them with such other things as came next to hand, but none of them armed as the [bill of complaint] alleged, to fetch away their cattle, without any manner of plot, no two of them knowing of any such occasion until the instant of their coming to the pen.

Violence erupted in William Gardiner's disordered attack. He advanced toward the women at the pen "with his knife drawn and his staff heaved up," and they had defended themselves. If Gardiner had suffered any

[58] Ibid., answer of defendants, 15 July 1622.   [59] Fisher, *Forest of Essex*, 182, 272–273, 277–280.

permanent injury, it was because his "very lewd and lascivious life" had resulted in "such a disease as with modesty they cannot express, which is his great hurt." In this account, Gardiner's diseased mind had transformed the vagaries of chance into misfortune, and the "lawful" and "peaceable" behavior of the villagers had thus ended in violence.

An understandable focus on the Caroline forest eyres has tended to blur the forest politics of the 1610s and 1620s. In 1617, James's plan to enlarge Theobalds Park caused violent disputes over access to commons and fears of enclosure in Cheshunt, a few miles southwest of Nazeing in Hertfordshire. Sir Fulke Greville, Chancellor of the Exchequer, complained that a "shower of shrews" had harassed the royal surveyor, Robert Treswell, as he attempted to complete his survey of local farms in Cheshunt.[60] Alongside local fears of the king's intentions, suspicions of Edward Denny lay behind this reaction. As lord of Waltham manor, where Cheshunt farmers contested rights of common in Waltham marsh, Denny was suspected of a scheme to enclose the disputed commons. As a result, the new enclosures for Theobalds Park "were much opposed by the people," who only relented "on lord Denny's assurance that he was enclosing nothing for himself and that they should lose nothing but have grounds given in exchange" for their commons.[61] Denny's involvement in a new survey of Waltham Forest only increased suspicions, as the lieutenant of Waltham responsible for the survey, Sir Thomas Edmondes, also handled the negotiations for new land in Theobalds as treasurer of the royal household.[62] In April 1617, when Denny and other forest officers started to survey the boundaries of Waltham, "the country began to mutiny, growing jealous of some further intention of enclosing their commons."[63] Greville advised Denny to suspend the survey until the work was finished at Theobalds and warned the Privy Council "how easily this tight sea of busy people is raised up with every wind, so as a tender proceeding with them can be no prejudice."[64] Denny's view of the forest jurisdiction in Nazeing in 1622 would seem to confirm this anxiety for the security of the commons, and local responses to the drift of the wood common become part of a major Jacobean political wrangle over the uses and meanings of the forest. Although Greville's unflattering reference to "busy people" in Waltham reveals his awareness of considerable practical

---

[60] *CSPD, Reign of James I*, 9 [1611–1618]: 462; Page and Round, *VCH Essex*, 2: 619.
[61] *CSPD, James I*, 9: 466; Powell, *VCH Essex*, 5: 157, 163; Manning, *Hunters and Poachers*, 205–207.
[62] Fisher, *Forest of Essex*, 36–37, 118–119.
[63] *CSPD, James I*, 9: 462; Fisher, *Forest of Essex*, 37; Page and Round, *VCH Essex*, 2: 619.
[64] Fisher, *Forest of Essex*, 37.

political activity, only fragmentary evidence survives to suggest how "the country" sustained this contest during the late 1610s and early 1620s.

According to a settlement of the disputed wood common in 1651, Nazeing parish contained 101 "ancient houses," a minimum of perhaps 480 inhabitants.[65] If these figures are accepted as rough estimates for the 1620s, the forty villagers cited as witnesses by the plaintiff and defendants, and the many others indirectly involved in the case as bystanders, servants, jurors, or sureties, become a substantial proportion of the adult population. A complex political system, defined by customary meeting sites, established institutional forms, and a network of local relationships, sustained the movements of this "tight sea." At some moments, this system was indistinguishable from forms of neighborliness. Before Denny's second drift on 14 June, Sarah Grave, one of those implicated alongside her husband in the attack on Gardiner, had visited the house of John Forde, another defendant, "on her own occasions and to speak with him and his wife to see if Denny's servants had made any drift of their cattle and sheep."[66] John Grave and John Forde were recognized as "tenants of the manor of Nazeing," clearly differentiated in status from the "strangers or dwellers in new erected cottages" accused of the disorders in Denny's bill of complaint.[67] Where the wood common was concerned, the tenants acted as a community of the propertied in Nazeing, and their deliberations in this case tended to exclude their poorer neighbors. John Tay, a local "gentleman" whose house bordered the wood common, described his "conference" before the drifts "with some of Denny's tenants" in Nazeing churchyard, a conference that included Robert Graves and Robert Keyes, "ancient" tenants aged seventy-one and seventy-three, respectively, whose depositions for both the plaintiff and defendants testified to their local authority.[68] This informal conference "concerning his lordship's selling away of timber in Nazeing wood" involved a substantial but unspecified number of tenants and may have followed routine church services in the parish. Tay revealed "that he was advised by counsel

---

[65] This agreement probably included the settlements of Nazeing and Nazeingbury, consolidated in the Denny estate and conveyed to James Hay, Earl of Carlisle, after his marriage to Edward Denny's daughter. See Northamptonshire Record Office: Wake Collection, Part 1, 213: Settlement of the Manor and Rectory of Nazeing, 1642; Powell, *VCH Essex*, 5: 141–144, 145. I thank John Walter for his abstract of the former document.

[66] PRO: STAC 8/125/16, Denny v. Tay, f. 37r; deposition of Sara Grave, 31 August 1622.

[67] Ibid., ff. 2r, 6r, 9r; depositions of Robert Keyes, 9 June 1623; Robert Graves, 11 June 1623; and Thomas Becke, 12 June 1623; bill of information, 9 July 1622.

[68] Ibid., ff. 2r, 6r, 56r–v, 67v, 70v; depositions of Robert Keyes, 9 April 1623 and 9 June 1623; Robert Graves, 4 April 1623 and 11 June 1623; and John Tay, 4 October 1622.

and had also read a statute concerning commons and found by that statute that no lord nor owner of any common might fell any manner of wood whatsoever in the common, other than for his own use, without the consent of the tenants that had right of common there."[69] Such informal meetings clearly served important political ends. Tay offered crucial information concerning the status of the wood common under the law. He advised the other tenants to "take counsel" on this information, and the literacy revealed by the depositions suggests the tenants' capacity to follow this lead.[70] Performances in the meeting doubtless solidified local reputations for leadership and integrity. According to Thomas Wilkinson and John Adams, Denny had declared Tay was "sicke but said he would not have him die until [Denny] had proved him a knave and left him not worth a groat." Tay responded passionately that "he neither had offended god, nor the king, nor his law, nor [Denny], but said that if his lordship spent his manor of Nazeing he should never prove him a knave, nor should make him not worth a groat, saying he would be still an honest man and have a groat in his purse when his lordship had spent what he would."[71] At this point, John Grave told the company of Gardiner's sickness, perhaps beginning a discussion that subsequently became a pillar of their answer to Denny's bill of complaint. Moreover, the informality of the meeting itself, as Tay addressed a diverse group of "tenants and some others in Nazeing churchyard," tended to promote the interrelationship of local neighborhood and a community of the propertied among the tenants, a relationship that became tactically significant in the deliberations of the manorial court. In practical politics, a faction of "tenants" became convinced of their authority to speak and act for the neighborhood as a whole.

Although recent work has approached manorial institutions as generic "forms of control" distinct from "political institutions," the experience of villagers in Nazeing during the 1610s and 1620s indicates the critical importance of the manor in their politics.[72] The manorial court served indisputably as the means to police and punish routine misdemeanors related to the wood common. According to local "custom," a group of "six or eight" of the "ancient tenants" acting on behalf of the manor court,

---

[69] Ibid., f. 56r–v; deposition of John Tay, 4 October 1622.
[70] Of the forty-three depositions taken in the case, eighteen (42 per cent) were signed. Of the men deposed, eighteen of twenty-eight (64 per cent) signed their statements. Of the women, all fifteen made marks rather than signing.
[71] PRO: STAC 8/125/16, Denny v. Tay, f. 56r–v; deposition of John Tay, 4 October 1622.
[72] Marjorie McIntosh, *Controlling Misbehavior in England, 1370–1600* (Cambridge University Press, 1998), 33.

held "at the will and discretion of the steward and ancient tenants of the manor," assessed and punished by fines any surcharge of cattle on the common.[73] Yet the court reached beyond such offences to determine "that tenants of the manor that are tenants of tenements of late erection have no right of common in the wood," thus reinforcing the political status as well as the economic power of the "ancient tenants."[74] As the most important local forum, more suited to the holding of discussions than the weekly assemblies in the parish church, the court served as a point of communication and negotiation between the lord and his officers and the tenantry. Before the drifts in June 1622, Denny's steward Lane used a session of the court to approach the "copyhold tenants" with a proposition "to sever, divide, and impropriate the wood and to enclose part of it to lord Denny's use and the rest to remain for the ancient copyhold tenants, either in severalty, every tenant to have a part, or the tenants to have that remainder in common."[75] After some deliberation, "when lord Denny understood that the copyhold tenants refused to consent to such division of the wood, he threatened to pull down the pale and suffer the wood to become forest or else to make a warren for conies."[76] The manorial court exercised a decisive influence on matters of belonging and status in the political community, witnessed such important initiatives as Denny's proposal to divide the wood common, and could become a site of political confrontation. Villagers found in the court a school of participation and experience vital in local politics. Robert Keyes had known the local customs of Nazeing and the procedures of its manorial court "by long observing" prior to his service on the jury of inquest that thwarted Denny's attempt to link William Gardiner's death to the disorders in Nazeing wood. Similarly, Robert Graves, a local elder cited as witness by both sides but opposed to Denny's view of the wood common as a part of Waltham Forest, "had for many years served as a juror at the courts held for the manor of Nazeing."[77]

Although Denny's initiative in the manor court and his circulation of rumors unflattering to John Tay reveal his appreciation of this local style of politics, his neighbors in Nazeing would have used the term "great man" to differentiate Denny's power and political resources from their own. Denny

---

[73] PRO: STAC 8/125/16, Denny v. Tay, ff. 2v, 6r, 9r; depositions of Robert Keyes, 9 June 1623; Robert Graves, 11 June 1623; and Thomas Becke, 12 June 1623.

[74] Ibid., f. 9r; deposition of Thomas Becke, 12 June 1623.

[75] Ibid., ff. 2v–3r, 6v, 9v; depositions of Robert Keyes, 9 June 1623; Robert Graves, 11 June 1623; and Thomas Becke, 12 June 1623.

[76] Ibid., f. 3r; deposition of Robert Keyes, 9 June 1623.

[77] Ibid., ff. 2v, 6r; depositions of Robert Keyes, 9 June 1623; and Robert Graves, 11 June 1623.

consistently carried the power and authority of formal office into his local dealings. As the chief forester of Newlodge Walk, Denny's threat "to pull down the pale and suffer Nazeing wood to become forest" evoked the substantial local power of the hierarchy of forest courts.[78] As justice of the peace for Essex, Denny could direct his servant to order John Tison, constable of Nazeing, to attend the drifts in Nazeing wood, although Tison seems to have taken his time, reporting that "all matters were ended, and all parties gone" before he arrived on the scene.[79] Denny's authority as justice also enabled him to summon the coroner to Waltham after William Gardiner's death and launch an investigation of its circumstances. Denny pressed so hard for a verdict placing the blame for Gardiner's death on the copyholders of Nazeing that the coroner, after reportedly consulting Denny, refused to record the jury's verdict of death by natural causes, claiming that Denny was "a great man and would complain against him" and that therefore "it was good for the coroner to walk straight."[80] Because Denny embodied the authority of office, the copyholders defined all the more carefully and explicitly the lawfulness of their responses to his actions, confronting him not as an association of individuals but as a community, confident in its possession of its customs under the law and sure of its broader integrity and loyalty to the king. This conflict between a "great man" and the "country" produced statements of principle as well as a politics of institutional forms.

Most historians would concede the increasing volume and distribution of news during the early seventeenth century as well as the tendency of much of the news to represent politics in terms of conflicts between opposed sides.[81] The contrast between "great man" and "country" political styles in Nazeing not only offers early evidence of this kind of adversarial politics in a rural setting, but also illustrates how the conflicts over land use and symbols of the forest, expressed in terms of these styles, could evoke profound concepts of good and evil, justice and oppression, loyalty and sedition, widening considerably the distance between political poles in the course of dispute. Both Denny and the copyholders used terms current in a discourse of national moral and political crisis to depict their local disagreement. In 1620, pamphlets had decried the "monstrous" assumption of

[78] Ibid., f. 3r; deposition of Robert Keyes, 9 June 1623.
[79] Ibid., f. 2r; deposition of John Tison, 16 May 1623.
[80] The accounts of Denny's response to the coroner and jury are ibid., ff. 1r–v, 4v; depositions of Jeremy Adam, 10 May 1623; and Robert Keyes, 9 June 1623.
[81] Richard Cust, "News and Politics in Early Seventeenth Century England," *Past and Present*, 112 (1986): 60–90.

masculine clothing by women and feminine attire by men, describing the inversion as "an infection that emulates the plague."[82] Despite consistent denials in the depositions, Denny's interrogatories implied that the women of Nazeing had been incited to attack William Gardiner by their husbands and other male copyholders "clothed and disguised in woman's apparel."[83] Both strains of plague apparently had struck the village, as this account featured a usurpation of leadership by the women involved in the attack and the monstrous adoption of feminine dress by local men. Although the direct influence of the pamphlets is impossible to prove, a more important point concerns Denny's evident conviction that the tenants identified as his opponents were "seditious" and therefore *must* be guilty of even more heinous offences. In like fashion, the tenants of Nazeing represented the "oppressions" of their lord as symptoms of a deeper corruption. Another pamphlet printed in 1620 had described the general crisis of morality and order in terms of "hic mulier," the forms of gender transgression and inversion criticized by earlier tracts, and had blamed the malaise on "senseless landlords" devoid of conscience, among other enemies of the commonwealth.[84] According to the tenants, William Gardiner stood for a similar replacement of authority by lust and power. Denny's schemes for the wood common had passed into the hands of this servant, who had "run away from his wife, full of corruption, and lay in an alehouse burned."[85] In this account, the "oppressions" of a lord reflected his deeper failure to select officers of integrity. The drifts of Nazeing wood in June 1622 stood to notions of good lordship as adultery stood to the principles of a well-ordered household. Both Denny and his tenants thus perceived profound moral concepts at stake in their dispute over the wood common, and the opposed sides embodied visceral assessments of social health and disease.

The evidence of conflict in Nazeing reveals the remarkable depth and sophistication of the "politics beyond parliament" during the 1610s and 1620s. This dispute over a wood common is precisely the kind of conflict often treated as a clash of economic interests in a rural politics defined by rival claims to resources. Yet the conflict in Nazeing suggests it was not only the intractable problems of reformation in the church, or the fiscal exigencies of the Stuart regime, that elicited a pattern of opposed sides and

---

[82] Anonymous, *Hic Mulier* (London, 1620), A3r, Bv–B2r; Anonymous, *Haec Vir or the Womanish Man: Being an Answer to a Late Book Entitled Hic Mulier* (London, 1620), Cr–C3r.

[83] PRO: STAC 8/125/16, Denny v. Tay, f. 75; interrogatories of plaintiff, 18 July 1622.

[84] Anonymous, *Muld Sacke* (London, 1620), Cv.

[85] PRO: STAC 8/125/16, Denny v. Tay, f. 56v; deposition of John Tay, gentleman, 4 October 1622.

political styles. A dispute over the enclosure of a wood common evoked contradictory understandings of forest symbols, distinct "country" and "great man" political styles and institutional tactics, and a political discourse that defined the opposed sides in terms of loyalty and sedition, justice and oppression, integrity and corruption, good and evil, that expressed the most significant criteria of political belonging. On both sides, the account of Gardiner's ordeal echoed the dominant concern over popery in the 1620s, as this concern often made a domestic crisis of morality and social order a chief cause of English vulnerability to popish stratagems. The effectiveness of "country" politics, and the capacity to sustain success across generations, are worthy of note. Denny's tenants succeeded for many years in opposing his schemes to divide and exploit Nazeing wood. Only in 1651 did James Hay, Earl of Carlisle, Denny's successor as lord of Nazeing, manage to negotiate a settlement.[86]

The evidence from Nazeing has equally important implications for understanding popular politics on the eve of civil war, particularly the "riotous assembly" of John Browne and his companions in April 1642. This form of political action and assertion of "no law settled" must be understood as a moment in a much longer history, indeed a "tradition," of political expression in the forest.[87] If claims of purlieu status often reflected efforts to negotiate gentility, the view of the forest in terms of its commons suggested an alternative understanding of forest law. According to this view, a forest comprised multiple claims to resources, and the justice of forest law lay in its power to adjudicate the legitimate claims of crown, nobility, and commoners, its power to protect both covert and pasture, deer and cattle. The most important sites of negotiation therefore shifted from the purlieus of the forest to the large wood commons, such as Nazeing wood, exempted by royal prerogative itself from the strict code of the forest. In 1622, this view of the forest and its boundaries surfaced in this vicious suit between Edward Denny and his copyholders in Nazeing. Although the immediate cause of the suit was the confrontation over the drift of Nazeing wood, the underlying controversy concerned Denny's claim that this wood amounted to no more than a park within Waltham Forest, subject to limitations of pasture prescribed by forest law and especially to the restrictions on the pasture of sheep, perceived as a great

---

[86] Powell, *VCH Essex*, 5: 145. According to the settlement, 100 acres of the wood common were reserved for the lord, and the remaining 420 acres were secured to trustees for the tenants of 101 "ancient houses" of Nazeing.

[87] HLRO: Main Papers, 1509–1700: 2 May 1642; HMC, *Fifth Report*, 20.

destroyer of the covert.[88] Denny's tenants viewed the wood as their free common, a liberty carved by prerogative from the forest that covered most of the manor and parish. As in purlieu cases, this dispute, and the violent satire of the protest in Nazeing, suggest an informed and principled understanding of the politics of forest law in local societies under its jurisdiction. The dispute unfolded in the context and terms of forest law, despite its rejection of the view that reserved primary place in the forest for matters related to the hunt. The festive violence of the Whitsunweek "revolt" in 1622 expressed a sophisticated idiom of protest in the forest that helps to account for the lawyerly taunts of 1642 and for the prison revels anticipated by Browne and his friends.

IV

The evidence from Waltham and elsewhere reveals a contentious Jacobean forest politics, routinely conceived in terms of a broader commonwealth. As the crown and such influential lords as Denny made greater use of the Star Chamber court to defend their interests in Waltham, these local disputes often came to resemble a competition of sides to express and serve the best interests of this commonwealth; it was not unusual for those involved to justify their behavior in terms of abstract political concepts or principles. In this limited sense, the Caroline regime of the late 1620s and 1630s did not *invent* ideological conflict in Waltham and other forests; such conflict existed in the 1610s and early 1620s.[89] Charles and his law officers did facilitate a diffusion of this forest politics through their revival of such institutions as the swanimote courts and courts of justice seat, disused in Waltham before 1630.[90] The revival of these courts in 1630 created a new set of arenas for the forest politics so evident in Nazeing and elsewhere during the 1620s. Much more than the occasional though spectacular case in Star Chamber, the revival of forest courts made the terms of forest politics – its conflicts and oppositions – more familiar among the neighborhoods or "walks" of Waltham Forest. John Browne's assertion of "no law settled" in 1642 suggests a view of law and tradition as negotiable aspects of a "settlement" rather than immemorial fixtures. As the statement of a moment in the history of forest politics, this view reflected the shifting

---

[88] PRO: STAC 8/125/16, f. 78, bill of information.
[89] Hammersley, "Revival of the Forest Laws," 88–89; Sharp, *In Contempt of All Authority*, 85–86, 208–9; Sharpe, *Personal Rule of Charles I*, 116–120, 242–245. Hammersley and Sharpe both argue for the rather haphazard nature of royal forest policy in the 1630s.
[90] Fisher, *Forest of Essex*, 80–81.

pattern of institutions used to adjudicate conflicts in Waltham and to determine forest justice during the 1630s.

This new forest regime had a substantial impact on local officers and societies in Waltham. Although the court of attachments held sessions during the 1620s, serving the local interests of such forest officers as the verderer Sir Bernard Whetstone of Woodford in 1622, the swanimote and court of justice seat had been discontinued.[91] On 14 September 1630, the crown revived the forest law and its courts through an impressive court of justice seat held at Stratford Langthorne, composed of courtiers and influential local families. Sir Thomas Edmondes presided as deputy of Robert Bertie, Earl of Lindsey, steward of Waltham; Edward Denny, Earl of Norwich, in perhaps his last public act before his death two weeks later, attended as chief forester of Epping, New Lodge, and Chingford Walks; Sir Robert Quarles, his former disputes over purlieu liberties behind him, now appeared in the court as chief forester of Leyton and West Hainault Walks.[92] Apart from the potent spectacle of this great assembly, the session of the swanimote court that accompanied the court of justice seat presented 396 offenders against the forest laws for punishment. But this court did not exceed the revival of tradition, using customary institutions to enforce the law within forest boundaries established in 1301. The forest eyre of 1634, famously reasserting bounds unknown in Waltham since the thirteenth century, challenged reasonable views of precedent and tradition.[93] Robert Rich, Earl of Warwick, who attended this court presided over by his brother Henry Rich, Earl of Holland, as chief justice of the forest, reported to the Council the provocative speech of Sir John Finch, the Attorney General, on Thursday, 2 October, to the effect that

he was come to let [Holland] and the country know he had found an ancient document of Edward I, whereby the bounds and meets of the forest of Essex had been from Bowbridge to Catway bridge in length, and in breadth from the river Thames to Stanstreet, and he would know how his master had lost every inch of it; and addressed also the lawyers there present, that if they were there for the country they should do well to prepare themselves for their defence.[94]

This "violent" speech served as a keynote for the presentation of 455 offences from the swanimote court's session in October 1634, and four

[91] PRO: STAC 8/298/21, Whetstone v. Hillary, bill and (3) answers; Fisher, *Forest of Essex*, 76, 80.
[92] PRO: C99/143, Perambulations of Waltham Forest: Rolls of Presentments in Swanimote Court, 14 September 1630; Fisher, *Forest of Essex*, 81; "Sir Anthony Denny (1501–1549)" in *Dictionary of National Biography*, 823–824. Edward Denny was Sir Anthony's grandson.
[93] Hammersley, "Revival of Forest Laws," 88–89; *CSPD, Charles I*, 7: 227–228; Fisher, *Forest of Essex*, 18–51.
[94] *CSPD, Charles I*, 7: 227–228; Fisher, *Forest of Essex*, 38–44.

years later, in 1638, the swanimote continued to manage a large and diverse caseload of 342 offences. This robust figure declined to eleven presentments in June 1639, and dwindled to a mere three in June 1640, as the administrative record of the forest courts all but vanished.[95]

The revival of the Waltham Forest courts in September 1630 resulted in the prosecution of numerous offences committed many years before, sometimes dating back to the early seventeenth century. John Browne, leader of the attacks in May 1642 on royal deer in Newlodge Walk, was presented and fined for a cottage and one-rood enclosure in Walthamstowe built in 1623 and for possession of an unexpeditated mongrel.[96] Because of the parish's proximity to London, land use in Walthamstow during the early seventeenth century had conformed more to the demands of the urban market than to the strictures of forest law. In 1607, John Russell had built a brick kiln on the waste in the manor of Higham Bensted in the north of the parish and, in 1621, had received a licence from the lord, Sir William Rowe, to dig pits for clay on three adjoining acres.[97] In 1630, the swanimote fined Russell for these activities and attempted to close his pits "for the making of brick and tile, which are open and very dangerous."[98] A widow named Overrell was presented for her occupation of a cottage on the waste in Walthamstow Sarum, one of four manors in the parish, built in 1600, thirty years before this session of the swanimote.[99] Among erstwhile defenders of the forest in the 1620s, Sir Bernard Whetstone of Woodford was fined for his exploitation of Hall Grove in Woodford, three acres of woodland that Whetstone had used for timber and pasture.[100] In this way, the revived court clearly signaled its willingness to confront vested interests in the forest and to transform unlawful uses into revenue through fines. In Chingford, Thomas Boothby had kept dogs harmful to the deer during the 1620s through the alleged complicity of the underkeeper of the walk. In 1630, the swanimote court fined Thomas's son Robert Boothby, esquire, for his illegal gun and brace of greyhounds, for his unlicensed gravel pits on the waste in Woodford, and, significantly, for a newly built house occupied

---

[95] Courts of justice seat were held for Waltham in 1630 and 1634; the sharp decline in presentments may reflect a tendency of prosecutions to cluster in the traditional three to four year intervals between sessions of the major forest court. See Fisher, *Forest of Essex*, 84–85. The records of the Waltham swanimote courts are among the Chancery papers for forest proceedings during the 1630s. The figures for presentments are based on PRO: C99/138–145, Perambulations of Waltham Forest: Rolls of Presentments in Swanimote Courts, 1630–1640.

[96] PRO: C99/144, Perambulations of Waltham: Presentments in Swanimote, 14 September 1630, m 1.

[97] W. R. Powell (ed.), *VCH Essex* (London: Oxford University Press, 1973), 6: 259, 268.

[98] PRO: C99/144, Perambulations of Waltham: Presentments in Swanimote, 14 September 1630, m 1.

[99] Ibid.   [100] Ibid., mm 3, 4.

by the keeper of Chingford Walk, Robert Sawyer.[101] The court did not spare high-ranking offenders and undertook several exemplary prosecutions. In Chigwell, Samuel Harsnett, Archbishop of York, was fined for building a house and for "cutting and stubbing the underwood and bushes" in Bishop's Grove.[102] Elizabeth Heneage, Countess of Winchelsea, was presented for constructing a house and brick enclosure in Epping and for failing to fence the eight acres of Orange Grove there, "suffering the grove to be spoiled with cattle." She also paid a penalty for "trestling" and spoiling two hedgerows on a three-acre parcel of land known as Gladwin's Farm in Waltham, leased from her friend Lionel Cranfield, Earl of Middlesex.[103] The swanimote and forest eyre of 1630 were nothing if not scrupulous in attention to detail.

Although vested interests came under attack in 1630, the revived forest courts recognized the traditional boundaries of the forest. Keepers in Waltham had long tolerated the hunting dogs kept by many local families; the swanimote's ambitious survey of this problem in 1630 confined its inquiry to customary forest hamlets. Among the owners of 173 unexpeditated dogs presented and fined in this survey from Waltham, Epping, Lambourn, Chigwell, Loughton, Chingford, Leyton, Wansted, and West Ham, only the two presentments from West Ham in Leyton purlieu exceeded the statutory bounds of the forest established in 1641.[104] In 1634, this revival became revolution, as the crown counsel, Sir John Finch, building on successes in the Forest of Dean, used the forest eyre in Waltham to incorporate most of the county in a new forest of Essex.[105] As described by the Earl of Warwick, this eyre began quietly enough; the Lord Warden and other officers "delivered up their horns to the justice and oyer on their knees" and handed in the swanimote's presentments "for hunting, building, cutting woods or not fencing them, for keeping dogs unexpeditated, and for making warrens in the forest." Warwick's comments suggest a local acceptance of the revived swanimote, but Finch's performance on the following day resulted in confusion and protest against his use of the forest eyre to attack and afforest the county. As Warwick assured the council,

if I had had the spirit of divination what mr. attorney would have been at by enlarging the bounds of the forest, myself and many of the lords and freeholders of the country would have been there with their evidences and charters to have given satisfaction to that court not to extend their bounds, as we might still enjoy with

---

[101] Ibid., mm 3, 12.   [102] Ibid., mm 20, 21.   [103] Ibid., mm 17, 18.   [104] Ibid., mm 25–27.
[105] Hammersley, "Revival of Forest Laws," 100–101; Fisher, *Forest of Essex*, 37–47.

quietness the possessions of our ancestors, which had been out of the forest for 330 years.[106]

Warwick's brother, as chief justice of the forest, adjourned the court until 8 April 1635, "wherein he would hear what the country can say in their defence," but in the final session Finch, now Chief Justice of Common Pleas and sitting as a judge of his own argument, delivered the decision of all the judges to enforce the new boundaries.[107] In his description of "grievous complaints" against this verdict, John Rushworth later reported a local account of

a drove of calves passing through [Stratford] to London, and, when they were at the open place in the town over against the justice seat, they sullenly made a stand and a great bleating, with such a united and unmeasurable noise as the court could not hear themselves to declare judgment, as if the dumb creatures understood that sentence was to be pronounced against the inhabitants in the forest in whose grounds they fed.[108]

The court's decision carried forest politics into hundreds of new households, as "many inhabitants were fined great sums of money, or forthwith [made] to depart from their houses and estates, for they were found by verdict to have encroached on the forests," and the swanimote court handled at least 797 presentments in the years 1634 and 1638 alone.[109] By 1638 and 1639, the court was convening as far afield as Chelmsford, Colchester, and Brentwood; the main purpose of its proceedings had become the collection of fines, rather than the protection of the woods and deer, for the latter were scarce in these new bailiwicks of the forest. In 1639, a swanimote at Brentwood heard only eleven presentments but levied £506 3s 4d in fines from 205 hamlets that refused to send a reeve and four assistants to the court of this new "forest of Essex."[110] In only a decade, the local communities in Waltham had experienced three distinctive regimes of forest law: the customary system of the 1620s, outside the highest courts and ruled by influential courtiers and local families; the regime of the revived forest courts after 1630, formed to confront these vested interests; and the new order of the "forest of Essex" after 1634, designed to raise revenue for the crown. Although crown and parliament addressed this new order as a grievance in late 1640 and early 1641, their negotiations reflected

---

[106] *CSPD, Charles I*, 7: 227–228; Fisher, *Forest of Essex*, 38–44.
[107] John Rushworth (ed.), *Historical Collections*, 8 vols. (London, 1721), 3: 1056–1057.   [108] Ibid.
[109] Ibid. These figures are conservative because based on the patchy records in PRO: C99/138–140, 145, Perambulations of Waltham: Presentments in Swanimote, 1634, 1638.
[110] PRO: C99/141, Perambulations of Waltham: Presentments in Swanimote, 10 June 1639.

an environment in which many could perceive in "justice" little more than a rationalization of interest; as a result, the reform statute in 1641 merely added a fourth variant to the unsettlement of law in Waltham.

V

On 16 March 1641, the Earl of Holland informed the House of Lords "that his majesty understanding that the forest laws are grievous to the subjects of this kingdom, his majesty, out of his grace and goodness to his people, is willing to lay down all the new bounds of his forests in this kingdom; and that they shall be reduced to the same condition as they were before the late justices seat held."[111] This concession followed by two months the impeachment drama of John Finch, then Lord Keeper, in January 1641, a drama reminiscent of the Nazeing dispute in both its terms and its rhetorical strategies. Addressing the House of Lords in support of the impeachment, Lucius Cary, Viscount Falkland, evoked the forest as metaphor and microcosm, describing how Finch

practiced the annihilating of ancient perambulations of particular forests, the better to annihilate the ancient perambulations of the whole kingdom, the meets and bounds between the liberties of the subject and sovereign power; he gave our goods to the king, our lands to the deer, our liberties to his sheriffs; so there was no way by which we had not been oppressed and destroyed if the power of this person had been equal to his will, or the will of his majesty had been equal to his power.[112]

As Gardiner's oppressions in Nazeing had been ascribed to malignant disease, Falkland compared Finch's machinations to the symptoms of

the plague, that the infection of others is an earnest and constant desire of all that are seized by it; and as [Finch's] design resembles that disease in the ruin, destruction, and desolation it would have wrought; so it seems no less like it in this effect, he having so labored to make others share in the guilt, making use of his authority and interest to persuade, and threatening [judges] in his majesty's name, whose piety is known to give that excellent prerogative to his person that the law gives to his place, not to be able to do wrong; [Finch] poisoned our very antidotes, making law the ground of illegality; he used the law not only against us but against itself, making it *felo de se*.[113]

Falkland's conclusion further echoed the language of the body politic used to express notions of loyalty and sedition, health and disease, in earlier local disputes; Finch had committed "a treason as well against the king as against

---

[111] Rushworth, *Historical Collections*, 4: 206.   [112] Ibid., 140.   [113] Ibid.

the kingdom, for whatsoever is against the whole is undoubtedly against the head."[114] It is not difficult to detect elements of the "great man" political style attributed to Lord Denny in Finch's approach to the forest eyres during the 1630s – the use of intimidation; the rejection of local custom, including chartered liberties, as a legitimate obstacle to political or fiscal interest; the tendency to represent responses other than submission as sedition – or to appreciate the similarities between the "country" style claimed by the villagers of Nazeing and the commonwealth rhetoric of the "whole" in Falkland's speech. Both parliamentary and village political arenas knew a language of ideological conflict, using the terms of natural bodies to describe opposed styles of political practice, long before civil war revealed its violent potential.

On 7 August 1641, a new statute embodied the royal concession, renouncing "late diverse presentments" in the forests, lamenting their "great grievance and vexation of many persons," and restoring the meets and bounds of the forests established in the twentieth year of James's reign. If in the preceding sixty years a place had held no justice seat, swanimote, or court of attachment, and had not received officers of the forest, it was considered "disafforested" and "free to all intents and purposes, as if the same had never been forest." Parliament was invited to appoint commissions of inquest under the great seal in order to establish the lawful meets and bounds of the forests.[115] On 8 September, the commissioners for Waltham conducted an inquisition at Stratford Langthorne to establish a new perambulation of the forest, more or less restoring the boundaries of 1301.[116] But this attempt to reach a settlement resulted in yet another variation on the forest regime, joining the forest territory of the 1620s to the revived judicial apparatus of the early 1630s; the commissioners William Conyers, Thomas Fanshaw, Carew Hervey als Mildmay, and Sir William Rowe, as well as many of their assistants, had acquired their knowledge of Waltham as officers of the Caroline courts.[117] This new regime could not escape the politics of the 1620s and 1630s in either the fluid rendering of forest conflicts in larger political terms or the perceived subservience of law to power and interest. As crown and parliament drifted further from political settlement in 1642, the hunt and its trophies, coveted

---

[114] Ibid.   [115] 16 Car. I, c. 16, in *Statutes of the Realm*, 5: 119–120.
[116] Although the commission included the Earl of Warwick, he does not seem to have participated in the inquisition. See Fisher, *Forest of Essex*, 50, 393–399, 400–403. In 1641, the commissioners excluded the liberty of Havering from the forest, a significant departure from the boundaries of 1301.
[117] PRO: C99/140, Perambulations of Waltham: Presentments in Swanimote, 1631, 1634; Fisher, *Forest of Essex*, 400–403.

markers of gentility, seemed to be loosed from their traditional moorings in forest law. The battlecry of "no law settled" offered by John Browne and his companions as a justification for killing deer in April 1642 likewise reflects the preceding generation of conflicts over land use and the meanings of forest in Waltham as well as the shifting judicial approaches to their settlement; the injunction from the House of Lords on 12 May, attempting to protect the deer in the absence of effective forest courts, only confirmed this politics of unsettlement.[118]

---

[118] HLRO: Main Papers, 1509–1700: 2 May 1642; Main Papers, 1509–1700: 3 May 1642; *LJ*, vol. 5: 37, 38, 61; HMC, *5th Report*, 20, 22.

Royal honor, great parks, and the commonweal in Windsor Forest, 1603–1642

PAGE   Why, yet there want not many that do fear in deep of night to walk
           by this Herne's oak. But what of this?
FORD   Marry, this is our device . . .

Shakespeare, Merry Wives of Windsor (1599)

The rude multitude have threatened to pull down the pales of the
park and lay it all to common, if they may not be satisfied of their
customs; and their late disorders in the destruction of his majesty's
red deer makes [the petitioners] justly fear that where they have a
colorable pretence they will not be less riotous and disorderly than
when they had no pretence at all.   Egham Petition (1642)

I

In the early 1600s, Michael Drayton described Windsor Castle and Forest
as "that supremest place of the great English kings," and few symbols of
English monarchy expressed so clearly the hunter in the king's heart.[1] The
first building of the castle lay in Arthurian mythology alongside the
invention of the English form of hunt, as Cockayne had attributed
the "first principles" of "the honorable sport of hunting" to "Sir Tristram,
one of the knights of King Arthur."[2] Such sources, not to mention
Shakespeare's *Merry Wives of Windsor,* have led to a greater interest in
Windsor's politics among literary critics than among historians. The search
for the social and political context of Shakespeare's play has explored the
"social dynamics" of Windsor itself, the conflicts between the corporation
of New Windsor and the royal domain of Windsor Castle and Forest, and

---

[1] Michael Drayton, *Poly-Olbion* (1612, 1622), Song XV: 314, in *Works of Michael Drayton*, 5 vols.
(Oxford: Basil Blackwell, 1933), 4: 311.
[2] William Harrison, *Description of England* (New York: Dover, [1587] 1994), 226; Sir Thomas
Cockayne, *A Short Treatise of Hunting* (London, 1591), A3r.

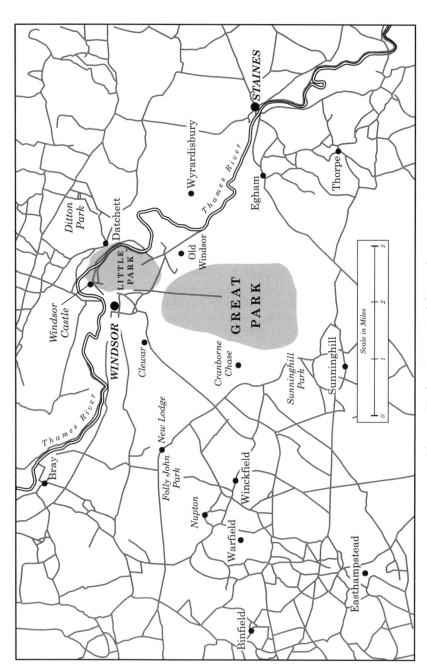

Map 4.1. Windsor Forest in Berkshire and Surrey

the plays on forest law and poaching in *Merry Wives* as a kind of poetics of order and property.[3] A history of the forest from the perspective of its courts both supports and opens a critique of this analysis of local politics. An important theme of work on Shakespeare's play has been the conflict between a bourgeois society and culture in the corporation of New Windsor and the aristocratic ethos of crown and court, defined by the properties of Windsor Castle and Forest. The power and presence of the crown in this analysis derive in great part from a view of Windsor Forest as an absolute royal property, a view reflected, for example, in Richard Helgerson's interpretation of John Norden's survey maps of the honor of Windsor, drawn in 1607, as the image of "an estate wholly amenable to the pleasure and possession of its proprietor."[4] The evidence of the forest court helps to define more precisely the nature of this royal property and reveals a more precarious politics in Windsor Forest, where the crown claimed authority over the woods and deer under the forest law but owned few of the forest's many estates.[5] As the crown's power appears less monolithic in the evidence of its court, the foresters assume greater importance, often serving in forest offices and shaping the court's enforcement of forest law in many ways. Seen from the perspective of the forest court, the security of the king's deer in Windsor during the early seventeenth century, and thus the defense of the forest as a hunting preserve, as a symbol of royal honor and power, resulted from a politics of negotiation among crown interests and those of local communities in Windsor Forest. Moreover, during the 1630s, when the crown did pursue its interests as if the forest was an absolute property, strictly enforcing the forest law, a covert – and later openly violent – local activism threatened to disafforest much of Windsor by the killing of the king's deer.

As a result of the historicist work on *Merry Wives*, it is clear the play contains an important view of the way forest matters intervened in local politics. The first scene reveals the competition for honor and status among noble families in the argument between Robert Shallow, esquire, and Sir John Falstaff over Falstaff's attack on Shallow's park and lodge in the forest. As Shallow, a justice of the peace, threatens to prosecute Falstaff in Star Chamber, this scene also introduces the important distinction, in both play and forest, between the major disputes removed from Windsor

---

[3] Richard Helgerson, *Adulterous Alliances: Home, State, and History in Early Modern European Drama and Painting* (Chicago: University of Chicago Press, 2000), 57–76; Berry, *Shakespeare and the Hunt*, 133–158; Jeffrey Theis, "The "Ill Kill'd" Deer: Poaching and Social Order in *The Merry Wives of Windsor*," *Texas Studies in Literature and Language*, 43 (2001): 46–73.
[4] Helgerson, *Adulterous Alliances*, 57.   [5] Thompson, *Whigs and Hunters*, 29.

and prosecuted before the council in the Star Chamber, and the local disputes resolved informally or handled in forest court.[6] Shakespeare's interest extended in later scenes of the play to a manner of political awareness and the political uses of the forest. Most famously, the Merry Wives build their attack against Falstaff on the local mythology of Herne's Oak in the Little Park, using the myth of the haunted oak as a "device" to defeat Falstaff's corrupt court scheme to seduce local women and usurp their property. Their skillful use of the forest landscape thus protects the integrity of the local community against the proprietary corruption of the court. Indeed, Falstaff's scheme might be interpreted more broadly to denote the subordination of local interests to the interests of court or crown.[7] In this context, the local capacity to enter the forest, its being commonly possessed and its meanings known, becomes a means to thwart Falstaff's design. Shakespeare appears to make use of elements identified in the "country" political style, playing on the political meanings of moral boundaries and on the fears of pollution embodied by Falstaff, in a manner reminiscent of the social dramas in Waltham Forest. Just as importantly, the play exploits the selfconsciousness of all these local "devices" and "pretences," its characters enacting both a practical politics, sustained by neighborly relations, and a set of political values.

During the early seventeenth century, John Norden's survey described Windsor Forest as seventy-eight miles in circumference, mostly in Berkshire and Surrey. The forest contained sixteen walks, each the responsibility of a keeper in the usual manner, although the boundaries between the walks remained vague. As Norden observed, "there is contention between every neighbor keeper, for the most part, for usurpation and intruding one into another's walk, for not one of them truly knows his own bounds."[8] Among these walks, and their archipelago of specially stocked parks, moved the king's deer. Although their numbers are difficult to estimate, of the important royal properties, Home or Little Park contained 280 acres and supported 240 fallow deer; Moat Park, enclosed in the Great Park by William III in 1701, contained 280 fallow deer in its 390 acres; and Great Park, the jewel in the crown of forest estates, boasted 1,800 fallow deer, spread among four distinct walks and 3,650 acres of "good ground."[9] As usual, a political hierarchy defined the "forest" as

[6] Berry, *Shakespeare and the Hunt*, 140–144.   [7] Helgerson, *Adulterous Alliances*, 60–61.
[8] Robert Tighe and James Davis, *Annals of Windsor*, 2 vols. (London: Longman, 1858), 2: 27–29.
[9] Ibid., 31, 35–36, 39.

much as its natural features. The hierarchy of forest officers exercised greater power in Windsor because, unlike Waltham Forest, the swanimote court held regular annual sessions. Among the important officers of the forest, the chief justice of the forests south of the Trent surmounted the hierarchy, joining the forest to the crown and royal council and presiding over the forest eyre, the high court of forest law. In Windsor, the foresters and keepers of walks and parks, supported by deputies, served under a constable of the castle and keeper of the forest, himself assisted by a lieutenant. In the swanimote, a forester and a bailiff, for the crown, two verderers, elected by the freeholders at the assizes in the manner of coroners, and twelve regarders from forest parishes served for each of the four major bailiwicks of the forest.[10] The swanimote court held separate sessions for the four bailiwicks named Battell's, Fyne's, Finchampstead, and Surrey, formed from the sixteen walks. Because of the scale of the archive, this chapter focuses on the evidence for Battell's bailiwick, the political heartland of the forest on the Berkshire side. This tract contained the most important royal hunting preserves – the Great, Little, and Moat Parks – as well as the vastness of Cranborne Chase, covered by 13,000 trees in a 1633 survey, and its troubled western border near Newlodge Walk, and the important parks of Sunninghill, Swinley Rails, and Folly John.[11] Apart from the trees and the deer, Battell's bailiwick contained the largest human settlements in Windsor Forest. In 1676, Braye and New Windsor contained adult populations of roughly 1,000 each, and four hamlets on the western border of the bailiwick, in Cranborne Chase, had a combined adult population of more than 1,500.[12] These substantial local settlements posed an enormous challenge to the institutions of the forest in their efforts to protect the royal hunt; the records of the swanimote court in Battell's bailiwick during the early seventeenth century reveal a complex political society under the flexible discipline of forest law.

---

[10] See J. Charles Cox, *The Royal Forests of England* (London: Methuen, 1905), 17–24; Thompson, *Whigs and Hunters*, 33–36, for descriptions of the forest hierarchy.

[11] PRO: C99, Chief Justice of the Forests South of Trent; Records of Forest Eyres, Charles I, 1632–1640: 128, Proceedings and Presentments in Swanimote Courts, Battell's Bailiwick, 12 June 1633 and 18 September 1633: survey of the King's Majesty's woods, 18 September 1633.

[12] These estimates pertain to the parishes of Braye (1,098), Clewar (371), New Windsor (1,025), Sunninghill (262), Warfield (650), and Winckfield (250). See Anne Whiteman (ed.), *The Compton Census of 1676: A Critical Edition* (Oxford University Press, 1986), 131–133. Because the Compton census returns yield uncertain estimates of even adult population, the figures are offered only for scale.

II

James I brought the same keen personal interest to affairs of the hunt in Windsor Forest that had animated his oversight of the keepers in Waltham. As Thomas Wilson famously said of James in 1603, "sometimes he comes to council, but most time he spends in fields and parks and chases, chasing away idleness by violent exercise and early rising."[13] In July 1603, James expressed his political priorities in a proclamation to forbid "any persons but noblemen or gentlemen of principal quality to enter the Little Park at Windsor, on account of injury done to the game, by inordinate resort of persons, since his majesty's arrival there."[14] Subjects should not come between the king and his prey. Yet this tenderness for his deer belied the subtle interrelationship of human interests and animal needs sustained by the forest regime in Windsor during the early seventeenth century. In contrast to the diminished courts of Waltham, the Windsor swanimote court held annual sessions and compelled the participation of influential local families as officers of forest and hamlet.[15] Star Chamber remained a powerful instrument for the furtherance of crown interests in the forest, and, when compelled to answer in Star Chamber for alleged challenges to those interests, factions in the neighborhood of Windsor evoked a divisive forest politics reminiscent of the battles over Nazeing wood common in Waltham. But the yearly sessions of the Windsor Forest courts offered a flexible institutional means to adjust the demands of forest law to the customs and shifting practices of local communities in the forest. Prior to the forest eyre of 1632, the Windsor swanimote protected both the interests of the crown and the customs of foresters.

During the early seventeenth century, the swanimote court intervened little in the everyday affairs or customary economies of the local communities in Windsor Forest, tending to follow the tithingmen from the forest hamlets and their assistants, whose declarations of *omnia bene* became a litany of the court sessions. These officers were often recruited for successive terms and became the faces of the forest hamlets in the court: Turners of Nuptowne in Warfield; Bakers and Mays of Sunninghill; Painters of Winckfield. Many years of experience in office inspired the confidence to chide the crown for such failures as the "decay and ruin" of Winckfield

---

[13] John Nichols (ed.), *Progresses, Processions, and Magnificent Festivities of King James I*, 4 vols. (London, 1828), 1: 188.
[14] *CSPD, James I, 1603–1610*, 18.
[15] The proceedings and presentments of the Jacobean swanimote court in Battell's bailiwick are in PRO: C154/8 and C154/10, records surviving for 19 of 23 regnal years.

bridge, decried by Thomas Painter in 1620 "as formerly presented but not amended."[16] Edward Matthew, Edward Baker, and Robert Lyde of Sunninghill used the swanimote in 1619 to prosecute Alexander Leviston, esquire, keeper of Sunninghill Park, "for enclosing a highway or lane, and laying the same to Sunninghill park, which has been a [common] way time out of mind."[17] Although the crown seldom acted on these complaints, the swanimote acknowledged the influence of local families by accepting their annual assurances of *omnia bene* regarding affairs of the forest. The court's primary task during these years involved its oversight of the keepers and woodwards responsible for Windsor's sixteen walks and parks. In 1606 and 1607, the woodwards and their deputies in Battell's bailiwick took 1,218 cartloads of wood from the forest, of the order of 60,900 cubic feet of timber, mostly for routine uses of deer browse and firewood, although the Earl of Nottingham licensed an additional twenty-three loads of timber in 1606 to support work on the pales of the Great Park and Sunninghill Park.[18] By 1623 and 1624, this yearly harvest had dropped to 651 cartloads – perhaps 32,550 cubic feet of wood – but the oversight of even these conventional uses of the forest continued to require the annual diligence of verderers and regarders in the swanimote court, and forest officers seldom looked beyond this great administrative task to present minor violations of forest law.[19]

Because the court pursued and prosecuted significant – and especially organized – violations of the forest law, this general pattern of relations between the swanimote and local communities in Windsor must be distinguished from the stereotype of an archaic forest law, barely remembered and poorly enforced.[20] A prohibitive system of fines and sureties, the

---

[16] PRO: C154/8/134, Court Proceedings and Presentments, 18 James I: presentments of Winckfield tithing. The forest hamlets consistently used the swanimote to petition the crown for repair of the local bridges in its jurisdiction. See PRO: C154/8/181, Court Proceedings and Presentments, 16 James I: presentments of East Oakley, Fyfield, Stroud, Winckfield tithings; C154/8/131, Court Proceedings and Presentments, 17 James I: presentments of Stroud, Winckfield tithings; C154/8/134, Court Proceedings and Presentments, 18 James I: presentments of Holyport tithing; C154/8/89, Court Proceedings and Presentments, 21 James I: presentments of Holyport, Winckfield tithings; C154/8/132, Court Proceedings and Presentments, 22 James I: presentments of Winckfield tithing; presentments of swanimote jury, 18 September 1624.

[17] PRO: C154/8/131, Court Proceedings and Presentments, 17 James I: presentments of Sunninghill tithing.

[18] These figures assume a standard "load" of 50 cubic feet. The regarders' presentments at the Windsor swanimote for 1606 and 1607 are in PRO: C154/8/91 and C154/8/55.

[19] PRO: C154/8/89, Court Proceedings and Presentments, 21 James I: regarders' presentments, Battell's bailiwick; C154/8/132, Court Proceedings and Presentments, 22 James I: regarders' presentments, Battell's bailiwick.

[20] Pettit, *Royal Forests of Northamptonshire*, 40–44.

ability to compel appearance in court and thus to control a person's time, secured the local power of swanimote courts against all but the richest among the accused, even in the absence of a forest eyre.[21] The court's willingness to defend the forest from spoliation is best illustrated by its enforcement of forest law on the western boundary of Battell's bailiwick. In 1618 and 1619, the swanimote jury presented John Avery and John Cooper of Warfield as ringleaders of a loose coalition organized "for the digging of turfs in Winckfield and the selling them to their neighbors in Warfield."[22] In 1623, following a complaint of "great spoil made in the Great Park by sturdy woodcarriers" and "disorderly cutting and carrying in this baili- wick," the "regarders, jurors, and the whole court" ordered "that none hereafter shall cut any turfs after the feast day of St. James the apostle; nor carry any turfs after the feast day of St. Bartholomew the apostle; nor at any time when the king is in the country."[23] Tensions on this score had reached such a pitch in July that John Goulding, a deputy underkeeper in the Great Park, "beat a poor man of Windsor, who trespassed by stealing wood, so severely that the man died."[24] During the following year, the scale of the problem became apparent, as William Yeeldall of Winckfield, a mariner, confessed to cutting and carrying twenty cartloads – 1,000 cubic feet – of Winckfield turfs for sale in Hurst, and the circle of prosecution broadened to include nineteen men from Warfield, Winckfield, and Braye.[25] Over this six-year span, the effectiveness of the court's enforcement of forest law is difficult to measure. Recidivism rates suggest its power to curtail the most serious encroachments. Although the swanimote did not defeat this steady attack on the forest covert, of the nineteen men prosecuted in 1624 only John Cooper, Richard Boyer, and Peter Montague of Warfield remained from the group of nine turfcutters prosecuted in 1618 and 1619.

Although the presentments resulting from local use of the woods were few in number, the court demanded a more strict annual accounting for

---

[21] Thompson, *Whigs and Hunters*, 36–39.

[22] Avery and Cooper were fined 50s each for their role in this black market for fuel; seven other Warfield men were fined 10s each. PRO: C154/8/181, Court Proceedings and Presentments, 16 James I: presentments of swanimote jury, 17 September 1618; C154/8/131, Court Proceedings and Presentments, 17 James I: presentments of swanimote jury, 15 September 1619.

[23] PRO: C154/8/89, Court Proceedings and Presentments, 21 James I: presentments of Windsor Great Park, Nether Walk; swanimote proceedings, 18 September 1623, court orders.

[24] After being sued for this beating, Goulding attacked the sergeant sent to arrest him and was condemned to a fine of £7 or imprisonment. See *CSPD, James I, 1623–1625*, 40, 43, 46; PRO: C154/ 8/89, Court Proceedings and Presentments, 21 James I: swanimote proceedings, 18 September 1623.

[25] Of the nineteen men presented, fourteen lived in Warfield, three in Winckfield, and two in Braye. See PRO: C154/8/132, Court Proceedings and Presentments, 22 James I: presentments of swanimote jury, 18 September 1624.

casualties among the king's deer. This usually did not entail much investigation of even the most suspicious circumstances, and few presentments named any neighbors suspected of illicit hunting, venturing only to record the owner of the land where the deer were found. In this way, Richard Staverton, keeper of New Lodge Walk, recorded "a sorrel found dead in Turner's ground that had been stricken by stealers, and not to be saved, but was hanged up."[26] When deer died by chance or under mysterious circumstances, forest officers might give the venison to the poor as an informal but customary act of charity and neighborliness. In 1606, a deer discovered in New Lodge Walk, "killed with dogs," was "given to the poor" without further inquiry. In another corner of the walk, the keeper Staverton found "a sorrel stricken, [which] was recovered and given to the neighbors, being pined away."[27] Across the walks and parks of Battell's bailiwick, the keepers and their deputies distributed eight deer in this way among "poor neighbors" in 1607 and 1608. This close interrelationship of the keepers and their neighborhoods meant that conflicts in the forest could bring down local retribution on the deer as symbols of the forest regime. In 1623 and 1624, as the swanimote attempted to limit turfcutting in Winckfield and Warfield, the keepers confronted a massive increase in deer "killed by chance" in the walks and parks of the forest. Although the number of these "chance deer" had increased from 169 in 1607 to 267 in 1619, the politics of chance generated an unprecedented 841 casualties in 1624, including 358 dead in the Great Park alone.[28] In 1624, "chance" was often a bullet from an unknown gun. Among the "deer killed by mischance" in Cranborne, William Smyth found "a doe shot through the paunch, by whom I know not, and a soken doe, with one of her legs broken by a bullet." Under these circumstances, the keepers led more rigorous inquiries and began to name individuals as "enemies" of the forest. Once he had identified Paul Harwood's dog and Henry Powney's shepherd's dog as deer killers, Smyth "caused [the dogs] to be hanged" as a warning to the owners and their employers.[29] After discovering a doe and five other deer "killed by stealth," Sir William Hewett, keeper of the Little Park, followed the trail to Richard Moore's house, found the dog, and tramped further afield to

---

[26] PRO: C154/8/91, Court Proceedings and Presentments, 4 James I: presentment of Richard Staverton, keeper of the New Lodge, Cranborne.

[27] Ibid.

[28] The keepers' presentments often indicated the impact of disease but offered no such explanations in 1624. Ibid., C154/8/131, Court Proceedings and Presentments, 17 James I; C154/8/132, Court Proceedings and Presentments, 22 James I.

[29] PRO: C154/8/132, Court Proceedings and Presentments, 22 James I: presentment of William Smyth, underkeeper of Old Lodge Walk, Cranborne Chase.

William Grace's house at Wyrardsbury in Buckinghamshire, uncovering a good store of venison.[30] In 1623 and 1624, local violence against deer in Windsor forest increased, and forest officers viewed the attacks with growing concern. As the swanimote prosecuted more turfcutters in Warfield and Winckfield, anonymous foresters and their "chance" bullets killed more deer, symbols of the forest as a royal hunting preserve. In 1624, forest officers thus confronted in stark form a question that was not to be satisfactorily answered before the Civil War: how were they to preserve the forest without challenging the fundamental assumptions of its politics?

The most serious conflicts in the forest were adjudicated not in the swanimote court but in Star Chamber.[31] As the more powerful court, Star Chamber gave pause to the wealthiest "enemies" of forest law, its crippling fines serving to inhibit organized attacks on the forest either by local gentry, those noisy suitors in the court of honor, or by other local groups seeking the forest's golden path, hoping to profit from the market in illicit venison or fuel. But because the swanimote court survived as an arbiter of crown and common interests in the forest, Star Chamber's political significance in Windsor differed in subtle but important ways from its impact on Waltham during the 1620s. Star Chamber removed disputes from their local context in Windsor Forest, the domain of the swanimote court, and isolated the defendants as offenders against the crown. In this way, Sir William Hewett's investigation of deer "killed by stealth" in the Little Park, which led him to the houses of Richard Moore and William Grace, though reported to the swanimote in 1623, became the basis of a Star Chamber prosecution.[32] This case separated the attack on the king's deer from the growing conflict over wood and turfs in the forest during the early 1620s, a judicial feat often impossible to achieve in a swanimote court recruited from the forest hamlets. After recognition of the king's "special affection and esteem" for the "red and fallow deer and other princely pleasures" offered by the royal parks at Windsor, "affording opportunity to your highness to recreate and refresh yourself upon any vacancy from your great and weighty affairs of the state, wherewith your majesty is continually pressed," Sir Thomas Coventry's bill of information included Moore and

---

[30] PRO: C154/8/89, Court Proceedings and Presentments, 21 James I: presentment of Sir William Hewett, keeper of the Little Park.
[31] Pettit describes a similar pattern of layered conflicts and courts in *Royal Forests of Northamptonshire*, 42.
[32] Ibid., STAC 8/29/7, Sir Thomas Coventry, Attorney General v. Thomas Habergill of Windsor, gentleman, and others, 1622, bill and answer. Perhaps because the Star Chamber action occurred after the swanimote session in 1622, Hewett reported the offences and investigation to the swanimote in 1623.

Grace among the "malefactors, lewd and desperate persons" induced by Thomas Havergill of Windsor, gentleman, to commit malicious "spoil and destruction" of the deer, "not regarding that duty they owe to your majesty." According to the bill, these attacks had occurred many times during the preceding five years, and Coventry included the usual array of weapons and rebellious zeal in order to stir the judicial pulse. But his account also charged a deadly avarice, describing how Havergill, Moore, and Grace had "wasted and destroyed your majesty's deer in so abundant and outrageous a manner that some have been salted, powdered, and layed up in their houses and barns, for the store killed was so great and plentiful that they were not able otherwise to have eaten and spent the same." Although the answer to these charges is insufficient to analyze the politics of this case, Coventry's bill of information reworked Sir William Hewett's investigation to evoke an immoral economy, casting the actions of Havergill, Moore, and Grace in terms of personal disloyalty to the crown and avarice in the hoarding of venison. To prosecute the case in these stark terms required its disentangling and distance from the local politics of Windsor Forest, and the Star Chamber served both ends.

These Star Chamber cases often involved attacks on the deer by the scions and servants of local gentry families, ambitious for the honor and status ascribed to tokens of the hunt. In 1607, Sir Charles Howard, lieutenant of the forest and keeper of the Ditton and Great parks, prosecuted Richard Hanbury of Datchett, gentleman, and others of his household for playing this "great man" style of politics in the parks under Howard's care.[33] The bill of information stressed the scale of this challenge to the forest regime, alleging Hanbury's orchestration of seven attacks on the forest between 1605 and 1607, including four hunting raids on Ditton Park, two on the Great Park, and one on the eastern border of the forest at Spelthurst. According to Howard, Hanbury avoided any direct involvement in these stealthy raids, five of the seven taking place under cover of darkness, but equipped and directed his servants William Glasbroke and Humfrey Mascoll and their friends to the king's parks for venison to grace his own table and to present as gifts, "greatly commending their misdoings." When summoned to answer Howard's suspicions, Hanbury "utterly neglected his duty to your majesty, not only refusing to bring his servants to [Howard at Windsor Castle] but sending them out of the country to places unknown, where they are kept at Hanbury's charges."

---

[33] PRO: STAC 8/182/26, Sir Charles Howard, lieutenant of Windsor Forest v. Richard Hanbury of Datchett, gentleman, and others, 1607, bill, [3] answers, and deposition.

Hanbury denied the allegations, but his young servant Glasbroke conceded much of Howard's case, only claiming royal pardon for his actions on the basis of Ditton Park's exclusion from Windsor Forest.[34] Glasbroke first described killing a doe in Ditton Park, dressing it with Humfrey Mascoll's help in one of Hanbury's outbuildings, then "putting the doe in a hamper and sending it down by water to London to Peter Dallowe, a tailor, dwelling in St. Martin's." Three years later, while walking in Ditton Park, Glasbroke "found a buck [killed by Mascoll with a crossbow] but still warm in the head, and there paunched and carried him to Hanbury's brewhouse." After Glasbroke dressed the buck, Hanbury's cook carried it to the larder, "and afterwards part of it was baked and eaten at his master's board." Hanbury did not lead the hunting raids but cultivated the "great man" style through the noble fare displayed on his table and perhaps through his power to settle debts by sending a haunch of venison.

The Star Chamber also provided an effective means of prosecution when these local gentry attacks on the forest undermined the forest regime itself. In 1609, the court accused Sir Richard Norton of a conspiracy to acquire venison by bribing the underkeeper of Lynchford Walk, on the Surrey side of the forest.[35] According to the information, Norton and his servant Henry Rogers

confederated together to hunt and kill your deer in the forest and to convert the flesh thereof to their wills and pleasures, but, knowing the penalties of your laws against offenders of this kind, thought it not safe to hunt or kill your deer themselves, but rather, in as secret and covert sort as they could devise, to subborn the underkeeper of the walk to kill the deer for them.

At Norton's direction, Rogers accordingly approached Thomas Montague, Sir Richard Weston's underkeeper in Lynchford Walk, and Montague's servant John Adams, offering them bribes to kill a stag in the walk.[36] When Adams delivered this "great stag" to Norton's house in Rotherfield, Norton paid him, gave him the agreed sum in trust for Montague, and asked him "to carry one quarter of the stag to a friend," keeping the remainder for his

[34] James routinely excepted offenders against the forest laws from general pardons. In 1607, John Norden included Ditton Park in the honor of Windsor, but the park's status in Windsor Forest remained unclear. At his interrogation in April 1608, Glasbroke gave his age as twenty-two years. See Tighe and Davis, *Annals of Windsor*, 1: 323–324; 2:3; PRO: STAC 8/182/26, Howard v. Hanbury: deposition of William Glasbroke, 4 May 1608.

[35] Ibid., 8/13/3, Sir Henry Hobart, Attorney General v. Sir Richard Norton, knight, and others, 1609, bill and answer.

[36] Norton allegedly offered Montague 13s 4d and Adams 3s 4d on the delivery of the stag. See ibid., Hobart v. Norton: bill of information.

own household. Norton's answer to these charges paints his actions in strikingly different colors and offers a subtle reading of politics on the borders of the forest. Norton attributed the misunderstanding first to his status as lord of Farmborough in Surrey, a manor adjoining Windsor Forest but customarily included in the Bishop of Winchester's chase. Because of its position near the forest, "great numbers of the king's deer used to come and feed in the demesnes of the manor," but lord and tenants "had always foresworn to hunt, kill, or chase any of the deer and suffered them quietly to depasture, without any trouble or molestation." This customary arrangement, Norton protested, had induced Rogers, his tenant, to request a stag from Montague for his landlord. Montague's servant Adams then delivered the news of the kill, unsolicited but much appreciated, to the house in Rotherfield, and Norton offered the sums of money charged against him "in some measure to show his thankfulness, as is usual in such cases." At Norton's instruction, Rogers then brought three quarters of the stag to Rotherfield and "sent the rest to a friend of [Norton's] dwelling near London." Norton's answer thus evoked a neighborliness and reciprocity of interests on the forest's borders. He "had no purpose to offend his majesty by receiving the stag" and prayed his answer might preserve his "reputation and credit" from the pall cast by the charges against him.

Star Chamber's broad jurisdiction could ease the prosecution of the networks involved in the illicit market for venison, networks sometimes extending as far afield as London. In 1615, an information against John Taylor of London, a brewer in Millford lane, described an elaborate scheme to take venison, based on Tileplace Farm in Old Windsor, a house conveniently located between the Great and Little parks and rented by Taylor in 1609 as a cover for his "business" in the forest.[37] Taylor and his servant John Steevens built their trade slowly over the ensuing four years, "awaiting such times as the keepers attended your majesty in other places," but ultimately "destroyed multitudes of your deer, with which Taylor not only fed himself and his family but sent to his friends at London and sold there many deer that he could not spend at home." By 1611, Taylor had become "so bold and impudent, as, instead of his former secret courses," he and Steevens began to use firearms in their attacks on the deer, once entering the forest near Taylor's house "with each of them a great gun, charged with a double bullet," to fire on a herd of red deer, killing a great stag and a hind calf and "wounding many of the herd." Taylor's wife Sara

---

[37] Ibid., 8/22/20, Sir Francis Bacon, Attorney General v. John Taylor and others, 1615, bill and demurrer.

then helped her husband "to fetch the stag and the hinde calf home," using "close and covered carts." Because Taylor conceded the charges against him, this information offers a rare detailed account of how the illicit trade in venison worked. According to Taylor, his activities in Windsor Forest had raised suspicions as early as 1611, and Charles, Lord Effingham, as lieutenant of the forest, had sent a pursuivant to summon Taylor and John Steevens to his house for questioning. Sir Richard Weston, a justice of the peace and now a chief ranger of the forest, had led the interrogation and secured a confession, resulting in Taylor's payment of a £10 fine. His demurrer simply objected to being "called again in question for the same charge," but his case illustrates the prosecutorial options available to forest officers in the absence of an eyre as well as the power of Star Chamber to prosecute offences extending beyond the limits of the forest.

Apart from their significance in the forest regime, Star Chamber cases often illuminate the subtleties of local conflict in Windsor Forest. Because the court required detailed statements from both sides of a case, its records often furnish the only evidence of how conflicts over forest matters took up the other important strands of local culture and politics. In 1609, a violent dispute between Simon Wilkes of Easthampstead and Ralph Scrope, both styled as gentlemen, may have begun as a disagreement over a church seat but ultimately included allegations of deer killing in the southern reaches of the forest.[38] In his bill of information, Wilkes claimed that Scrope and his servants had attacked him repeatedly after Wilkes, as a churchwarden in Easthampstead parish, had presented Scrope and his wife Mary in the consistory court for "not having received the holy communion for the space of five years together." Scrope then moved beyond beatings, using his influence as an underkeeper of Easthampstead Walk to paint Wilkes as "a common stealer of deer," knowing that Sir Charles Howard, the keeper of the walk, "was very careful to preserve your majesty's deer and would severely punish any person that should steal or kill the game." Howard took Scrope's word for these offences and imprisoned Wilkes for "a long time" before finally looking into the matter, releasing Wilkes, and allegedly rebuking Scrope for his malice. Although Wilkes brought the case to Star Chamber, Scrope answered the charges with the same sense of accumulated grievance and injury. In this account, Scrope and Wilkes had quarreled over a seat in their parish church formerly occupied by Scrope's father-in-law, Sir Richard Coningsby. Wilkes had refused to make peace and once

---

[38] Ibid., 8/290/11, Simon Wilkes of Easthampstead, gentleman v. Ralph Scrope, gentleman, and others, 1609, bill and [2] answers: answer of Ralph Scrope and William Yealdall.

followed Scrope in his keeper's rounds, "being then by reason of his office to attend the king's majesty in the park and walk." Scrope admitted to beating Wilkes with a hunting staff on this occasion, only "to be rid of him, the better and quieter to perform his service to the king." But Wilkes had been imprisoned because, for the third time, his "mongrel dogs, between greyhounds and mastiffs," had attacked the deer in Easthampstead. Scrope denied any misuse of his office and defended himself and his wife against the charge of "popish recusancy or refusal to receive the sacrament," implicit in the consistory court presentment. The case reveals once again the subtle but potent politics of honor. Wilkes and Scrope argued over a place in church, a form of dispute so often perceived in terms of honor and dishonor, the defence and usurpation of rank, and their grappling produced rippling accusations of a more general dishonor, including allegations of killing the king's deer and abusing the power of office in the forest.

As in Waltham Forest, the most significant cases in Windsor involved conflicts that resulted from the failure of the swanimote court to protect local customs and the response of foresters to this perceived usurpation of their place in the forest. This politics of custom marked the fluid western border of Windsor Forest, particularly in Bear Wood Walk, where the holders of "ancient houses or lands" in Arborfield, Barkham, Hurst, and Wokingham parishes had traditionally shared common of pasture in Bear Wood.[39] During the first half of the sixteenth century, Bear Wood or Bishop's Bear Wood had been the Bishop of Salisbury's chase, exempted from the forest jurisdiction. The crown acquired the chase along with Sonning manor in 1574, and Bear Wood then became a walk in the forest of Windsor, subject to the laws and officers of the swanimote court.[40] These changes made the newcomers in Windsor Forest more watchful of their customs, but peace ruled until 1613, when James decided to build a new lodge and an enclosure for the deer in Bear Wood, suddenly renamed Newland Coppice. Sir Francis Knollys, the keeper of Bear Wood Walk and scion of a powerful court family, and Richard Arrowsmith, a yeoman of the chamber, had a patent to build on the fifty-two acres of woodland now designated as Newland Coppice and proceeded, in February 1614, to set up a mound and hedge, perhaps seven feet high, around 330 poles of land in

[39] Ibid., 8/20/22, Sir Francis Bacon, Attorney General v. William Allwright of Barkham, and others, 1614, bill, [2] answers, interrogatories, and [3] depositions.
[40] Ibid., 8/20/22, Bacon v. Allwright: answer of William Allwright and others; William Page and P. H. Ditchfield (eds.), *VCH Berkshire* (London: St. Catherine Press, 1923), 3: 250.

Bear Wood, nearly completing the enclosure.[41] After an informal meeting among the families living nearest to the works, as many as sixty neighbors assembled on 9 February to break the mound and its ditch, "quietly in the night time, for fear of the displeasure of Sir Francis Knollys, who countenanced the enclosure and is a great man in that country, some of them having women's apparel about them to keep them the better from discovery."[42] This gathering resembled a collection of loosely organized work groups more than a unified crowd, but its success in pulling down a large, sturdy hedge appears to owe something to the leadership of the Allwrights of Barkham and Hurst, styled as yeomen.[43] Several women of the Allwright family later became involved in a second action against the new lodge. As Margaret Allwright declared,

on 2 June [1614], being Ascension day, she being by chance at play with other young maidens and children at a place not far from the enclosure, some speeches were used by the young people there that Arrowsmith had brought freestones to the enclosure and threatened very insolently to build a house on the common there, enclosing a great part of Bear Wood to his own use in despite of all men and debarring the inhabitants thereabouts from their common. Upon which speeches, [Margaret] and others, conceiving that by such courses their parents or masters, and consequently themselves, should be impoverished, and not understanding that Arrowsmith had any lawful right to enclose the common from his poor neighbors, but imagining that he endeavored the same out of his own head and authority, the young maidens and children went to the place in the woods where the stones lay and, with three or four axes, broke some of the greatest stones and scattered others, then departing away to their former pastimes.[44]

These local youths thus used the occasion of Rogation Week and Ascension Day or Holy Thursday, a church festival customarily marked by processions

---

[41] An initial grant in November 1613 confusingly referred to the lodge as if it already existed. A second grant in March 1614 then licensed the enclosure and the new building on the renamed site. See *CSPD, James I, 1611–1618*, 209; PRO: STAC 8/20/22, Bacon v. Allwright: bill of information; answer of William Allwright and others; W. Harry Rylands (ed.), *The Four Visitations of Berkshire* (London: Harleian Society, 1907), 1: 103 (Knollys of Stanford and Reading, 1623).

[42] PRO: STAC 8/20/22, Bacon v. Allwright: answer of William Allwright and others. James Allwright, Robert Avery, Henry Webbe, William Webbe, and Richard Edwards described themselves as "dwelling near the [enclosure], holding small tenements and houses in the parish of Hurst, and having lawful title of common there."

[43] The bill of information and supporting documents named six members of the Allwright family; William and Joane figured as leaders, but Agnes, James, Margaret, and Robert were accomplices. The only depositions in the case came from Joane Allwright, William's wife, aged sixty years, Agnes Allwright, a seventy-year-old widow, and her twenty-six-year-old daughter Margaret, all avowed participants in the actions against the lodge and enclosure. See PRO: STAC 8/20/22, Bacon v. Allwright: bill of information; interrogatories; depositions.

[44] Ibid., answer of Agnes Allwright, Joane Allwright, and Margaret Allwright.

around the parish boundaries and prayers for blessings on the fields, to remove an improper boundary from a common pasture.[45]

Although these actions were doubtless less spontaneous than Margaret's account suggested, her description faithfully rendered key elements of the local justification for them, particularly the moral defense of custom and common in the forest, under the law, against the "great man" style of enclosure ascribed to Knollys and Arrowsmith. The king had impressed William Allwright and his neighbors during the early years of his reign by appearing to understand that the forest was more than a royal hunting preserve. According to their answer in Star Chamber, James had confirmed the "diverse privileges and immunities" of Bear Wood in 1604 under the privy seal, in exchange for local support of efforts to increase his deer in the walk, "which the inhabitants of the four parishes, to give contentment to his majesty and to show their loyalties and sincere love to him, do suffer most freely and quietly to eat their corn and grass and to crop and spoil their woods."[46] Indeed, this settlement resembled the king's grant in 1608 of exemption from purveyance to the inhabitants of Surrey bailiwick "on condition of preserving the king's deer in the forest."[47] Although the foresters of Bear Wood did not use "commonweal" to describe their politics, their notion of fair practices in a lawful and just forest regime had many of that term's overtones. The forest law, in this view, ought to preserve the customs of foresters as well as the king's hunting privileges, because a forest devoid of just balance among these interests fell prey to "great men" and such political cronies as Richard Arrowsmith, who "unlawfully and without warrant" usurped their neighbors' livelihood. But the law in this case had missed the Wood for the trees. Knollys and Arrowsmith had received their patent to build on a site under "the new and feigned name" of Newland Coppice, "given to a piece of waste ground which never had any such name." Allwright and his neighbors could not accept that their common had disappeared beneath this name, and begged royal favor either to preserve their privileges or to allow a right to sue for recovery, but "nevertheless, since they have been better advised [of the law], are very sorry and much grieved for their acts and error, being committed ignorantly, and not with any contempt of the king's laws or authority."[48]

---

[45] See Brand, *Observations on the Popular Antiquities of Great Britain*, 1: 197–212, for the customary beliefs and practices surrounding Rogation Week, leading up to Ascension Day.

[46] PRO: STAC 8/20/22, Bacon v. Allwright: answer of William Allwright and others. The deer had increased from a mere thirty-four in 1604 to a herd of more than 200 in 1614.

[47] *CSPD, James I, 1603–1610*, 394.

[48] PRO: STAC 8/20/22, Bacon v. Allwright: answer of William Allwright and others.

In this case, the "voice of the country" assumed an ambiguous tone, expressing the common esteem for crown, law, and custom. The foresters of Bear Wood Walk made a principled submission in Star Chamber, marked by a reverence for the law and a willingness to take action against challenges to the rule of law in the forest.[49]

If not for the records of the swanimote court, a monument to the successful preservation of a mundane peace, the moments of conflict could easily dominate accounts of Windsor Forest during the early seventeenth century. The records of the swanimote in Battell's bailiwick reveal a court keeping a close eye on its officers and adapting the forest law to local realities in Windsor Forest. Apart from the evidence of conflict in Star Chamber, James himself sometimes spoke and behaved in ways that belied the administrative and political successes of forest institutions in Windsor. In 1624, when officers from the Windsor borough council approached the king during a hunt in Moat Park to request an augmentation of their vicarage, James reported the complaints of a few keepers, demanding of an embarrassed mayor and aldermen "why you vex me by suffering your poor to cut down and carry away my woods?" The mayor should order these offenders as well as the buyers of their wood to be publicly whipped.[50] These words were spoken as the swanimote struggled to curtail the destruction of covert in Winckfield and escalating mortality among the deer. At the same time, however, the Earl of Middlesex revealed in a letter that "diverse poor men are set on work, by his majesty's special commandment, for draining and conveying the water which now overspreads diverse parts of the Great Park of Windsor, making it unfruitful."[51] Under James, forest officers generally tried to sustain the forest as hunting preserve by this kind of negotiation, acknowledging local realities in Windsor and attempting to incorporate the diverse interests and uses of the forest. When the needs of the royal hunt and these other uses were mutually exclusive, such negotiations became impossible and Star Chamber adjudicated the matter, but this occurred in only a handful of cases. These conflicts were important not because of their numbers but because of their political qualities, revealed in the statements routinely collected by the court. Only the Star Chamber cases now remain of the keen competition among Windsor's influential families for tokens of honor in the forest, and these cases also illuminate matters of principle in forest politics, elegantly enfolding local claims to forest resources in a reverence for the authority of law. This rule of

---

[49] Ibid., deposition of Margaret Allwright of Hurst.
[50] Tighe and Davis, *Annals of Windsor*, 2: 82–83. [51] Ibid., 87–88.

law demanded and justified an active response to transgressions in the form of petition and direct action. In 1630, the commoners of Bear Wood complained to the Earl of Holland, constable of Windsor Castle, that Richard Arrowsmith had enclosed an additional 100 or 120 acres of their pasture, "converting [his previous enclosure] into tillage," and petitioned "for the preservation of their right of common." In 1655, the foresters again offered "to prove by records" that Bear Wood "is chase, not forest, and belonged to the bishops of Salisbury, under whom they enjoyed herbage," and once more "begged the demolition" of Arrowsmith's lodge and enclosure.[52] According to this politics, to preserve the rule of law in the forest, a key aspect of authority's dignity and a warrant for the reservation of the forest as a hunting preserve under king or commonwealth, demanded the participation of foresters as defenders of custom and legal rights in the courts and in their local communities.

III

In September 1632, the first pleas of the forest for many years began quietly at Windsor and at Bagshot, on the Surrey side of the forest. More than any of the other eyres held during the 1630s, the Windsor eyre attempted to reform and preserve what Sir John Coke had described in 1623 as the forest's significance for the "honor and power" of the crown.[53] The major officers of the court viewed the many fines imposed as punishments, intended to bring order to a major royal seat and hunting preserve.[54] This concern for order in Windsor dated from the appointment of Henry Rich, Earl of Holland, as the constable of Windsor Castle and keeper of the forest in 1629. In April 1630, eight months after his appointment, Holland had received a certificate from Sir Arthur Mainwaring, the lieutenant of the forest, Sir Richard Harrison, one of the verderers, and Sir Charles Howard, the ranger, lamenting the appearance of cottages and encroachments in Windsor as "the ruin and destruction of the woods and game, and the shelter of deer stealers and all disorderly persons."[55] In 1631, Sir William Noy, the Attorney General, had examined the records of the forest eyres held in Windsor under Edward III, Henry VIII, and Elizabeth I and, concerning the boundaries of the forest, had expressed his opinion

---

[52] *CSPD, Charles I, v. 4 (1629–1631)*, 278; *CSPD, Commonwealth, v. 9 (1655–1656)*, 149.
[53] Pettit, *Royal Forests of Northamptonshire*, 66; Sharpe, *Personal Rule*, 243.
[54] The relative insignificance of fiscal concerns in the Windsor eyre is well known. See Hammersley, "Revival of the Forest Laws," 89; Sharpe, *Personal Rule*, 243.
[55] *CSPD, Charles I, v. 4 (1629–1631)*, 53, 247–248.

that the bailiwick of Surrey remained forest rather than purlieu of Windsor Forest.[56] In 1632, Holland, as chief justice in eyre of forests south of Trent, and Noy, as crown counsel, directed an eyre in Windsor marked by an insistence on the formal ceremonies and traditions of forest law, as the keepers and woodwards kneeled to present their horns and hatchets and paid fines for the return of these insignia of office.[57] As an attempt to reform the state of the forest in Windsor, this eyre reacted against the forms of negotiation practiced under James and the adaptation of forest law to local circumstances. In 1632, the court included Surrey bailiwick in the forest as a matter of law, rejecting an earlier politics that had secured local favor for the king's deer in exchange for such privileges as an exemption from purveyance of provisions.[58] This reformed regime would enforce the law more rigorously; the swanimote would confront interests and uses of the forest not sanctioned by law. As distinct from the forms of local accommodation used under James, the Caroline forest eyre in Windsor asserted and enforced royal interests in the preservation of deer and woods as the highest purpose of the forest and its institutions.

This reform initiative in Windsor Forest had an enormous impact on the swanimote court. After decades of oversight focused primarily on forest officers, the court prosecuted hundreds of local violations of forest law during the 1630s, the offences ranging from petty encroachments to the organized attacks on the deer formerly prosecuted in Star Chamber. The sheer scale of activity dwarfed a generation of judicial routine in the forest. During the first sessions of the eyre in 1632 and 1633, the swanimote court in Battell's bailiwick alone prosecuted 394 violations of forest law and imposed £474 in fines.[59] Of these cases, the court investigated 225 purprestures, involving enclosures and cottages or other buildings in the forest, ninety-eight acts of waste, or removal of the forest cover, and twenty-five assarts, the more serious offense of converting the forest permanently to arable land or pasture. As Kevin Sharpe has suggested, the court's fines hardly solved the fiscal problems of the Caroline regime, but individual punishments revealed a harsh attitude towards such offenders as

---

[56] H. E. Malden (ed.), *VCH Surrey*, 4 vols. (London: Archibald Constable and Company, 1905), 2: 568.
[57] Cox, *Royal Forests*, 297–298; Hammersley, "Revival of the Forest Laws," 89; Sharpe, *Personal Rule*, 243.
[58] *CSPD, James I, 1603–1610*, 394.
[59] These figures remain tentative, as individual cases often involved multiple offences and a fine is sometimes lost in the damaged margins of the court's records. See PRO: C154/10/149, Court Presentments, 8 and 9 Charles I; C154/10/190, Court Presentments, 9 Charles I; C99: Chief Justice of the Forests South of Trent; Records of Forest Eyres, Charles I, 1632–1640: 126, Regarders' Presentments, Battell's Bailiwick, 14 September 1632; C99/128, Proceedings and Presentments in Swanimote Courts, Battell's Bailiwick, 12 June 1633 and 18 September 1633.

Christopher Smith, gentleman, fined £40 for "converting the earth to tile and brick in two great pits in Old Windsor wood, to the annoyance of his majesty's hunting there."[60] Although unlawful hunting did not figure prominently in the early sessions of the eyre, the court's presentment of seventy-one "unlawed" (unexpeditated) dogs signaled its intention to protect the king's deer against the most common forms of attack. In addition to prosecuting these cases, officers of the court reported the routine actions of woodwards and keepers, surveyed the crown woods and the coppices in the bailiwick, and walked the boundaries of both the Berkshire side of the forest and the bailiwick in an attempt to resolve jurisdictional conflicts. The result of this broad administrative effort, as indicated by the evidence of a single forest bailiwick, did not make Windsor a mirror of forest law, but the eyre did establish the crown as the dominant political force in Windsor and subordinated other uses to royal interests in the forest.

Many of the enclosures and buildings presented in the swanimote had affected the welfare of the king's deer and thus symbolized the deterioration of royal honor and power in the forest. A keeper complained that William Wheatly's house, built on his freehold land in Winckfield, was an "annoyance to his majesty's game." In nearby Warfield, William Turner had raised a fodder house next to "a great covert called Holtshott, to the disturbance of his majesty's red deer." His neighbor Edward Stafferton, esquire, had set up "six pole of pale" on his land in Warfield, "straighting the fall of the deer," while another unidentified neighbor had "railed up a strait passage near Warfield field, where the deer had formerly liberty to pass, that the deer cannot pass."[61] But the buildings presented also reveal the tendency of the eyre to interpret the adaptation of forest law to local uses and interests in terms of encroachment. Many barns, stables, and warehouses in New Windsor incurred fines under this new regime. Nicholas Rance used a sliver of the king's waste in Clewar to build a blacksmith's shop that the regarders found "no hurt to the king's pleasure," but the court fined Rance twenty shillings. John Robinson, clerk of Sunninghill, paid a lesser fine of two shillings for an acre of forest land enclosed to build a schoolhouse. In Winckfield, "four small cottages on the king's waste" sheltered "four poor widows, who pay no rent, neither are

---

[60] PRO: C99/126, Regarders' Presentments, Battell's Bailiwick, 14 September 1632: presentments of Old Windsor parish; Sharpe, *Personal Rule*, 242–243.

[61] Ibid., presentments of Winckfield parish, Warfield parish; C99/128, Proceedings and Presentments in Swanimote Courts, Battell's Bailiwick, 12 June 1633 and 18 September 1633: presentments of Warfield parish; C154/10/149, Court Presentments, 8 and 9 Charles I: presentments of Warfield parish.

able to pay by reason of poverty, being altogether relieved by the parishioners." Although the regarders claimed "these cottages [are] no annoyance to his majesty's pleasure," the court demanded five shillings per house.[62] Yet this attack on encroachments could also defend common interests from the destructive acts of individuals, a traditional strength of forest law. When George Sherwood and Thomas Barton of Clewar damaged a watercourse and a pedestrian way in the process of making "a clam of brick" and transporting bricks and coals, the court fined them £10 and required them to make repairs. In like fashion, Ralph Dell's sawpit in Winckfield, made "to the peril of men and destruction of traffic in Free Lane," was made the subject of a fine and then filled in by the court's order.[63]

The prosecutions for waste more clearly reflected the conflicts between human and animal economies in the forest, as the court used the forest law to curtail the impact of individual interests and local customs in Windsor on the subsistence of the royal deer. John Gurnett of Winckfield, a tenant of the local "brick keele," received a £5 fine for digging pits in the forest "to the prejudice of his majesty's hunting." Brickmakers were not the only source of potential danger to the undergrowth used by the deer for cover and for food: a diverse market supported the sale of coppice wood for building and as fuel for households as well as for brick- and tile-making enterprises. Thomas Finch had planted an illegal coppice of "120 small oaks and saplings" in Uptown that, according to the underkeeper, "destroyed the covert of underwood." Among the more ambitious foresters, it was difficult to ignore growing markets for produce in New Windsor and Braye. In addition to the five orchards and ten gardens prosecuted as enclosures, the eyre punished acts of waste that converted the forest to arable land. In the Great Park, symbol of royal aspirations in Windsor, the regarders complained of six acres illicitly "sown with oats and peas" in Edward Norwood's walk, and the court fined Norwood for negligence. Henry Sawde of Warfield received a £5 fine for "grubbing and assarting a coppice" of three acres "and sowing it with French wheat."[64] The most difficult of these cases touched on local custom, as the eyre confronted the same claims to take the covert for fuel in such hamlets as Warfield and

---

[62] PRO: c99/126, Regarders' Presentments, Battell's Bailiwick, 14 September 1632: presentments of Clewar parish, Sunninghill parish, Winckfield parish.

[63] PRO: c99/128, Proceedings and Presentments in Swanimote Courts, Battell's Bailiwick, 12 June 1633 and 18 September 1633: presentments of Clewar parish, Winckfield parish.

[64] PRO: c99/126, Regarders' Presentments, Battell's Bailiwick, 14 September 1632: presentments of Winckfield parish, Sunninghill parish, Great Park; c99/128, Proceedings and Presentments in Swanimote Courts, Battell's Bailiwick, 12 June 1633 and 18 September 1633: presentments of Warfield parish.

Winckfield as those the swanimote had struggled against since the 1610s. In 1633, the reeve asserted once again "that the parishioners of Winckfield have usually taken turf for their own burning" but questioned the authority of neighbors in Warfield to do the same.[65] The matter was seldom this simple, as foresters in Winckfield often violated the custom by selling turfs to neighbors in Warfield. In Warfield, a proprietary relationship to the Nevilles of Wargrave, whose grant of "parks, warrens, chases, purlieus, and wild beasts" from Edward VI had mirrored the liberties of the bishops of Winchester in Wargrave, allowed such turfcutters as William Horsenayle and Henry Sawde to justify their actions.[66] Under these circumstances, the eyre passed over the Winckfield custom but took a stand against Warfield, imposing fines on the widows Bowyer and Hawthorne, the husbandman Gilbert Walden, and the yeoman William Wise, foresters of Warfield who "had dug turfs in Winckfield, owning no lands in the hamlet, contrary to the laws of the forest."[67]

Despite the small number of cases prosecuted, the eyre successfully transferred the violence of unlawful hunting from the Star Chamber to the swanimote, and a variety of other presentments affirmed the primacy of the royal hunt in the forest. The eyre cracked down on hunting in those tracts of the forest inclined to view their status in terms of purlieu, such as Warfield, and to defy forest law. In response to the eyre's articles, the regarders presented Leonard Peade of Warfield "for hunting and coursing a stag in the walk with a greyhound, a beagle, and a spaniel," and his neighbor John Hawthorne of Tilehouse "for coursing a great stag with a mongrel." The court also took notice of traps set by the foresters, prosecuting John Larchin of Braye, yeoman, "for setting an engine made of a cord to take the king's deer at Waltham Hill."[68] But the attack on warrens and dogs expressed the eyre's broader concern to limit hunting in Windsor. Among the ten warrens prosecuted and removed from Battell's bailiwick, the court ordered the destruction of a particularly egregious cony warren at Conduit Head in Winckfield, "planted these many years" by Sir Richard Harrison, lord of Hurst and Winckfield and a verderer of the forest, and maintained by "the hands of diverse tenants of Winckfield and the keeper

---

[65] PRO: C154/10/149, Court Presentments, 8 and 9 Charles I: presentments of Winckfield parish.
[66] See Page and Ditchfield, *VCH Berkshire*, 3: 185, 193, for the manors of Wargrave and Warfield. Horsenayle and Sawde were prosecuted by the swanimote in 1624 and by the eyre in 1632.
[67] PRO: C99/128, Proceedings and Presentments in Swanimote Courts, Battell's Bailiwick, 12 June 1633 and 18 September 1633: presentments of Clewar, Warfield, Winckfield parishes.
[68] PRO: C154/10/149, Court Presentments, 8 and 9 Charles I: presentments of Warfield parish; C154/10/190, Court Presentments, 9 Charles I: presentments of attachment court, 13 April 1633 [Larchin of Braye].

of Swinley Walk."[69] Although the officers who broke their oaths killed many deer indirectly, the foresters who kept unlawed dogs posed a more serious challenge to the new order in the forest, and the court acted to remove this threat. The list included such great offenders as Edward Staverton, esquire, a prominent landholder in Warfield, who received a £2 fine for his pack of twelve beagles, and the reeve of Winckfield presented John Henry, esquire, for his kennel of fourteen "harehounds." In a definitive statement concerning the primacy of the hunt under statute and forest law, a special jury and the reeve of New Windsor, in response "to certain articles [from the eyre] touching the forest of Windsor," presented eighteen neighbors, including the alderman Thomas Havergill, for keeping unlawed mastiffs.[70]

The court used the exemplary punishment of great offenders, including the punishment of forest officers for negligence and corruption, to establish the effective power of this new order in Windsor. The king's powerful neighbors had to be brought to understand the coercive power of the forest court. Thomas Havergill, alderman of New Windsor, was summoned for enclosing six acres of meadow in Datchet Mead, "ploughing and sowing it with barley," for building an orchard on a patch of meadow near Frogmore, and for enclosing two acres of forest next to the Great Park. Thomas Erskine, Earl of Kelly, received £80 in fines for "destroying much covert for his majesty's game" near Braye, felling "a hedgerow of great wood," containing eighty trees, assarting and clearing a further six acres of forest, and cutting down "a grove of [120] great trees."[71] In 1632 and 1633, the eyre investigated twelve officers in Battell's bailiwick, including the ranger Sir Charles Howard and his deputy, Simon Avery als Bernard, presented for more than ten acres of illegal enclosures used to set up three "salteries" or salt works in New Lodge Walk. In response to the eyre's articles of enquiry, the reeve of Old Windsor presented John Leavar,

---

[69] PRO: C99/126, Regarders' Presentments, Battell's Bailiwick, 14 September 1632: miscellaneous presentments. This conduit in Winckfield carried water to Windsor Castle. See Tighe and Davis, *Annals of Windsor*, 1: 599.

[70] Those presented for New Windsor included two gentlemen, two yeoman, one baker, two brewers, five butchers, two tanners, and one fellmonger. PRO: C154/10/149, Court Presentments, 8 and 9 Charles I: presentments of New Windsor parish, Winckfield parish; C99/128, Proceedings and Presentments in Swanimote Courts, Battell's Bailiwick, 12 June 1633 and 18 September 1633: presentments of Warfield parish.

[71] PRO: C154/10/149, Court Presentments, 8 and 9 Charles I: presentments of Old Windsor parish, Braye parish; C99/126, Regarders' Presentments, Battell's Bailiwick, 14 September, 1632: presentments of New Windsor parish, Braye parish; C99/128, Proceedings and Presentments in Swanimote Courts, Battell's Bailiwick, 12 June 1633 and 18 September 1633: presentments of Old Windsor parish. In 1622, Havergill had been prosecuted in Star Chamber for complicity in deer stealing.

a regarder, for sixteen acts of waste and corruption, including the destruction of a twenty-four-acre coppice called Friends Grove and the use of his office to protect neighbors from charges in the swanimote court. In 1633, the eyre sequestered the office of Edmund Sawyer, deputy woodward of Clewar Wood under Sir Thomas Aylsbury, for "negligently keeping the wood, permitting diverse persons to fell and carry away loads of wood, as much as they can carry on horseback, and permitting others with hatchets and axes to cut short the great oaks, which afterwards fall and die, to the destruction of the wood and the damage of the king."[72] Although few officers lost their places in this way, the signal must have been clear. If the court's investigations could touch Howard and Sir Richard Harrison, the verderer prosecuted for his warren, none of those who helped themselves to the king's woods could count on safety.

The forest eyre served the crown well in Windsor during the 1630s, using the power of the forest courts to support an ambitious refurbishment of royal amenities. Because of the reforms made among officers and subjects, the forest's resources became more dependably available to the crown in pursuit of its interests in Windsor, especially the security of the parks and forest as royal hunting preserves. Indeed, Charles liked to keep Windsor's venison for his own use. Most of his gifts to "ambassadors and agents of princes" and to high officers of London came from Waltham Forest and from the parks near London, but deer from Windsor seemed to belong especially to the king's service, such as the four does carried to "his majesty's house" at Whitehall from the Great Park and New Lodge Walk for the Christmas festivities in 1640.[73] Among other expensive signs of his interest in Windsor, in 1636 Charles had enclosed the east end of the terrace near his lodgings "with a handsome wall and gate," including an image of Diana, leading into the Little Park.[74] The value of the new order in the forest became apparent during the rebuilding of the Great Park in 1638. Sir Arthur Mainwaring and Sir Robert Bennett, surveyor of the king's works in

---

[72] PRO: C154/10/149, Court Presentments, 8 and 9 Charles I: presentments of Braye parish, Old Windsor parish; C99/126, Regarders' Presentments, Battell's Bailiwick, 14 September, 1632: presentments of Braye parish; C99/128, Proceedings and Presentments in Swanimote Courts, Battell's Bailiwick, 12 June 1633 and 18 September 1633: miscellaneous presentments, Clewar parish. Sawyer subsequently served in important offices during the 1630s.

[73] Between 1638 and 1640, the king offered forty-two bucks annually as political gifts, but only four from Windsor: one buck from the Great Park for the French ambassador, one buck from the Little Park for the Venetian ambassador, and two bucks from the Great Park for the Lord Mayor, aldermen, and recorder of London. See PRO: SP 16/384, Orders and Warrants Concerning Forests, ff. 10r–11r, 30r–v, 47r, 53r–v.

[74] H. M. Colvin (ed.), *History of the King's Works* (London: HMSO, 1975), vol. 3 (1485–1660), part 1: 330–332.

Windsor, presented the pale of the park as "very ruinous and greatly decayed" and "needful to be new set for the better preservation of his majesty's deer in the park." On the basis of their survey, the Earl of Holland allowed 173 loads of wood from the Great Park itself, Old Windsor Wood, and Cranborne Wood, providing the material and £92 in funds for the work entirely from the honor and forest of Windsor. In the spirit of his eyre's reforms, Holland indicated to Mainwaring and Bennett,

> because these proportions both of timber and money are very great, considering the present condition of his majesty's revenue and woods there, I cannot but put you in mind of the care you ought to take of this service, and require you accordingly to perform it with as much husbandry and ease of charge to his majesty as may be, selling the lops, tops, and offal wood from the felled trees to his majesty's best advantage, and the price to go to the charge of the work, upon account of the whole to be given in the usual manner.[75]

As this work went forward, in October 1639, Holland ordered Bennett to secure the gates of the Great Park and "to alter the locks," in order "to disappoint the multitude of keys by which the park is made in a manner common, as well to the disturbance and hazard of the king's deer there as to the filling of the park with horses and cattle of persons unknown."[76] Of course, many "persons unknown" to Holland, particularly in the parish of Egham on the Surrey side of the forest, claimed a customary right to pasture in the park, to make the park "common" in a manner unsuited to the new order in the forest. In 1640, the rebuilding spread to other walks of the forest, always tending to reinforce Windsor's significance as a royal domain. Buoyed by accounts of the "great store of deer" in New Lodge Walk, Holland allowed timber from Braye Wood for work on the New Lodge as well as "the pale enclosing the little park about the house and the pond heads."[77] On the Surrey side of the forest, more firmly included in Windsor during the eyre, Holland supported Bennett's survey in June of "decays" at Seas Lodge, authorizing new "tiling, walling, and other brick-work, the ovens in the bakehouse [being] newly roofed," and carpentry work in the barns and stables.[78] Apart from these planned works, Bennet undertook such unforeseen but significant projects as £27 in assorted repairs to Bagshot Lodge, a favorite royal retreat damaged "by the last great wind," in order "to make it something fitting for his majesty against his coming thither."[79] These were the major concerns of the forest officers in Windsor during the summer of 1640. Although Holland's decision to

---

[75] PRO: SP 16/384, Orders and Warrants Concerning Forests, ff. 2v–4r. [76] Ibid., f. 33r–v.
[77] Ibid., ff. 36r–37r. [78] Ibid., ff. 38v, 41r–43r. [79] Ibid., f. 48r–v.

drive the Great Park in July appears to have caused some anxiety among the keepers, the impression remains of a gradual but successful expansion of effective royal power in Windsor during the late 1630s. In the absence of a national crisis, it seems likely that political conflicts in Windsor would have remained local matters for the local courts. Under different circumstances, historians might see the key evidence of local reform in the noble gifts presented by the corporation of Windsor to the royal children, Charles and James, in August 1640. A delegation of the mayor and aldermen bestowed on the children

> two hunter's horns, tipped and adorned with silver and gilt of goldsmith's work, and two fair taffeta scarfs to hang them at, richly embroidered with gold, and edged with a very great gold and silver bone lace at the ends of them, also a fair tassel of silk and gold to each of the horns, fastened with great broad ribbon.[80]

This gift recognized the interplay of the hunt and royal honor that Charles had attempted to restore in Windsor. Before the parliamentary presentment of the Caroline forests as a national grievance, before the last scattered sessions of the forest court on the eve of civil war, one could hardly find more persuasive evidence of local submission to royal authority in Windsor.

IV

The violence in Windsor Forest during the late 1630s and early 1640s resulted from political conflicts intensified if not created by the forest eyre. Although most understood the law whereby the crown sequestered the forest as a royal hunting preserve, such local communities as Warfield, on the western border of the forest, and Egham, on the southeastern border, continued to believe in the justice of their customs as legitimate claims to the forest's resources, and many local aspirants to gentility, status, and office continued to believe in a necessary competition for honor expressed in trophies of the hunt. The royal hunt had traditionally existed, however uneasily, alongside these other notions of forest, but the eyre had unequivocally insisted on the primacy of those elements of forest law most conducive to royal interests. Moreover, the eyre had reformed the swani-mote as the judicial force behind the new order, removing the boundary between major conflicts formerly adjudicated in Star Chamber and the local matters handled in the swanimote. Under the Caroline regime, the swanimote court became the primary forum for all manner of conflicts in

---

[80] The corporation spent more than £20 on these gifts. See Tighe and Davis, *Annals of Windsor*, 2: 146.

the forest, summoning the enemies of both deer and covert to face the same fines before the same tribunal.

In 1638, the main business of the swanimote concerned attacks on the king's deer by local gentlemen and entrepreneurs, the kinds of cases removed to Star Chamber during the 1610s. Of those prosecuted for hunting raids, Hercules Trew served as chamberlain of Windsor corporation in 1638 and as mayor in 1639. As an alderman, Trew was chosen for the delegation that presented the corporation's gift to Charles and James in 1640.[81] Trew hunted in many styles, using a dog, a net, or a crossbow as the occasion or company seemed to require, accumulating £72 in fines for his convictions.[82] Like the Dayrells in Stowe, Trew and his friends could not resist the theater of honor in the Little Park. During the late 1630s, the forest eyre and swanimote defined hunters and woodcutters as common enemies of the forest, destroyers of deer and covert. In this spirit, the court prosecuted Trew's friend Thomas Bromley in 1638, fining him £5 for killing deer in New Lodge Walk, and, in the same session, levied a £5 fine on a certain William W for felling fifteen oaks on his customary land in Warfield, "without a viewing by the foresters."[83] Although this decision to prosecute all forest offences in the same way made for judicial efficiency, politically it also created a common grievance in the forest court for a range of offenders not used to defining their activities in the same terms. The process whereby these common grievances were formed is evident in Holland's order book, containing notes on select swanimote cases. Thomas Bromley's friend John Elliot, an innkeeper in New Windsor, petitioned Holland in November 1638, having been imprisoned and fined £12 "for carrying stolen venison to London, dressing stolen venison in his house, and receiving the skins of four does brought to him by a notorious malefactor." In his own words, Elliot "justly deserved" punishment but could not pay the fines that kept him in gaol and begged "compassion for his poor wife and children."[84] The court's strictness became a common theme of petitions. In January 1639, Robert Wilkes of Warfield complained of a £5 fine imposed by the regarders of Battell's bailiwick for twenty elms felled on his copyhold land in Warfield. Wilkes

---

[81] Ibid., 1: 235; 2: 135, 146.
[82] PRO: C154/18/122, Swanimote Courts, 10–14 Charles I: court presentments, Battell's bailiwick, 17 September 1638.
[83] Ibid.
[84] Thomas Bromley's friend William Piggot, the servant of an underkeeper of New Lodge Walk, was the "notorious malefactor" dealing in the skins. See PRO: C154/18/122, Swanimote Courts, 10–14 Charles I: court presentments, Battell's bailiwick, 17 September 1638; SP 16/384, Orders and Warrants Concerning Forests, ff. 14v–15r.

argued that the previous copyholder had obtained a license from Holland himself to remove these trees, but the officers had ignored the licence, presented him in the swanimote, and assessed the fine. Wilkes petitioned Holland to uphold his own prior order.[85]

During late spring and summer 1640, local irritations in Windsor began to find expression in the broader politics of national grievances. In July Holland elected to challenge notions of custom in the Great Park, having received information "that one Eastwick takes upon him the power to dispose of the herbage of the park, and by color thereof depastures there great numbers of horses and other cattle, to the great damage of the park and his majesty's deer." Holland ordered the keepers to drive the park and to certify both the numbers and owners of all the horses and cattle, a tactic often understood, in the manner of Nazeing wood, as the prelude to a stint of the commons.[86] This drive exacerbated a local dispute that had larger implications, as the foresters in such hamlets as Egham viewed their common pasture in the Great Park as a legitimate claim under the law. Because a political tradition in the forest defined conflict in these terms of protections and claims under the law, it is not surprising to find Windsor's grievances being included in a broader political defence of "established laws" in 1640. In July, the famous petition of the Berkshire grand jury made Windsor's predicament part of the larger injustice committed "by officers deriving their authority from your majesty, but being directly contrary to your laws established in this kingdom." Although modestly leaving redress to the king's mercy, the petition encouraged Charles to show his subjects,

and especially those of the privy council and other officers and ministers of justice, that your majesty is resolved to give them all their rights and liberties which they desire by their petition of right, and were confirmed by you in the third year of your reign.[87]

The list of grievances included the illegality of ship money, the distress caused by "undue means to enforce the payment" of the "new tax of coat and conduct money," and "the infinite monopolies on everything almost that the countryman has to buy." The petition implicitly criticized the priority of the royal hunt in Windsor, complaining that "your forest of Windsor is particularly burdened with the innumerable increase of deer, which, if they shall go on so fast, in ten years more will neither leave food nor room for any other creature." The forest officers deepened this

---

[85] Ibid., f. 22r–v.
[86] Ibid., f. 46r–v.   [87] *CSPD, Charles I, v. 16 (1640)*, 466–467.

hardship by their "rigid execution of the forest laws" and the "exaction of inordinate fees" under the justice in eyre.[88] Attacks on the "red and fallow deer" in Windsor began during the summer, "certain persons living in the forest being suspected," and Holland lost confidence in the swanimote. In November, he issued a license to Sir Arthur Mainwaring and Sir Richard Harrison "to repress this disorder before time and impunity give it growth and encouragement." Mainwaring and Harrison took the place of the swanimote, receiving new powers, as "principal officers of the forest," to summon, examine, and punish offenders "as shall be agreeable to the forest laws."[89]

Although the Berkshire petition did not mention religious grievances, the hints of religious faction in Windsor may figure in the disposition to view local conflicts in broader terms. There is slight evidence of a godly faction led by John Martin, vicar of New Windsor during the 1620s and early 1630s, but, following Martin's death in 1633, Matthew and Christopher Wren, as deans of Windsor, and Godfrey Goodman, as canon of St. George's chapel, introduced significant Laudian reforms to "beautify and adorn" the parish church. In the usual Laudian style, this "beautification" involved such projects as the repaving of the chancel and setting up of rails around the communion table, the installation of an organ, and, more dramatically, the rebuilding of the market cross in 1635, surmounted by a crucifix "erected in colors." The mayor and corporation of New Windsor opposed the building of "a new crucifix, where never was any before, in the heart of our common market place," and demolished the cross in 1641. The major concerns of these factions, needless to say, were not those of the forest, but the politics of religion in 1640 and the familiar indictment of popery in the Caroline church may have sharpened local perceptions of royal injustices in the forest. In September 1640 Christopher Wren wrote from Windsor to Laud's secretary, William Dell, that "the defeat of the king's horse and the surprise of Newcastle have made the Scots here [the godly faction] so insolent, it is not to be imagined what words have passed some of them, and those of our society are miserably cast down."[90]

---

[88] Ibid.

[89] These attacks in the summer and fall 1640 may explain the report in December of "great decay" in the "pale and rails" of the Great Park, "so as neither the course can be kept several for the male deer, which is their only relief, nor can the deer be brought to their standings." See PRO: SP 16/384, Orders and Warrants Concerning Forests, ff. 49r–v, 53v–54r.

[90] *CSPD, Charles I, v. 17 (1640–1641)*, 6–7; Tighe and Davis, *Annals of Windsor*, 1: 234–235; 2: 77–79, 98–111.

When the Earl of Holland announced to the House of Lords in March 1641 that the king was "willing to lay down all the new bounds of his forests in this kingdom, and that they shall be as they were before the late justices seat," he signaled the return of a traditional style of political negotiation in the forests.[91] In Windsor, this meant an effort to settle the borders of the forest. On 16 March, the same day as his speech in the Lords, Holland issued a license to Sir Richard Harrison and his tenants in Finchampstead, Winckfield, and Wittingham, on the troublesome western border of the forest, "for liberty to cut turf and peat on his own soil in these parishes, forasmuch as I confide in his discretion and fidelity as a verderer of the forest to govern this liberty with such moderation and care as becomes the trust reposed in him." Although Holland stipulated the cutting of turf in "moderate quantities, convenient places, and at seasonable times, not in the [fence] month nor to the exile and destruction of the deer," this license clearly restored the negotiation of interests in forest politics.[92]

The negotiations were tougher on the southeastern border, where the drift of the Great Park in August 1640 had polarized local politics by appearing to indicate the crown's intent to break the custom of common pasture. In May 1642, seventeen inhabitants of Egham described their petition to Holland in the familiar terms of negotiation, as "the desire of those who have a respect as well to his majesty's right as to their own." But the drift had also evoked a style of politics overtly hostile to crown interests in the forest. As these petitioners reported, "the rude multitude have threatened to pull down the pales of the park and lay it all to common, if they may not be in some measure satisfied in this particular [of their common pasture]." These "rude" neighbors had expressed their view of the forest by "their late disorders in the destruction of his majesty's red deer, despite the best means of either the messengers of parliament or the magistrates of the county to prevent it." Although the petitioners renounced the deer killing, they agreed with their neighbors about the principle of the common, "justly fearing that where they have a colorable pretense [of defending their customary rights] they will not be less riotous and disorderly than when they had no pretense at all." Among their terms, the petitioners requested their "ancient custom" of pasture in the Great Park from 10 May until Lammas day on 1 August, and from the feast of All Hallows on 1 November until Christmas, an arrangement justified "in respect that a great part of the park has been taken out of the commons of

91 Rushworth, *Historical Collections*, 4: 206.
92 PRO: SP 16/384, Orders and Warrants Concerning Forests, ff. 57v–58r.

Egham parish." In return, the crown would have the customary service of "carrying in hay" for the deer during the winter and "sending in treaders" to press down the soil around new covert. "Though by their ancient custom none paid above three halfpence a week," the petitioners would accept a rate of 4d per head of cattle and 6d per horse, "in respect that the price of land as of all other commodities are since that time much increased." Holland seems to have been unprepared for this detailed proposal, declining to give "any positive order concerning this without advising with his majesty's counsel at law." Although not accustomed to negotiation, Holland ordered "that some person or persons to be trusted by those inhabitants do attend the attorney general, who is hereby desired to take their demands into consideration and, having informed himself how the same are grounded, to certify to me what course he thinks convenient to be held."[93] In the absence of an effective forest court in Windsor, a desperate hope was placed in the power of these petitioners to deliver peace in Surrey bailiwick.

Peace did not return to the forest before the war, despite the new statute of August 1641 renouncing the "late presentments" and restoring Jacobean boundaries.[94] Sir Arthur Mainwaring wrote to Holland in October that "the law and the House of Commons order preventing destruction had been published in churches and the swanimote courts, and lately at the commission in Egham for setting the bounds of Surrey bailiwick," but the "insolent killing of deer in Egham walk" had not ceased. In September and early October, "the rude multitude" in Egham had seceded from the forest, "pretending they were out of the bounds," and "a great number of people entered the woods there, killed the king's stags and other deer, and divided them amongst them." Of the four leaders of this action, William Purse bore the name of a substantial forest family and took an active part, threatening to stab or shoot Robert Box, and the other keepers of Egham Walk, "if they came into them." Participants claimed the new statute had removed Egham from the forest and justified their proceedings under the law. When a parliamentary messenger tried to arrest Purse and his friends in early November, their supporters rescued them.[95] Apart from direct local actions of this kind, the violent politics of reaction against the symbols

---

[93] Ibid., ff. 62r–63r.
[94] 16 Car. I, c. 16, in *Statutes of the Realm*, 5: 119–120.
[95] HLRO: Main Papers, 1509–1700: 27 October 1641; *LJ*, vol. 4: 406–407, 434, 547. William Purse of Egham, a leader of these attacks, may have been related to the Pursey family of nearby Sunninghill, often recruited for swanimote juries during the 1630s. See PRO: C154/18/122, Swanimote Courts, 10–14 Charles I: court presentments, Battell's bailiwick, 17 September 1638.

of the Caroline forest regime remains shadowy. In April 1642, Holland received a letter claiming "that the *people* of Berkshire, adjoining Windsor forest, have a *resolution* speedily to come in a tumultuous manner and pull down the pales of the Great park."[96] The references here to the "people" and a "resolution" suggest a political process and perhaps an element of organization, at least in the form of local meetings, but this dimension of the "rude" politics of violent activism remains as dark as the process that resulted in the petition of the Egham commoners a month later.

The few scraps of evidence produced by local activism in 1641 and 1642, usually a result of parliamentary efforts to suppress it, reveal a sketchy but coherent pattern of political intentions behind the violence in Windsor. In Surrey bailiwick, the accounts of attacks on the deer in Egham Walk and the petition of the Egham commoners reveal local convictions concerning their status in the forest and the security of their customs under forest law. As Purse and his faction in Egham placed their actions "out of the bounds" of the forest, presumably in the purlieu, the attacks on the deer more generally suggest a practical disafforestation, claiming the liberties of purlieu in disputed tracts of the forest and, in others, destroying the deer to remove what had become under Charles the primary justification for the enforcement of forest law. During the 1630s, the forest eyre had elevated the royal hunt and the king's deer as symbols of the "honor and power" of the crown in Windsor. As local customs on the western and southeastern borders seemed to disappear beneath the weight of this symbolism, and as the boundaries of forests became a national grievance worthy of a parliamentary remedy, attacks on the deer make sense as a rejection of the Caroline high forest and as a local, practical solution to the problem of disafforestation. If the deer vanished from the forest, in the calculus of this "rude" politics, their law might follow. Sir Arthur Mainwaring had seen this politics of disafforestation clearly in the attacks on Surrey bailiwick and urged Holland to adopt "some speedy course to restrain ... the rest of that condition or else if it shall be adjudged forest hereafter there will be no deer to keep in it."[97]

Perhaps because the swanimote had been discredited in its execution of the forest eyre, the parliament began as early as January 1642 to shift the

---

[96] *LJ*, vol. 5: 25, 33, 35. The petition of the Egham commoners was submitted after a parliamentary investigation of this rumor in May 1642.

[97] HLRO: Main Papers, 1509–1700: 27 October 1641. See Pettit, *Royal Forests of Northamptonshire*, 93, for a similar explanation of attacks in Whittlewood Forest in 1640 as the tactics of a practical disafforestation, conveyed in a letter from the lieutenant of the forest to Henry, Lord Spencer, the master of the game.

judicial authority for the enforcement of the new statute to sheriffs and justices of the peace.[98] But the sheriff of Berkshire failed to deter "the great destruction and killing of his majesty's deer in the New Lodge," on the western border of the forest, in February 1642, "where the people of the country, in a riotous and tumultuous manner, have lately killed a hundred of his majesty's fallow deer, and red deer besides, and threaten to pull down the pales about the lodge."[99] When those suspected in this action refused to obey Holland's warrants, the parliament began to intervene in a style similar to that of Star Chamber, ordering the sheriff of Berkshire "to attach and deliver" the suspects "to the gentleman usher of this house" for presentation before the House of Lords to answer the charges.[100] Of the five leaders of this action from Warfield, Easthampstead, and Ockingham arrested, Aminadab Harrison and Thomas Patey of Easthampstead were confined in the Berkshire house of correction in March, "there to be kept to work until the pleasure of this house be further known."[101] In April and May, parliament took increasingly strong measures to suppress these "riots and disorders" in both Windsor and Waltham forests, "being a blemish to government, and of a dangerous consequence in the example, thus to violate and deface his majesty's parks and forests."[102] Parliament had an obvious political stake in the enforcement of the "known bounds as now limited" by the statute, and a further ordinance in May formally empowered sheriffs and justices of the peace to confront this "force and violence as scandalous to the public justice of the kingdom, if not punished, and dangerous for the future."[103]

The disafforestation of Windsor continued, however, and parliament could not enforce the statute or the ordinance before the arrival of Colonel John Venn and twelve companies of soldiers in October 1642 to take possession of Windsor Castle as a parliamentary garrison.[104] In May, John Barnes, the constable of Windlesham, a forest parish next to Egham Walk, reported an attack by William Crockford, Thomas Bishop, and Nicholas Buckridge of Cobham and Chertsey. Barnes had received a warrant from a Berkshire justice of the peace to apprehend deer stealers in Swinley Walk and, after gathering a few assistants, had met the suspects on the highway. "When [Barnes] charged them in the king's name to stand and obey his warrant, they answered they cared neither for king nor parliament, neither would obey his warrant." As Barnes chased them

---

[98] *LJ*, vol. 4: 547.   [99] Ibid., 595.   [100] Ibid., 602.   [101] Ibid., 653.   [102] *LJ*, vol. 5: 35.
[103] HLRO: Main Papers, 1509–1700: 12 May, 1642; *LJ*, vol. 5: 38, 61.
[104] Tighe and Davis, *Annals of Windsor*, 2: 168.

down the road, one of the suspects shot and killed Barnes's horse, ending the pursuit, and later "made his brags in an alehouse at Chertsey that he killed the constable's horse or else they had been taken."[105] This manner of indifference to the authority of king and parliament, as the crisis approached civil war, provoked a martial response from the parliament. After the Earl of Holland had issued a warrant to Ralph Madison, esquire, the keeper of Battell's and Easthampstead walks, to search the houses in Winckfield, Warfield, Sunninghill, and Easthampstead and to impound dogs, guns, crossbows, nets, "or other engines meet to kill the deer," the parliament authorized the sheriff of Berkshire in July "to raise the power of the county" to arrest any suspects named by Holland "for destroying the king's woods in Windsor forest."[106]

At this juncture, the separation and hostility of king and parliament, the assembly of armies on both clearly formed sides, undermined the power of local officers to enforce the forest statute in the divided communities of Windsor Forest. The new political landscape challenged the authority and honor of the Earl of Holland himself. In July, amidst his peace mission from the parliament to the king in Yorkshire, Holland found his patent to the lodge and walk in the Great Park challenged by Edward Terringham, esquire, an underkeeper of the park and son of Sir Arthur Terringham, an underkeeper during the early 1620s and a prominent servant of the Caroline regime in Ireland.[107] Holland claimed the lodge from his patent as constable of the castle and keeper of the forest, but Terringham obtained a new patent from the king, a token of Holland's loss of favor.[108] Holland complained in the House of Lords of Terringham's declaration "that he would present his case to the king, to know his pleasure." Francis Young and Thomas Symonds, underkeepers of the Great Park and Holland's servants, offered evidence of Terringham's distrust of the parliament in order to undermine his claim. According to Symonds, Terringham had rejected any role for parliament in the most disdainful terms. As a matter of law, Sir Robert Heath "and others about the king" had already declared Holland's patent worthless. According to Symonds, Terringham avowed

that whosoever came from the House to lay hand on him, he had that should speed him, he was a man of that mettle. If the king and parliament were in a union, he

[105] HLRO: Main Papers, 1509–1700: 21 May 1642.
[106] PRO: SP 16/384, Orders and Warrants Concerning Forests, ff. 64r–65r; *LJ*, vol. 5: 199.
[107] *CSPD, Charles I, v. 18 (1641–1643)*, 359–362; Tighe and Davis, *Annals of Windsor*, 2: 167–168; Hugh Kearney, *Strafford in Ireland, 1633–41: A Study in Absolutism* (Cambridge University Press, 1959), 47, 251–252.
[108] *CSPD, Charles I, v. 18 (1641–1643)*, 188, 192.

would refer his cause to them before any court of justice in the world, but, being as it is, he held it as no court of justice.[109]

Terringham's arrest and confinement by the House of Lords in November is beside the point. If Holland could not sustain the authority of his offices, local forest officers became leaves before the political storm. The circumstances of civil war offered new sources of power and protection – the royal court, the parliament, the armies of both sides – and made a restoration of the Jacobean forest settlement impossible. Holland had Hercules Trew, alderman and former mayor of Windsor and a proper icon of this new politics, arrested in 1642 and committed to Newgate as "a ringleader and constant disturber and destroyer of the forest, parks, and king's deer in Windsor." Trew promptly "broke prison," made his way to Windsor Castle, and enlisted under John Venn's command in the parliamentarian army. Although the hunt's code of honor led often enough to royalism among the nobility, the forest politics of the 1630s and early 1640s in Windsor makes sense of deer killing as a qualification for killing royalists. In the ethics of popular political action that allowed the removal of the king's deer to bring about a just disafforestation, the destruction of the king's armies might by the same means lead to political reformation.[110]

---

[109] Tighe and Davis, *Annals of Windsor*, 2: 167–168. In October, Holland appointed Young "to take custody of the Great Park, its lodges and deer," including the power to appoint and dismiss keepers according to the king's interest. PRO: SP 16/384, Orders and Warrants Concerning Forests, ff. 66v–67r.

[110] HLRO: Main Papers, 1509–1700: 10 May, 1643; *LJ*, vol. 6: 39.

Venison and the politics of honor in
Corse Lawn Chase, 1620–1642

I need not complain of the times; every traveler tells them; they are as
clear to see as an Angel in the sun.   Henry Osborne, October 1642[1]

I

In early October 1642, a tract of forest and deer chase in the Severn valley
northwest of Gloucester, known as Corse Lawn, became the site of a grisly
spectacle. Many of the words and techniques used in this grim performance
reprised the incidents in Stowe, Waltham, and Windsor earlier in the year.
Richard Dowdeswell, steward of Corse Lawn Chase, described the scene in
a letter to Lionel Cranfield, Earl of Middlesex, the absentee owner resident
in Great St. Bartholomew in London. Dowdeswell delivered terrifying
news of how "a rising of neighbors about Corse Lawn" destroyed more
than 600 of Middlesex's deer in a "rebellious, riotous, devilish way," a
hideous consequence of what Dowdeswell termed "this time of liberty."[2]
Dowdeswell rode to the site from his estate at Pull Court, a few miles from
the chase, and "appeased the multitude, yet some scattering companies
gave out in alehouses that they would not only destroy the remainder of
deer but rifle your lordship's house at Forthampton and pull it down to the
ground and not let a tree or bush stand in all the chase."[3] The deer massacre
became an assault on the chase, the forest, and the manor house of
Forthampton, an estate close to the chase but not included in the meets
and bounds of the forest. Middlesex's tenant at Forthampton Court,
his brother-in-law Henry Osborne, prudently moved his household to

---

[1] CKS: U 269, Sackville Mss/4/2/1 (Correspondence of Lionel Cranfield, Earl of Middlesex): Henry
Osborne to Lionel Cranfield, Earl of Middlesex, 24 october 1642. Osborne was Middlesex's brother-
in-law and his tenant at Forthampton Court, on the border of Corse Lawn Chase.
[2] CKS: U 269 Sackville Mss/4/2/1: Richard Dowdeswell to Middlesex, 18 october 1642.
[3] Ibid.

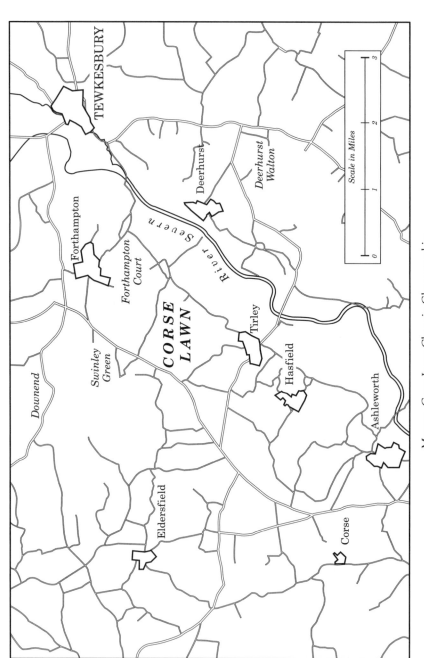

Map 5.1. Corse Lawn Chase in Gloucestershire

Gloucester until Dowdeswell acquired a formal certificate of protection from the Earl of Essex to defend the forest, the deer left in the chase, and the house in Forthampton.

This violent theater in Corse Lawn has received mixed reviews from historians uncertain of its genre, main players, and context. Menna Prestwich described the incident as an example of *jacquerie* or peasant rebellion, evidence of Middlesex's unpopularity as a landlord, but also noted the anomalous involvement of rich gentlemen.[4] In an effort to fit the incident into the series of attacks on parks and other hunting preserves, Brian Manning drew on Prestwich's work to depict the massacre as a typical example of that "peasant hostility towards the king and the great landlords" in the late summer and early autumn of 1642, a symbol of the political transformation among the "middle rank of men" in rural society. But this example does not support Manning's general view of conflict between gentlemen and commoners, because a faction of gentlemen led the attack, and Middlesex's property in Corse Lawn was described as a "chase or forest" rather than a park, and lacked the symbolism of enclosure important for Manning's case.[5] These accounts borrow from Richard Dowdeswell's explanation of the massacre in his letter to Middlesex, yet leave unexplored the subtle interrelationship of assaults on separate properties: the forest and chase in Corse Lawn, and the manor house in Forthampton. What caused the issues of the chase, the forest, and the Forthampton estate to coalesce in this massive assault on Middlesex's deer? Dowdeswell made no allusion to the local market for venison, at first glance a likely commercial motive for the attack, and referred only to the "destruction" of the animals.[6] He promised "if the kingdom stand your lordship will have ample reparations" from "rich and able men," described as "prime delinquents" in the massacre and perhaps in the series of raids on the chase Middlesex had attempted to prosecute in the 1630s.[7] A small-scale battle among rich gentlemen for the deer in Corse Lawn had existed for decades, but the involvement of "the mean and middle rank of men" and

---

[4] Menna Prestwich, *Cranfield: Politics and Profits Under the Early Stuarts* (Oxford: Clarendon Press, 1966), 568–570. Prestwich overestimates the impact of civil war on the chase in 1643 and 1644. A letter from Dowdeswell to Middlesex adduced as evidence of only six deer *left* in the chase in June 1644 states, rather, that only six deer have been *lost* since the massacre. See CKS: U 269, Sackville Mss/4/2/1: Dowdeswell to Middlesex, 9 June 1644.

[5] Manning, *The English People and the English Revolution*, 207–212, 258–259. See PRO: STAC 8/23/25, Sir Francis Bacon, Attorney General v. Sir William Throckmorton of Tortworth and others, 1616: bill of information, 10 February 1616, for references to the "chase or forest" of Corse Lawn.

[6] CKS: U 269, Sackville Mss/4/2/1: Dowdeswell to Middlesex, 18 October 1642.

[7] Ibid.

the sheer scale of the assault on the chase represented new developments. Dowdeswell did not explain how the small bands of gentlemen poachers in the 1630s became the crowd of "neighbors" recruited in local alehouses for the massacre in 1642, but described the new atmosphere in incendiary terms. "Since those times of combustion have happened in the countries hereabouts," Dowdeswell intoned, "and most places full of soldiers and volunteers or cavaliers, the countenances of men are so altered, especially of the mean and middle rank of men, that the turning of a straw would set a whole county in a flame and occasion the plundering of any man's house or goods, although much against the hearts and endeavors of all in authority."[8] This chapter explores how the straw came to be turned in Corse Lawn. The deer massacre reveals – more succinctly than any other single event – how a common cultural idiom, the symbolism of the hunt and its related notions of nobility and honor, could join and simplify complex social and political problems. Seen through this cultural lense, disputes over the forest and chase in Corse Lawn and the estate in Forthampton became skirmishes in the noble struggle against popish despotism, and the disparate properties of an absentee aristocratic landlord in London became the object of violent activism.

II

A symbolism of honor imparted meaning and power to the circulation of the products of the hunt in Gloucestershire. Middlesex, as the master of the chase and the feast, dominated this network of exchange from his distant household in London, using the animal resources of Corse Lawn to create lines of communication and influence among law officers of the crown, courtiers, bishops, justices of the peace, and a variety of useful local friends in the 1630s. Middlesex offered "a brace of bucks" as a gift to Henry Rich, Earl of Holland, chief justice in eyre of the forests south of the Trent, on his arrival in Gloucester for the forest eyre in 1634, in a public display of support for the reclamation of royal forests.[9] In 1639, Middlesex honored a request for a doe "at new year's tide" from a Mr. Bridges, a Gloucestershire client of Edward Sackville, Earl of Dorset, Middlesex's close friend and contact at court in the 1630s.[10] Another friend on the venison circuit was William Jones, a justice of the king's bench solicitous of Middlesex's

---

[8] Ibid.   [9] CKS: U 269, Sackville Mss/4/2/1: William Hill to Middlesex, 8 July 1634, 22 July 1634.
[10] CKS: U 269, Sackville Mss/4/2/1: William Hill to Middlesex, 15 December 1639; Prestwich, *Cranfield*, 538.

interests at the Gloucester assizes.[11] This friendship involved several convivial exchanges of venison, such as the feast offered at Worcester assizes in 1639, where Jones was disappointed not to meet Middlesex and "would have bid [him] welcome, for [Jones] had great store of fat venison, whereof Sir Henry Spiller had his share every meal, and [Spiller and Jones] drank to your honor and heartily wished your presence."[12] Sir Henry Spiller of Laleham in Middlesex, a veteran officer of the Exchequer, a justice of the peace for Middlesex and Worcestershire, and a prominent catholic, held the manor of Eldersfield in Worcestershire, on the border of Corse Lawn and, on frequent visits to the country from London in the 1630s, presided as lord of Eldersfield Court.[13] Spiller performed many local favors for Middlesex in return for pleasures of the chase. These favors included the solicitation of depositions in a court case related to the chase, mediation between Middlesex and his neighbors in Corse Lawn in 1637, and service as a ranger of the chase in 1640.[14] As a mark of this friendship, Spiller received a fallow doe from Corse Lawn for the Christmas holidays in 1637 and 1638 and apparently drank frequent healths to Middlesex in return.[15] In 1637, Middlesex presented half a buck to Richard Dowdeswell, a local attorney useful in a variety of business affairs and eventually appointed master of Corse Lawn Chase in 1640.[16]

Middlesex used the venison of Corse Lawn to construct an extensive network of friends in Gloucestershire. In 1637, a visit from Godfrey Goodman, Bishop of Gloucester, necessitated the preparation of "a fat buck" for his entertainment.[17] In August, 1637, a flurry of gifts followed the death of Sir Richard Tracy, the master of game in Corse Lawn. Anne, Countess of Middlesex, presented half a buck to Lady Tracy in the week

[11] CKS: U 269, Sackville Mss/4/2/1: William Hill to Middlesex, 9 July 1638.
[12] CKS: U 269, Sackville Mss/4/2/1: William Hill to Middlesex, 19 August 1639.
[13] *Calendar of the Committee for Compounding, 1643–60*, v. 2 (1643–1646): 1145–1149; J. W. Willis-Bund (ed.), *VCH Worcester*, 4 vols. (London: Dawsons, 1971), 4: 78; J. W. Willis-Bund (ed.), *Worcestershire County Records: Calendar of Quarter Sessions Papers*, 2 vols. (Worcester, 1900), 1: 394–396, 610–611, 617, 653, 659, 2: xxiv–xxv, xxix, cxv, ccxxii. Spiller's catholicism, career in the Exchequer, and connections to Henrietta Maria's court in the 1630s are discussed in M. C. Questier, "Sir Henry Spiller, Recusancy, and the Efficiency of the Jacobean Exchequer," *Historical Research*, 66 (1993): 254–255.
[14] In 1639, Spiller even offered Middlesex the use of his house in Eldersfield. CKS: U 269, Sackville Mss/4/2/1: William Hill to Middlesex, 7 January 1637, 9 July 1638, 19 August 1639; Richard Dowdeswell to Middlesex, 2 March 1640.
[15] Spiller petitioned Middlesex for some venison in the summer of 1638, as the fallow doe promised for the previous holiday season had not been delivered. CKS: U 269, Sackville Mss/4/2/1: William Hill to Middlesex, 7 January 1637, 9 July 1638, 19 August 1639.
[16] CKS: U 269, Sackville Mss/4/2/1: William Hill to Middlesex, 30 August 1637; Richard Dowdeswell to Middlesex, 2 March 1640, 10 August 1640.
[17] CKS: U 269, Sackville Mss/4/2/1: William Hill to Middlesex, 2 August 1637.

after Sir Richard's death, and hard on this gift Middlesex bestowed the "great favor" of a fallow buck on Sir Humphrey Tracy.[18] These noble gifts honored Sir Richard Tracy's service in Corse Lawn and solicited Sir Humphrey Tracy's goodwill in matters related to the property. In the late 1630s, Middlesex used the dividends of the chase to cultivate the friendship of the Tracys, the Duttons, the Cookes, and the Stephenses, the major parliamentary families in Gloucestershire. In addition to gifts bestowed on the Tracy family, Middlesex opened his chase to the courses of John Dutton, Sir Robert Tracy's election manager in March 1640, and Sir Robert Cooke received rare permission to hunt and kill "a very fat buck" for presentation to the Stephens family in September 1639.[19] Yet Middlesex did not hold a monopoly of the hunt, and the circulation of venison could also express the interrelationship of aristocratic networks and competition for status. In 1639, William Hill, the town clerk of Tewkesbury and Middlesex's local solicitor, boasted to Middlesex of a "venison feast" planned by the Tewkesbury borough council. This banquet featured "a brace of bucks," the gifts bestowed on the town by Spencer Compton, Earl of Northampton, from his stock in Compton Park, and by Thomas Lord Windsor, and the guest list included such notables as the inevitable Sir Henry Spiller.[20]

The restrictive laws of the hunt increased the value and prestige of this flow of noble gifts, the safest source of venison for commoners excluded from the chase. Middlesex used the venison of Corse Lawn as a mark of favor, as a reward for loyal service, and sometimes as a substitute for money in the satisfaction of debts. In August 1637, William Hill was embarrassed to have only twenty shillings from Middlesex to pay Cresfield, the recorder of Tewkesbury, for the preparation of an important lease, "but, having occasion to speak of venison, I was bold to tell him your lordship would bestow half a buck on him, as I presume you will."[21] Middlesex himself presented a fallow buck to a Mr. Tully, presumably in return for services rendered in Tully's place of employment, the office of the Seal of Green Wax in the Exchequer.[22] In 1637, Middlesex shipped a deer to a Mr. Ingram in

---

[18] Lady Tracy uncharacteristically refused her half buck but returned her "humble thanks." Ibid., William Hill to Middlesex, 30 August 1637; Humphrey Tracy to Middlesex, 6 September 1637, 7 September 1637.

[19] *CSPD, Charles I*, v. 15 (1639–40), 580–583; CKS: U 269, Sackville Mss/4/2/1: William Hill to Middlesex, 30 August 1637, 2 September 1639.

[20] Ibid., William Hill to Middlesex, 19 August 1639.

[21] Ibid., William Hill to Middlesex, 25 August 1637, 30 August 1637, 19 August 1639.

[22] William Hill also described Tully as "a special friend" of Nicholas Herman, a trusted relative and "confidential servant" to Middlesex over many years. Ibid., William Hill to Middlesex, 25 August 1637, 30 August 1637; Prestwich, *Cranfield*, 238.

Worcestershire, perhaps a connection to James Ingram, deputy warden of the Fleet, as the animal settled the accounts of a Colonel Billingsley, a relative of Middlesex imprisoned in the Fleet for debt.[23] Middlesex's servants coveted the pleasures of his chase. William Hill offered to send the first buck killed in 1638 to Middlesex's country house in Warwickshire, then solicited a gift as a reward, for "my wife desires to beg one half haunch, which will satisfy her for the whole year."[24] Hill had an unfortunate tendency to present gifts from Corse Lawn without asking Middlesex for approval. In addition to the half buck given to Cresfield in 1637, Hill extended this favor to John Golding, an obstreperous tenant Middlesex wanted to remove from Forthampton Court in 1639. Hill "in plain terms did move Mr. Golding to leave the house and for such a courtesy to expect no further requital than a buck to warm his own house, which I would beg of your lordship."[25]

The practice of the hunt and the distribution of its trophies as noble gifts reveal an important cultural dimension of the deer massacre in 1642. These trophies of the chase flowed from noble stock to its loyal servants, and the treasures of noble largess were, in theory, not available to commoners for exchange.[26] If the prescriptive literature of the hunt furnishes reflections on the nature of the hunted deer as a symbol of nobility and source of honor, the correspondence between Middlesex and his friends and servants in Gloucestershire offers insight into the practical uses of venison as a gift of power and influence. The destruction of deer in Corse Lawn in October 1642 harmed Middlesex in several interrelated ways. The attackers reduced a stock of political capital, the deer in the chase, prudently invested by Middlesex to secure friendship, service, and loyalty. Yet the value of the deer lay in the mystique of the hunt, its symbolism of nobility and honor, and the massacre, as an inversion of the conventional assumptions and

---

[23] CKS: U 269, Sackville Mss/4/2/1: William Hill to Middlesex, 6 February 1637, 11 April 1637, 30 August 1637; *CSPD, Charles I*, v. 11 (1637), 242, 433–434. In April 1637 William Hill, the attorney appointed to manage Billingsley's law problems, prepared a "release" to the warden of the Fleet and reported a principal debt of £250. On 18 December 1637, Hill wrote to Billingsley at Middlesex's house in London to report the difficult circumstances of Billingsley's children in Gloucester, suffering from "extreme want of money to buy them necessities, and Mr. Nelmes is most importunate for money for their clothes." CKS: U 269, Sackville Mss/4/2/1: William Hill to Middlesex, 18 December 1637.

[24] Ibid., William Hill to Middlesex, 24 July 1638.

[25] Golding accepted the gift but refused to leave the house in Forthampton without a reduction of his rent. Ibid., William Hill to Middlesex, 2 September 1639.

[26] When John Hullins of Gloucester ventured to dispatch a deer already "mortally wounded with an arrow," William Hill described the deed as "a very saucy part." Ibid., William Hill to Middlesex, 11 September, 1637.

techniques of the hunt, mocked Middlesex's aristocratic honor and pride.[27] Perhaps the scattered carcasses on Corse Lawn chase offer a glimpse of the "grotesque realism" characteristic of Bakhtin's carnivalesque style in early modern culture.[28] In sharp contrast to the hunter's reverent dispatch of a noble and unique animal, Middlesex's deer were killed in the manner of "cows, oxen and swine" slaughtered in the "blood month" of November, as farmers reduced their herds, and animals the farmers could not afford to keep for the winter were butchered and salted or consumed in feasts.[29] As Bakhtin observed, "laughter degrades and materializes," and the indiscriminate killing of hundreds of deer appears in this sense to render Middlesex's aristocratic pretensions in gargantuan form.[30] At the very least, the massacre struck at a symbol of Middlesex's aristocratic dignity and attempted to deny him the genealogy of noble power implicit in the hunt. This act of mockery and hatred was expressed in a cultural idiom as familiar in Gloucestershire alehouses as in the prescriptive literature of courtiers and country gentlemen, the royal court, and the mansions of the aristocracy. It remains to be seen how Middlesex's neighbors in Corse Lawn came to hate him so.

III

The deer massacre of 1642 was performed in the great theater of Corse Lawn Chase, a vast open territory of four walks, distributed across eight parishes and thousands of acres on the western bank of the Severn.[31] The crown

---

[27] This element of inversion lends the massacre a formal resemblance to rites of *charivari* and rough music described in Burke, *Popular Culture in Early Modern Europe*, 198–201; Robert Darnton, "Workers Revolt: The Great Cat Massacre of the Rue Saint-Severin," in *The Great Cat Massacre and Other Episodes in French Cultural History* (New York: Basic Books, 1984), 74–104; Martin Ingram, "Ridings, Rough Music and the 'Reform of Popular Culture' in Early Modern England," *Past and Present*, 105 (1984): 79–113; E. P. Thompson, "Rough Music," in *Customs in Common* (New York: New Press, 1991), 467–538; Peter Sahlins, *Forest Rites: The War of the Demoiselles in Nineteenth-Century France* (Cambridge, MA: Harvard University Press, 1994), 29–60.

[28] Bakhtin, *Rabelais and His World*, 18–24.

[29] Although Middlesex's deer were killed in the first weeks of October, this seasonal transition from autumn to winter in the rural economy remains important in the general context of the massacre. The forms of animal husbandry and festive activities centered on 11 November, the feast of St. Martin, are described in Brand, *Observations*, 1: 399–404; Ronald Hutton, *The Rise and Fall of Merry England: The Ritual Year, 1400–1700* (Oxford University Press, 1994), 45; Hutton, *The Stations of the Sun: A History of the Ritual Year in Britain* (Oxford University Press, 1996), 386.

[30] Bakhtin, *Rabelais and His World*, 20.

[31] CKS: U 269, Sackville Mss/4/2/1: Richard Dowdeswell to Middlesex, 2 March 1640; Christopher Elrington (ed.), *VCH Gloucester*, 9 vols. (Oxford University Press, 1968), 8: 274–275. The forest and chase included land in the parishes of Ashleworth, Chaceley, Corse, Eldersfield, Hartpury, Hasfield, Maisemore, and Tirley.

owned Corse Lawn "forest and chase" until Charles I granted the property in trust to the Earl of Middlesex in 1629.[32] Yet the chase had suffered since the early seventeenth century from numerous raids and feuds among factions of the Throckmorton and Tracy families in northern Gloucestershire.[33] In September 1620 Sir Richard Tracy of Stanway acquired the office of master of the game in Corse Lawn from the crown, an office he held until his death in 1637.[34] After years of battle against the Tracys and other gentlemen poachers in the neighborhood, Sir William Throckmorton had surrendered his patent for the office in return for a settlement of £200.[35] Under Sir Richard Tracy's regime, continued after Middlesex acquired the property, a keeper patrolled each of the four walks of the chase, and the office of keeper was reinforced by a warrant from the chief justice in eyre of the forests south of the Trent to search all suspicious houses.[36]

The first reports from Corse Lawn after Middlesex's acquisition of the chase in 1629 described a peaceful administration and abundant deer, but problems that had disturbed the chase as a royal property soon surfaced in Middlesex's correspondence.[37] In a now familiar practice, the farmers in Corse, Hasfield, and Tirley, parishes included in the chase, took fuel from the forest as their common custom, a destruction of the covert essential to local families in winter but harmful to the deer in the chase; in addition, the farmers complained that the deer ate their corn.[38] Small groups of commoners, often friends and relatives of the keepers, also poached from the chase to supply an active local market in venison, and their nocturnal raids resulted in violence.[39] In March 1634, six poachers from the Barnard, Beale, Morse, Stocke, and Underhill families killed John Beale, a keeper

---

[32] *CSPD, Charles I*, v. 3 (1628–29), 65, 100, 106; Elrington, *VCH Gloucester*, 8: 275. Prestwich mistakenly ties the chase to the manor of Forthampton and assigns Middlesex's acquisition of the property to 1622. See Prestwich, *Cranfield*, 411.

[33] PRO: STAC 8/23/25, Sir Francis Bacon, Attorney General v. Sir William Throckmorton of Tortworth and others, 1616, bill and answer; STAC 8/34/14, Sir Thomas Coventry, Attorney General v. Sir Richard Tracy of Haresfield and others, 1624, bill and (2) answers; Manning, *Hunters and Poachers*, 151–152.

[34] *CSPD, James I*, v. 10 (1619–23), 179; CKS: U 269, Sackville Mss/4/2/1: William Hill to Middlesex, 25 August 1637.

[35] *CSPD, Charles I*, v. 3 (1628–29), 62.

[36] CKS: U 269, Sackville Mss/4/2/1: William Underhill to Middlesex, 1 April 1639.

[37] Ibid., William Hill to Middlesex, 26 March 1633.

[38] William Hill "sent for process" to the Council in the Marches of Wales to stop the "destruction" of the forest. Ibid., William Hill to Middlesex, 23 September 1634, 16 March 1635; Elrington, *VCH Gloucester*, 8: 101, 278, 286.

[39] The state of the local venison market is described in CKS: U 269, Sackville Mss/4/2/1: William Hill to Middlesex, 22 October 1637.

of the chase, but could not be apprehended to stand trial for the murder at the assizes.[40]

Another layer of conflict and violence resulted from local gentlemen's raids on the chase to seize the honor represented by trophies of the hunt. In 1637, a particularly violent group of this kind, prosecuted by Middlesex in Star Chamber, consisted of Edmund Harris of Deerhurst Walton, a gentleman; Giles Long, a relative of Sir William Throckmorton's ranger in the 1610s; and Richard Horsame, a keeper employed by Sir Richard Tracy in the 1630s.[41] Harris and his cronies used violence and threats of violence to silence the other keepers and, according to Tracy, continued their nocturnal assaults on the deer even after Middlesex had initiated his Star Chamber suit.[42] In defense of the keepers, Tracy beseeched Middlesex to seek an additional warrant from the lord chief justice and to "have a care that these poor men may walk in peace, otherwise we shall have no order in Corse Lawn."[43] Before the administrative reform of the chase in the late 1630s, these inveterate conflicts over the uses of the forest, and the activities of commercial and gentlemen poachers in the chase, were treated as separate problems and clearly involved distinct groups in the neighborhood. The key to the great deer massacre was the creation, in the late 1630s, of explicit interrelationships between the political issues and symbolism of the forest, the chase, and, finally, the manor house in Forthampton.

In 1637, Sir Richard Tracy and William Hill attempted to resolve the problems of the forest and the destruction of crops by mediation.[44] Tracy proposed Sir Henry Spiller, Godfrey Goodman, Bishop of Gloucester, and Henry Brett, Middlesex's brother-in-law, as mediators between Middlesex and "the country," authorized to receive the "humble suit" or petition of the countrymen and then to collect the sum of money negotiated on Middlesex's behalf.[45] This hopeful project lapsed after the sickness and death of Sir Richard Tracy himself later in the year.[46] Tracy's death shifted

---

[40] Ibid., William Hill to Middlesex, 10 March 1634. John Beale was a kinsman to one of the poachers and familiar to the other five in the group, and Stocke, Beale, Morse, and the two Underhills apparently tried to persuade Barnard to spare the keeper's life.

[41] GRO: Will 1645/34; PRO: STAC 8/34/14, Coventry v. Tracy of Haresfield, 1624, answer of Sir Richard Tracy; CKS: U 269, Sackville Mss/4/2/1: Sir Richard Tracy to Middlesex, 15 June 1637; Walter Long to Andrew Long, 4 June 1638; Elrington, *VCH Gloucester*, 8: 275.

[42] CKS: U 269, Sackville Mss/4/2/1: William Hill to Middlesex, 6 June 1637; Sir Richard Tracy to Middlesex, 15 June 1637.

[43] Ibid., Sir Richard Tracy to Middlesex, 15 June 1637.

[44] Ibid., William Hill to Middlesex, 7 January 1637.   [45] Ibid.

[46] Tracy had health problems in the 1630s. In 1635, William Hill reported Tracy "dangerously sick of a fever and likely to die, but now we hope the danger is past, for he begins to recover." This concern for Tracy's health was mingled in Hill's letters with concern for the health of Middlesex's chase. See ibid., William Hill to Middlesex, 22 March 1635, 2 August 1637, 25 August 1637.

concern from the forest to the chase. Hill warned of a few "desperate companions" likely to exploit the situation in raids on the deer, and as a result the keepers received reinforcements from Tewkesbury. But the voice for mediation of local claims to the forest had died, although Hill did inform Middlesex of Tracy's final wish to pardon the poachers being prosecuted in Star Chamber and presumed to advise Middlesex that "love will do more good than force in Corse Lawn."[47]

Middlesex disagreed and clearly doubted the integrity of the officers in Corse Lawn. After Tracy's death, Middlesex made his first major effort to reform the administration of the chase. Hill rode to Corse Lawn himself, five days later, to announce the end of Tracy's patent as master of the game and to demand a strict account from the keepers.[48] Middlesex tried to use his extensive family network to regain control of the chase. Henry Brett became the new ranger, and James Cranfield, Middlesex's eldest son, joined Brett in a mission to ascertain the true condition of the property.[49] Yet efforts to reform the chase could not even produce reliable estimates of its population, only the suspect reports of interested parties. In 1637, Middlesex received an estimate of 150 deer from Brett, estimates of 160 deer and 400 deer from neighbors in the vicinity of the chase, and reports of 200 and 300 deer from the keepers and their assistants.[50] "If your Lordship hold not your hands two years at least," Brett disingenuously lamented, "you need not sell your chase, for it is almost killed."[51] Middlesex found it impossible to replace Tracy's keepers, and Sir Humphrey Tracy, baronet, not only defended his father but demanded Middlesex's "favor" to protect Lady Tracy's "great rents" in the manor of Hasfield, on the eastern border of Corse Lawn, from "the spoil of the deer."[52] The Tracy presence remained palpable, but these probes into the condition of the chase in 1637

---

[47] Tracy wanted to pardon the poachers named in Star Chamber on condition of their paying the charges of the suit. Hill believed this show of mercy would "preserve the game for time to come." Ibid., William Hill to Middlesex, 25 August 1637, 30 August 1637.

[48] Hill boasted that his heroic action after Tracy's death ensured only two deer were killed in the chase, both authorized by Middlesex. "I have appointed the keepers to make a note of every particular deer killed this year and how disposed of," Hill added, "and for my part I protest I have not had one piece for myself nor friend." Ibid., William Hill to Middlesex, 30 August 1637.

[49] Ibid., William Hill to Middlesex, 30 August 1637; James Cranfield to Middlesex, 30 August 1637; Henry Brett to Middlesex, 30 August 1637.

[50] Ibid., James Cranfield to Middlesex, 30 August 1637; Henry Brett to Middlesex, 30 August 1637; William Hill to Middlesex, 6 September 1637, 11 September 1637.

[51] This report from Brett is not supported by the accounts of substantial numbers of deer in the chase from many parties in the late 1630s. Ibid., Henry Brett to Middlesex, 30 August 1637; William Hill to Middlesex, 24 July 1638.

[52] Ibid., James Cranfield to Middlesex, 30 August 1637; Humphrey Tracy to Middlesex, 7 September 1637.

created mild consternation among the keepers, and Richard Jelfe, keeper of Woolridge walk in the parish of Maisemore, a southern tract of the chase described in 1638 as the heartland of poachers, rather hurriedly attempted to resign his post.[53]

The problems of Corse Lawn persisted in 1637, and Middlesex, under pressure to find the dowry for his daughter Frances, began to consider the sale of the property.[54] Before his death, Sir Richard Tracy had hinted the local gentlemen most likely to bid for the chase were also the active poachers in the neighborhood.[55] In October 1637, William Hill approached Middlesex in secret to report an offer made to Richard Dowdeswell. An anonymous party had contacted Dowdeswell and offered to buy Corse Lawn for the same price Middlesex had paid in the late 1620s. Dowdeswell cited the decay of the woods and the increased activity of poachers as causes of the decline in the value of the property.[56] Apparently Hill and Dowdeswell had their usual difficulties keeping Middlesex's secrets, as Henry Brett received from his cousin Andrew Saunders a report of John Dutton's keen interest in the property. Dutton was a friend of the Tracys, a regular visitor to Middlesex's chase in the 1630s, and a poacher prosecuted for raids on the royal deer at Woodstock in 1638.[57] This effort to sell the chase ultimately failed, perhaps because Middlesex could not command a price equal to his personal and financial investment in the property. In 1637, Middlesex could neither sell Corse Lawn nor reform its administration.

A small but complex network of poachers was the main obstacle to reform. In addition to the nocturnal hunts of Edmund Harris and other gentlemen, poachers allied to the keepers of the walks used violence to dominate the chase and supply venison to the local market. Walter Long of Ashelworth, ranger of Corse Lawn under Sir William Throckmorton in the

---

[53] Hill hinted darkly at "some mystery" in Jelfe's desire to leave his place, although Jelfe protested a desire "to follow his own private business" and offered to recommend an "honest" replacement. Ibid., William Hill to Middlesex, 11 September 1637; Walter Long to Andrew Long, 4 June 1638; Ordnance Survey, *Cheltenham*, SO 82/92; Elrington, *VCH Gloucester*, 8: 275.

[54] CKS: U 269, Sackville Mss/4/2/1: William Hill to Middlesex, 13 September 1637, 22 October 1637; Prestwich, *Cranfield*, 541–542.

[55] CKS: U 269, Sackville Mss/4/2/1: Sir Richard Tracy to Middlesex, 15 June 1637.

[56] Dowdeswell attributed this increase in the activities of poachers to the local scarcity of venison. Ibid., William Hill to Middlesex, 22 October 1637.

[57] Dutton also served as an undertaker for Sir Robert Tracy in the contested county election of March, 1640. *CSPD, Charles I*, v. 15 (1639–40), 580–583; CKS: U 269, Sackville Mss/4/2/1: James Cranfield to Middlesex, 30 August 1637; Andrew Saunders to Henry Brett, 22 October 1637; William Hill to Middlesex, 27 April 1638, 2 September 1639.

1610s, described this covert politics of the chase in a letter to his son Andrew Long, a servant in the household of Henry Brett, the new ranger, in 1638.[58] The most powerful gang of poachers on the chase operated under the leadership of Dennis and Walter Compton, Giles Long and Anthony Long, both cousins of the former ranger, and prowled the neighborhood of Longridge End in the parish of Ashleworth, a tract of the chase known as Woolridge Walk, patrolled by Richard Jelfe, the keeper so anxious to leave Middlesex's service before the investigation of the chase in 1637.[59]

The keepers moved easily across a fluid boundary between the poachers and the officers of the chase. Andrew Long, a cousin to the most prominent of the poachers, served in the household of Henry Brett, the new ranger.[60] Anthony Long, Andrew's cousin, openly killed deer in the chase and threatened to shoot uncooperative keepers, but Brett reportedly "did nothing" when informed of the mayhem created by the Comptons and Longs.[61] Walter Long described the keeper Richard Horsham as an embattled hero of Corse Lawn in 1638, a loyal servant "at his wit's end about [the poachers'] dealing" and "about to have come to my Lord to show him how the world goes," yet Sir Richard Tracy had identified Horsham as Edmund Harris's confederate in raids on the chase in 1637.[62] Middlesex held back the keepers' wages in the late 1630s, perhaps from suspicions of their loyalty, and this meanness may have sharpened incentives to join the poachers' lucrative enterprise.[63]

The power of this network of poachers extended into the courts in Gloucester. Despite the friendship between Middlesex and justice William Jones and their cooperation on issues related to the chase, the Gloucester assizes proved an unsuccessful arena for trials of poachers in Corse Lawn.[64] A relative of the murdered keeper John Beale, reluctantly indicted by the grand jury for Beale's murder in 1634, could not be apprehended for trial before his voluntary submission in 1638, and the

[58] Ibid., Walter Long to Andrew Long, 4 June 1638; PRO: STAC 8/34/14, Coventry v. Tracy of Haresfield, 1624, answer of Sir Richard Tracy.

[59] CKS: U 269, Sackville Mss/4/2/1: William Hill to Middlesex, 11 September 1637; Walter Long to Andrew Long, 4 June 1638; Ordnance Survey, *Cheltenham*, SO 82/92.

[60] CKS: U 269, Sackville Mss/4/2/1: Walter Long to Andrew Long, 4 June 1638.

[61] Ibid., William Underhill to Middlesex, 1 April 1639; William Underhill to Anne, Countess of Middlesex, 21 October 1639.

[62] Ibid., Walter Long to Andrew Long, 4 June, 1638; Sir Richard Tracy to Middlesex, 15 June 1637.

[63] The keepers' complaints of their lack of wages are expressed in ibid., William Underhill to Middlesex, 1 April 1639, 21 October 1639, 14 April 1640, 25 May 1640.

[64] Ibid., William Hill to Middlesex, 10 March 1634, 10 March 1638, 9 July 1638, 19 August 1639.

jury then convicted him only of manslaughter.[65] Middlesex, Jones, and William Hill suspected a manipulation of the jury and the influence of the Tracys in this case, and, according to Middlesex, Sir Humphrey Tracy conceded "Beale's deliverance by art."[66] The local respect or "countenance" afforded to officers of the chase was further weakened in the late 1630s by the lapse of a warrant from the Earl of Holland, the chief justice in eyre, to search suspicious houses, an important instrument of the keepers' authority under Sir Richard Tracy's regime.[67] In March 1639, three keepers followed a blood trail left by the poachers Dennis and Walter Compton to the door of the Compton house but could proceed no further for lack of the warrant.[68] Middlesex renewed this warrant before June 1639, and a lawsuit in Star Chamber then led to a declaration of outlawry against the Comptons, but this costly assault in the prerogative courts foundered on the local alliance of poachers and officers of the chase. At the moment the warrant and the outlawry were delivered, the local assistant to Henry Brett in the office of ranger, a man named Maddox, later identified as part of the network of poachers, opted for an extended journey to London to sell oxen, and the Comptons escaped to the Isle of Wight.[69]

Middlesex failed to reform the chase in the late 1630s and could not even deter poachers in the courts, although the Star Chamber suit dispersed the Comptons, the most "insolent" raiders of the chase in 1639.[70] After the effort to sell the property stalled in 1637, the problems of the forest and chase remained unresolved, as William Hill chased poachers from Cheltenham to Cheshire in 1638 and 1639 and approached Maddox, the ranger's assistant, at the Gloucester assizes to discuss how to make examples of the "chiefest offenders" among the local woodcutters.[71] The economic

---

[65] This Beale had been present at the scene of the murder for the purpose of poaching but claimed he had attempted to persuade Barnard, who did the shooting, to spare the keeper's life. Despite the precedent of Lord Dacre's case in the sixteenth century, an argument for considering death caused in the course of an unlawful act as murder committed by all the participants in the act, the jury refused to convict Beale for anything other than manslaughter, a clergiable offence. Ibid., William Hill to Middlesex, 10 March 1634, 9 July 1638.

[66] This quotation is taken from William Hill's letter in acknowledgment of Middlesex's statements to this effect. Ibid., William Hill to Middlesex, 2 August 1638.

[67] Ibid., William Underhill to Middlesex, 1 April 1639; Margaret Brett to Middlesex in William Hill to Middlesex, 2 April 1639.

[68] Ibid., William Underhill to Middlesex, 1 April 1639.

[69] Ibid., William Hill to Middlesex, 2 April 1639, 7 May 1639, 7 June 1639; Richard Dowdeswell to Middlesex, 10 August 1640.

[70] Ibid., William Hill to Middlesex, 7 May 1639.

[71] As usual, the pursuit of poachers offended vested interests in the neighborhood of the chase, and in April 1638 Sir Humphrey Tracy expressed anger over the prosecution of his tenant Middleton for deer stealing. In May 1639, Hill lamented, "It is not God's will to grant me deliverance" in the tricky

difficulties and international strife of the late 1630s also created new problems in Corse Lawn. In March 1638, William Hill reported the "great affronts" to the keepers made by "desperate persons going beyond sea," and in April 1639 "men pricked for soldiers and other desperate persons" killed some deer in the chase.[72] The morale and loyalty of the keepers, hardly stalwart at the best of times, suffered further from Middlesex's failure to pay their wages.[73]

In 1639 and 1640, the new pressures on the resources and administration of Corse Lawn threatened to undermine Middlesex's use of the chase to entertain the many local gentlemen drawn to the hunt, such as the Duttons, the Cookes, and the Stephenses, recipients of Middlesex's favors in September 1639.[74] The noble gifts of venison and flow of hospitality from Corse Lawn carried Middlesex close to the influential families in county politics and formed connections particularly important in December 1639, as Middlesex launched a scheme to elect either his son James or his son-in-law Edmund, Lord Sheffield, to the next parliament representing a Gloucestershire borough.[75] The guests on Middlesex's chase and the beneficiaries of his largess in September 1639 ranked among the most powerful players in the parliamentary election for Gloucestershire in March 1640: John Dutton as an undertaker for Sir Robert Tracy, the Stephens brothers as candidates and undertakers, and Sir Robert Cooke as a candidate.[76]

As the assaults on his animals became more serious in 1639, Middlesex made a second and more ambitious attempt to reform the chase. The first phase of this reform resulted in the removal of Henry Brett, his assistant Maddox, and the keepers in residence since Sir Richard Tracy's mastership. In July 1639, William Hill complained because his "good friend" Maddox failed to keep exact accounts of the deer killed, and the keepers could not be trusted to present accurate accounts.[77] Maddox's loose accounts concealed

business of arresting poachers. Ibid., William Hill to Middlesex, 10 March 1638, 26 April 1638, 24 May 1638, 24 July 1638, 29 July 1638, 7 May 1639, 16 July 1639; William Underhill to Middlesex, 1 April 1639; 21 October 1639.

[72] Ibid., William Hill to Middlesex, 10 March 1638, 2 April 1639. These assaults influenced Middlesex's decision to renew the warrant from the Earl of Holland in 1639.

[73] In May 1640, William Underhill loaned forty shillings to the keepers, described as "poor men in great want of [their wages] now against the times." Ibid., William Underhill to Middlesex, 1 April 1639, 14 April 1640, 25 May 1640; Margaret Brett to Middlesex in William Hill to Middlesex, 2 April 1639; William Underhill to Anne, Countess of Middlesex, 21 October 1639.

[74] Ibid., James Cranfield to Middlesex, 30 August 1637; William Hill to Middlesex, 6 September 1637, 16 July 1639, 2 September 1639.

[75] Ibid., William Hill to Middlesex, 15 November 1639.

[76] *CSPD, Charles I*, v. 15 (1639–40), 580–583.

[77] CKS: U 269, Sackville Mss/4/2/1: William Hill to Middlesex, 16 July 1639.

a multitude of family sins: Richard Dowdeswell, the overseer of the chase appointed in March 1640, lamented "the spoil and waste made by Mr. Maddox's brothers-in-law, who were a kind of licentious, debauched libertines."[78] According to Dowdeswell, the keepers had agreed to remain silent about the trespasses of Maddox's relatives because Maddox then indulged the keepers in their own raids on the chase.[79] Dowdeswell proceeded to reform the structure of authority in the chase and to change its personnel. The new system recruited prominent rangers, such as Sir Henry Spiller, to police each of the four walks in the chase, and each walk received a new group of keepers subordinate to the rangers.[80] Dowdeswell served as the overseer of this new structure and revived the jurisdiction of the forest law in Corse Lawn, a court of dubious authority since Middlesex had acquired the chase and in any event not held since the 1610s.[81] An early casualty of this war on the traditional politics of the chase was the distinction between woodcutters and poachers, a distinction lost in a broader notion of the chase's enemies. As Dowdeswell reported to Middlesex in August 1640,

I will be as careful as if all were mine own, both by myself and my bordering friends, and I doubt not but the game shall flourish. I have kept court twice this vacation in the Lawn and do threaten much and promise all fair respect where it's due. Truly if it had not been taken in the nick, between wasters of the covert and woods and base destruction of the deer, all had fallen to ground in a moment, for I perceive now all things posted that way.[82]

Dowdeswell's decision to involve several assistants of rank in the government of Corse Lawn, and his determination to create a record of his administration in the forest courts, departed from earlier patterns of leadership in the chase. The spirit of this new administration was evident in the army of forty horsemen and six footmen, "such as I could all safely trust," used to create the most ambitious survey of the chase in the first half of the seventeenth century. Previous surveys had understated the number

---

[78] Ibid., Richard Dowdeswell to Middlesex, 2 March 1640, 10 August 1640.

[79] Ibid., Richard Dowdeswell to Middlesex, 10 August 1640.

[80] There is a parallel here between Sir Henry Spiller's participation in the reform of Corse Lawn Chase and his earlier involvement in efforts to increase efficiency in the collection of recusancy fines in the Exchequer. See Questier, "Sir Henry Spiller, Recusancy, and the Jacobean Exchequer," 261–262.

[81] Gloucester City Library: Gloucestershire Collection: forest court presentments, Wycombe Gate, 19 April 1616. The transfer of forest authority from crown to subject required a special grant. In the absence of this grant, the property became a chase. See Manwood, *Laws of the Forest*, ff. 34r–35r.

[82] CKS: U 269, Sackville Mss/4/2/1: Richard Dowdeswell to Middlesex, 10 August 1640.

of deer in the interests of the rangers, but Dowdeswell's survey in 1641 made the new overseer responsible for 408 deer.[83]

A crucial aspect of reform in the chase was the link between poachers and woodcutters, a connection made first in Star Chamber, then in the forest court of Corse Lawn itself. As late as July 1639, the actions of farmers in search of fuel, and the depredations of poachers, remained distinct problems in the conversation between William Hill and Maddox at Gloucester assizes.[84] The destruction of the covert harmed the animals in the chase, but claims to wood from the forest in winter had never been prosecuted in the same way as armed assaults on the chase. Perhaps the success of the Star Chamber suit against the Comptons in 1639 induced Middlesex to undertake the joint prosecution of poachers and wood-cutters, small farmers and gentlemen, in Star Chamber in February 1640. Star Chamber became the executive instrument to resolve the problems of the forest and chase and to make an example of the enemies of Corse Lawn. In a letter to Middlesex, William Hill discussed the advantages and disadvantages of this strategy.

And the truth is the [woodcutters'] offence of itself deserves not the censure of the Star Chamber, neither is proper for that court, but punishable elsewhere, yet now being joined with high offenders for deer stealing and as confederates with them, they are at your lordship's mercy, and cannot avoid the expence of much money without remedy, yet I wish the keepers had been honest, to have named the principal offenders, wherein I doubt they have dealt corruptly and for reward sake have spared the chief offenders, and complained either of poor men or innocent men.[85]

Middlesex's attempt to reform the administration of Corse Lawn in 1639 and 1640 thus created an alliance between poor farmers and gentlemen, woodcutters and poachers, named as defendants in the same Star Chamber suit and in cases before the local forest court. This conflation of conflicts over the forest and chase was a necessary prelude to the massacre in 1642, and made sense of the stated determination to kill every deer and to cut down every tree and bush in Corse Lawn.

---

[83] Dowdeswell reported that approximately 100 of the 408 deer counted were males, and a substantial number of animals had died of the rot in the winter, although fewer than expected. Ibid., Richard Dowdeswell to Middlesex, 30 March 1641.

[84] Ibid., William Hill to Middlesex, 16 July 1639.

[85] The accused woodcutters pooled their resources to hire Richard Dowdeswell, the attorney soon to be appointed as Middlesex's overseer in Corse Lawn, to defend their case. Ibid., William Hill to Middlesex, 8 February 1640.

IV

The Earl of Middlesex's interest in broad policy issues related to the forest antedated his service as Lord Treasurer, years before his practical involvement in the administration of Corse Lawn. As an active supporter of disafforestation in the early 1620s, Middlesex helped to remove royal forests in Worcestershire, Somersetshire, and Wiltshire from the jurisdiction of the forest law, a prelude to the clearance of the land for enclosure and an increase in rents.[86] Crown law officers explored this policy as well as the revival of forest law in the 1630s, and Middlesex continued to support both the reclamation and the exploitation of the royal forests.[87] At the same time that Middlesex tried to reform Corse Lawn and to tighten his control over its woods and deer, he publicly endorsed the attempts to punish encroachments on royal forests and to reserve the resources of the forest for the crown. If the hunt and the circulation of its trophies are viewed as elements in the local politics of nobility, Middlesex's support for royal forest policy and his approach to the administration of Corse Lawn in the 1630s tended to a more strict control, if not a local monopoly, of these sources of honor and gentle status.

Middlesex's support for the revival of forest law in the 1630s was evident in his response to the forest eyre, the high court revived in 1632 to prosecute the encroachments at Windsor and then extended to the forests of Dean and Waltham in 1634.[88] The Forest of Dean eyre included Middlesex's friend William Jones as an adviser to Henry Rich, Earl of Holland, the chief justice in eyre.[89] In July 1634, William Hill apprised Middlesex of the eyre's arrival in Gloucester "in great state." On Middlesex's orders, Holland received from Sir Richard Tracy "a brace of bucks, being large fat deer," as a gift and as a token of Middlesex's "tender of the game in Corse Lawn."[90] Holland did not exploit this public invitation to make use of the chase but "kindly accepted" the gift of deer and "returned many thanks" for the show of welcome.[91] As the justice in eyre, Holland

---

[86] Prestwich, *Cranfield*, 345; Sharp, *In Contempt of All Authority*, 85–86.
[87] Hammersley, "Revival of the Forest Laws," 88–89; Sharp, *In Contempt of All Authority*, 208–209; Sharpe, *Personal Rule*, 116–120, 242–245.
[88] CKS: U 269, Sackville Mss/4/2/1: William Hill to Middlesex, 22 July 1634; Hammersley, "Revival of the Forest Laws," 86–102; Sharp, *In Contempt of All Authority*, 209–211; Sharpe, *Personal Rule*, 116–120. A detailed account of the politics behind the forest eyre, entitled "The Iter of Deane, 1634," can be found in GRO: D 2700, Berkeley Mss, KI, 504.M14.31, No. 19.
[89] Ibid.; Hammersley, "Revival of the Forest Laws," 94.
[90] CKS: U 269, Sackville Mss/4/2/1: William Hill to Middlesex, 8 July 1634, 22 July 1634.
[91] Ibid.

proceeded to an ambitious extension of the royal forests in Gloucestershire and imposed heavy fines for encroachments.

The forest eyre convened in the aftermath of bitter conflict and violence over abuses in the Forest of Dean, and this conflict received a powerful religious interpretation in the eyre of 1634.[92] A favorable account of the "justice seat" in Gloucester represented catholic magnates among the chief enemies of the forest and invoked the protestant memory of a Spanish plan in 1588 to destroy the Forest of Dean, nursery of the "wooden walls" of England, if the general invasion and conquest of England proved unsuccessful.[93] A petition to the eyre from justices of the peace in the forest lamented the destruction of young timber "as if men had feared the posterity of England had been armed against their enemies."[94] Despite many small fines of £200 and £300 for gentlemen and even smaller sums of £5 and £10 for the peccadilloes of small farmers, William Hill described the political effect of this eyre as a division between "the forest men" and great gentry – the allegedly catholic faction involved in the exploitation of the forest – and "the country," concerned over "transcendent offenses" in the forest and hopeful the eyre would preserve the woods "for succeeding generations."[95] The new perambulation of the forest, "beyond all expectation and contrary to 300 years usage," extended its boundaries north to Gloucester bridge and now included the estates of "diverse gentlemen," such as Sir Robert Cooke's land and park.[96] Hill also reported the £86,100 in "great fines" imposed on Sir Basil Brooke, George Mynne, Sir John Winter, and John Gibbons, secretary to Richard Weston, the Lord Treasurer.[97] In 1634, Middlesex thus supported a forest administration in Gloucestershire harmful to the interests of this sinister faction of prominent gentlemen in the county but "acceptable," in William Hill's opinion, to many commoners and even to Sir Robert Cooke, "who has as yet no

---

[92] Sharp, *In Contempt of All Authority*, 82–125.

[93] GRO: D 2700, Berkeley Mss, KI, 504.M14.31, No. 19.   [94] Ibid.

[95] CKS: U 269, Sackville Mss/4/2/1: William Hill to Middlesex, 8 July 1634, 22 July 1634.

[96] Cooke, a justice of the peace in the forest division, had expressed support for the forest eyre in its early days and had joined his "reputation" and "heart" for "the generality of my country" to endorse a petition from the mayor and commonalty of Bristol to preserve the forest from the violence of the magnates. Cooke served as foreman of the jury for damages at the eyre and thus provoked "the embittered spirits of the farmers [of the forest] and their friends." After the jury delivered its verdict and the eyre assessed its fines, Cooke also joined Sir Baynham Throckmorton and Sir Richard Catchmay, justices of the peace in the forest, in a petition "for preservation of the forest." See the account of the eyre in GRO: D 2700, Berkeley Mss, KI, 504.M14.31, No. 19.

[97] Hill sent Middlesex rounded figures rather than exact fines in CKS: U 269, Sackville Mss/4/2/1: William Hill to Middlesex, 22 July 1634. The fines are reported in GRO: D 2700, Berkeley Mss, KI, 504.M14.31, No. 19. See also Hammersley, "Revival of the Forest Laws," 95–98.

other benefit by that great action than to have much of [his] estate involved in the common calamity of the new perambulation."[98]

This politically important distinction between great offenders and commoners disappeared in the late 1630s. In 1634, Hill described Exchequer commissions as an effective means to deter the more ambitious of the woodcutters, but, in 1639 and 1640, Middlesex began to prosecute woodcutters and poachers as "confederates" in Star Chamber and in the forest court at Witcombe Gate in Corse Lawn, revived in the summer of 1638 for "preservation of the woods and severe punishment of the offenders."[99] As injustice in the forest and hints of popish conspiracy had been joined in the forest eyre of 1634, this new style of administration in Corse Lawn may have acquired a darker cast from the recruitment of Sir Henry Spiller, a known catholic and friend of the papists, to serve as a ranger in the reformed hierarchy of the chase.[100] During the 1630s, Spiller had acquired an evil reputation as a supporter of priests and their machinations in southern Worcestershire.[101]

The offences prosecuted in this new manner were not limited to the encroachments of gentlemen. Hill believed the keepers concealed the names of "chief offenders" and "complained either of poor men or innocent men."[102] In January 1640, William Underhill, Middlesex's bailiff in Forthampton, lamented the case of Thomas Carpenter of Eldersfield, "a poor man" and "a very honest tenant to your Lordship, by wrong information of your keepers questioned in the Star Chamber for cutting wood

---

[98] The prosecution of spectacular encroachments on the forest effectively preserved resources for other commoners, even if small farmers received fines for their own offenses. Hill's view of the forest eyre is supported by the account in GRO: D 2700, Berkeley Mss, KI, 504.M14.31, No. 19, a description of the eyre as a disappointment only for a few magnates "of the popish side." See Hammersley, "Revival of the Forest Laws," 87–88, for the distribution of fines.

[99] Hill doubted whether the prosecution of woodcutters was a legitimate use of Star Chamber, but acknowledged the court's power to terrify the defendants. CKS: U 269, Sackville Mss/4/2/1: William Hill to Middlesex, 9 September 1634, 23 September 1634, 29 July 1638, 2 August 1638, 16 July 1639, 8 February 1640; Richard Dowdeswell to Middlesex, 10 August 1640.

[100] As an officer of the Exchequer in the 1610s and 1620s, Spiller had advocated a moderate course against recusants in order to discourage conversions and to ensure a steady flow of fines into the Exchequer. As a justice of the peace in Middlesex and Worcestershire in the 1630s, Spiller continued to oppose abuses in the enforcement of laws against recusants. According to Spiller and others, such abuses encouraged conformity and reduced the revenue collected from fines. See *CSPD, Charles I*, v. 9 (1635–36): 326–29; Questier, "Sir Henry Spiller, Recusancy and the Efficiency of the Jacobean Exchequer," 254–55, 261–62.

[101] See Willis-Bund, *Calendar of Quarter Sessions*, 2: cxv, for Spiller's local reputation. On 21 November 1640, the parliament ordered Spiller's arrest and confinement "for releasing and conniving at popish priests." See Rushworth, *Historical Collections*, 4: 54, 59, 74.

[102] CKS: U 269, Sackville Mss/4/2/1: William Hill to Middlesex, 8 February 1640.

in the chase of Corse Lawn."[103] Small farmers on the border of the forest, such as Carpenter, were treated in the same way as gentlemen poachers on the chase, such as Edmund Harris and his cronies.[104] In August 1640, Richard Dowdeswell, the new ranger, classified "wasters of the covert and woods" and poachers as indistinguishable enemies of Corse Lawn.[105] After 1639, Middlesex's administration conflated the problems of the forest and chase and facilitated the cooperation of gentlemen and commoners in the deer massacre of 1642, an alliance hardly visible on the political horizon at the forest eyre in 1634.

V

After the deer massacre, Richard Dowdeswell reported the determination of "the multitude" to "pull down" Middlesex's house in Forthampton, on the border of the chase, as the final act of their drama. These statements raise the difficult question of how Forthampton Court came to be joined to the forest and chase in a grim mockery of Middlesex's nobility. The simple connection of ownership doubtless played a part, and the motive for some may have amounted to little more than a broad attack on Middlesex's property in the neighborhood; but evidence of local hostility to the ornamentation of the house in 1642 indicates the attack may have signified more than a personal assault on Middlesex's honor. A letter to Middlesex written in April 1642, six months before the massacre, described a local impression of Forthampton Court as a symbol of popery, a memory of the dark centuries when a Benedictine monastery ruled the northern Severn valley like an empire from Tewkesbury. As a set of interrelated performances, the assault on Corse Lawn and the dramatic threats against Forthampton Court thus acquired the overtones of an attack on a style of administration and abuse of power understood in terms of popery.

Middlesex acquired the manor of Forthampton, described in 1633 as "a goodly lordship, the like of it not in Gloucestershire," in slow phases between 1619 and 1634.[106] The property finally passed to Middlesex from Edward Cotton, a substantial householder in Forthampton and a leaseholder of the previous owner, in a difficult process of settlement recorded

---

[103] Ibid., William Underhill to Middlesex, 27 January 1640.
[104] Thomas Carpenter held Middlesex's farm in Eldersfield for the small yearly rent of £12. Ibid., William Underhill to Middlesex, 27 January 1640.
[105] Ibid., Richard Dowdeswell to Middlesex, 10 August 1640.
[106] Ibid., William Hill to Middlesex, 17 June 1633.

in January 1634.[107] Middlesex's style of lordship in Forthampton in the 1630s reflected the heavy demands on his income. He scrambled to provide a dowry for his daughter Frances in 1637 and to construct "a complete seat" at Sezincote in the northern Cotswolds in 1639. The extraordinary royal demand for revenue in the 1630s compounded the personal financial pressures, as Middlesex unhappily faced the collections for ship money in 1635, 1637, and 1640 and for coat and conduct money in 1640.[108] These economic vicissitudes, and the subsequent efforts to manipulate the customs of the lordship for financial advantage, help to explain the often wary and occasionally hostile relationship between Middlesex and the copyholders of Forthampton.

Soon after his acquisition of the estate in 1634, Middlesex became embroiled in a series of debates over the relative duties of lord and tenant to maintain the common ways and structures of the manor. As part of an effort to make the manor of Forthampton pay for its own maintenance, Middlesex confronted his tenants on such vexed questions as the obligation of copyholders to contribute "teams and servants" to repair the "banks, stanks and pitched highway" built to protect the arable and pasture from the Severn floods.[109] Yet these conflicts over the responsibilities of the lord and tenants of Forthampton in the 1630s were not discussed or negotiated in the formal assemblies of the manor. Middlesex used his power over the assembly of the manorial court to deny his tenants this important site of deliberation on issues of custom. In 1638, William Terrett, an exasperated copyholder of Forthampton, petitioned Middlesex

that we may have a court at Forthampton, as by the custom of the manor we have usually had and as I do believe we ought to have. That so I and some other may be admitted tenants in court, according to the tenure of our copies. That so our wives may likewise enjoy their widow estates, as by the custom they ought to do. And if it please you, I will be at the charge to purchase a court for the doing thereof.[110]

---

[107] Elrington, *VCH Gloucester*, 8: 201; CKS: U 269, Sackville Mss/4/2/1: William Hill to Middlesex, 26 March 1633, 17 June 1633; Edward Cotton to Middlesex, 10 January 1634.

[108] These financial demands on Middlesex's estates in the 1630s are evident in ibid., William Hill to Middlesex, 8 December 1635, 6 February 1637, 15 February 1637, 4 March 1637, 13 September 1637, 22 October 1637, 7 June 1639; Richard Bravell to William Hill, 9 March 1637; John Golding to Middlesex, 27 February 1637; Henry Osborne to Middlesex, 25 April 1640; William Underhill to Middlesex, 28 December 1635, 25 May 1640; Humphrey Tracy, sheriff of Gloucestershire, to Middlesex, 8 July 1640; Prestwich, *Cranfield*, 541–542, 544–545.

[109] Ibid., William Hill to Middlesex, 26 March 1633, 25 February 1634; Middlesex to his "loving friends and tenants, the inhabitants of Forthampton," 20 February 1634; John Fitzherbert to Middlesex, April 1634.

[110] Terrett was described as "a very honest religious man" in 1633, and his evident concern over Middlesex's approach to the problems of the lordship may indicate a broader anxiety among the copyholders. Ibid., William Hill to Middlesex, 26 March 1633; William Terrett to Middlesex, 26 May 1638.

The controversy over customs assumed a strikingly different form in disputes over assessments for the poor and ship money in 1635 and 1637, as John Barnard of Swinley Court, his neighbor Thomas Smarte, and a faction of the tenants in Swinley, a western hamlet of the manor, attempted "to alter the ancient custom" and base the assessments on the *value* of land rather than on the uniform measure of the yardland, "on pretence their yardlands are not so good as those in Forthampton."[111] This local campaign to make value the basis of assessments involved Middlesex in a conflict between the tenants of Forthampton, a hamlet settled on the rich alluvial lands in the eastern tract of the manor, and the tenants of Swinley and Downend, hamlets situated on the less valuable western lands, closest to the deer chase in Corse Lawn.[112] On the financial advice of William Underhill and William Hill, Middlesex consistently demanded the "customary" use of the yardland to determine assessments in the 1630s, but Underhill remained worried about the "covert" efforts of Barnard, Smarte, and other tenants in Swinley to shift a greater proportion of the burdens of ship money and poor rates to the richest lands of the manor.[113]

In addition to the major conflicts over custom and copyholds in Forthampton, Middlesex and his bailiffs placed the reputation of the lordship at risk in the everyday politics of the estate, in such sordid local affairs as the sale of Middlesex's hops and the prosecution of petty thefts among his servants.[114] In 1637, Middlesex prosecuted his hopman, William Price, before justices of the peace in Tewkesbury for stealing two or three pounds of hops "for his necessity," although Price claimed, and subsequent testimony supported, the complicity of Merlin, the former hopman, in a conspiracy to lure Price into this theft of hops "and a hatful of apples" from a storeroom at Forthampton Court.[115] Middlesex involved himself directly in the prosecution of Price, Merlin, and Lowe, a boy who lived in the same house as Merlin and acted as his accomplice in the deception, although Price evidently received a pardon and continued in the office of hopman

---

[111] Ibid., William Hill to Middlesex, 3 March 1637, 4 March 1637, 16 March 1637; William Underhill to Middlesex, 28 December 1635, 24 July 1637.

[112] Ibid., John Barnard to Middlesex, 6 November 1637; William Underhill to Middlesex, 12 November 1637, 27 January 1640 (and attached schedule of tithes for the "Forthampton side" and the "Swinley and Downend side" of the manor).

[113] Ibid., William Hill to Middlesex, 3 March 1637, 16 March 1637; William Underhill to Middlesex, 28 December 1635, 24 July 1637.

[114] Ibid., William Hill to Middlesex, 27 February 1635, 16 March 1635; William Underhill to Middlesex, 5 October 1635, 26 January 1637, 22 February 1637; Thomas Vaughan to Middlesex, 3 January 1637; John Golding to Middlesex, 8 February 1637.

[115] Ibid., Thomas Vaughan to Middlesex, 3 January 1637; William Underhill to Middlesex, 26 January 1637.

for another month.[116] If this strict treatment of the household servants at Forthampton Court did not exceed the conventional prerogatives of a lord, Middlesex's behavior was more remarkable in his humiliation of prominent estate officers in his service.[117] In 1637, Middlesex accused William Underhill, the bailiff of Forthampton, of dishonesty in the estate accounts and then contrived to embarrass Underhill before his neighbors in the matter of a lucrative leasehold. As Underhill lamented after the loss of the lease,

> Besides this I suffer in that which is most precious, to wit, my good name, which being once lost is hardly recovered. And it was my lord's promise that he would not discredit me. And this tends not a little to my disgrace, being now laughed at and derided for it. I hoped my lord would not deal so with me, I having done him faithful service, which was not for wages but freely performed.[118]

In August 1637, William Hill suffered the humiliation of a painful ride north from Gloucester to Tewkesbury on "a bad horse, who almost endangered my life, wherein, under favor, I conceive I was discourteously used," because Middlesex had inexplicably denied the use of his gelding for the journey.[119] Hill became a virtual bond servant in the late 1630s. He had borrowed money from Middlesex early in 1637 and could never afterwards persuade him to allow payment for services in law, financial business, or the administration of Forthampton and Corse Lawn.[120] Middlesex thus made tactical use of fear, humiliation, and debt to protect his political and financial interests among the officers, servants, and tenants of Forthampton in the 1630s.

In 1642, the political conflicts on the estate only intensified a fundamental problem related to the house itself, Forthampton Court. In the early sixteenth century, this house had belonged to the Benedictine monks of Tewkesbury Abbey; it had served as a residence of the abbots, and contained a chapel built for their use. In 1540, the crown had granted the

---

[116] In February 1637, Price was imprisoned for debt in Tewkesbury and removed from office. Ibid., Thomas Vaughan to Middlesex, 3 January 1637; William Underhill to Middlesex, 26 January, 1637, 22 February 1637.

[117] This process of alienation is reflected in the series of affronts and silences recorded in ibid., William Hill to Middlesex, 9 January 1637, 6 February, 1637, 14 January 1637, 30 August 1637, 1 September 1637, 11 September 1637; William Underhill to Middlesex, 28 December 1635, 26 January 1637; 2 February 1637; William Underhill to the Countess of Middlesex, 17 August 1637, 21 October 1639.

[118] Ibid., William Underhill to the Countess of Middlesex, 17 August 1637.

[119] Ibid., William Hill to Middlesex, 1 September 1637.

[120] Hill's experience is an evocative illustration of Middlesex's use of debt as a political instrument. Ibid., William Hill to Middlesex, 9 January 1637, 6 February 1637, 14 January 1637, 30 August 1637, 1 September 1637, 11 September 1637.

house to John Wakeman, last abbot of Tewkesbury and first bishop of Gloucester.[121] Wakeman carried a few fragments of his shattered monastery across the Severn to decorate Forthampton Court and, in particular, appears to have rescued a crusader's tomb, built in the fourteenth century, from the ruins of the Lady Chapel in the abbey.[122] The precise location and use of the artifacts are difficult to determine. But the house and its lands preserved the shards and memories of a catholic past in northern Gloucestershire, and the monastic history of Forthampton Court could not have pleased the small but vocal faction of protestant nonconformists in the village, led by Humphrey Fox, the curate of Forthampton suspended in 1630 for his repeated rejections of clerical vestments, the Book of Common Prayer, and the Thirty-Nine Articles.[123]

This connection to the abbey became a public issue early in 1642, as parliament created its ordinance against superstitious relics and images in parish churches. The ordinance established May 1642 as the deadline for the removal of the offensive objects, and, in London, its execution famously extended beyond parish churches to include such "superstitious images" as the sign of Charing Cross at a local tavern.[124] In April 1642, local hostility to Forthampton Court as a remnant of popery surfaced in a letter to Middlesex from his sister Margaret Osborne, the wife of Middlesex's tenant in the house. "As for the imagery here about your Lordship's house," Osborne wrote in a mood of frustration and cold resentment,

Mr. Dowdeswell does what he can, that as much may be saved as is without offence, but we are here very precise and would down with all. Your Lordship must be pleased to put a gentle restraint to the business. I am not allowed to speak a word in it.[125]

---

[121] *Letters and Papers, Foreign and Domestic, of the Reign of Henry VIII*, 21 vols. (London: HMSO, 1864–1920) v. 15 (January–August, 1540): 19.

[122] There are detailed architectural descriptions of the house in David Verey and Alan Brooks, *Gloucestershire: The Vale and the Forest of Dean* (New Haven: Yale University Press, 2002), 369–371, and Elrington, *VCH Gloucester*, 8: 199, 201, 202.

[123] Humphrey Fox had become the curate of Forthampton in 1616, after suspension from the cure of Tewkesbury in 1602, and served the cure intermittently until Bishop Goodman suspended him for the last time in 1630. Fox held property in the neighborhood and lived in Tewkesbury after his suspension. He sent his sons, Help-on-High and Hopewell Fox, to the University of Edinburgh to be educated, and the Privy Council ordered a search of Fox's study in 1639. See GRO: GDR 115, v. 2, Visitations, 1612–19: Episcopal Visitations, 1616, 1619: 333, 479; GDR 146, Episcopal Visitation, 1622; GDR 157, Episcopal Visitation, 1625; GDR 166, Episcopal Visitation, 1628; Gloucester City Library: Survey of Abbey Lands in Tewkesbury, 1632, 7; *CSPD, Charles I*, v. 14 (1639): 159, 198–9, 266–7; v. 15 (1639–40): 582.

[124] Rushworth, *Historical Collections*, 4: 558.

[125] CKS: U 269, Sackville Mss/4/2/1: Margaret Osborne to Middlesex, 25 April 1642.

Unfortunately, the details of the architectural correctness enforced at Forthampton Court were not recorded, but this evidence of local hostility to the "imagery" of the house suggests the assault on Corse Lawn in October 1642, and the related threats against the house in Forthampton, may be read as a dramatic expression of the subtle interrelationship of local grievances and parliamentary concerns over constitutional issues and the insidious influence of popery. Middlesex had attempted an unprecedented administrative reform of the chase and had used Star Chamber to prosecute both gentleman poachers and plebeian woodcutters as the common enemy of the forest. His sharp practices in Forthampton had fostered an adversarial relationship with his tenants and alienated even his local servants. Yet the link between Forthampton Court and the symbolism of popery made Middlesex infinitely more hateful than any bad landlord. These overtones of popery joined Middlesex's pettiness and opportunism to broader afflictions of the nation and sanctioned the use of violence as a necessary response to evil.

VI

The deer massacre and its attendant threats communicated serious grievances and violent hatred from the neighborhood of Corse Lawn to an absentee aristocratic landlord in London. As a performance, the massacre was drawn from a common stock of assumptions and symbols related to forms of mockery or criticism, the hunt, and the significance of deer as a source of honor. As the previous micro-histories have suggested, these assumptions and symbols were not the exclusive domain of either the gentlemen and commons of the Severn valley or their aristocratic landlord in London. The power of venison and the politics of hunt and forest reflected a broad appreciation of this cultural idiom as a source of status and influence, a means to communicate notions of honor. Middlesex's neighbors scorned his nobility and mocked his honor in powerful and familiar terms. The symbolism of honor became a political arena, as the mass destruction of Middlesex's deer conveyed local convictions of the injustice, the lack of nobility, the absence of the most common form of neighborliness from his administration of the chase. The political culture and mentality of the Severn valley, the creative sources of the deer massacre, did not differ fundamentally from the metropolitan world of the absentee aristocracy in London. If the Earl of Middlesex differed from his neighbors in northern Gloucestershire, it was in the innovative use of such institutions as Star Chamber to achieve his local political objectives.

The symbolism of the deer massacre joined local and national grievances in 1642. As the assault on the chase mocked Middlesex's claims to nobility and spread the dark smoke of popery over his possessions in the Severn valley, the parliament rejected the royal forest policy of the 1630s, a policy supported and, in several important respects, emulated by Middlesex in Corse Lawn Chase, as "a great grievance and vexation" and as a species of "arbitrary and tyrannical government."[126] This guilt by association profoundly affected Middlesex's political and economic relationship with his tenants. As early as May 1643, before the sustained demands of royalist and parliamentarian armies brought hardship to the Severn valley, William Underhill reported the general refusal of Middlesex's tenants to pay their rent.[127] Although the episode in Corse Lawn Chase in October 1642 appears to support the familiar pattern of riot or "disorder" in the early years of civil war, the political qualities of the performance may help to explain the persistence of such subtle forms of "disorder" as this refusal to pay rent.[128] Richard Dowdeswell reported that the participation of local gentlemen in the assault on the chase was a matter of alehouse gossip in Forthampton and Corse Lawn. As gentlemen had assumed the lead in the deer massacre, the subsequent refusal to honor Middlesex's property claims was easily justified as an extension of this legitimate local resistance to despotic policies and their supporters. Once the straw had been turned in Corse Lawn, few of the fixtures in Middlesex's complex relationship to his neighbors could be saved from the flames.

---

[126] These words are drawn from the impeachment of John Finch, Lord Keeper, in January 1641 before the House of Commons, and from the 1641 statute to halt the expansion of the royal forests. Finch, a pillar of the protestant interest in the anti-catholic forest eyre at Gloucester in 1634, was accused, among other high misdemeanors, of the expansion of the royal forest in Essex in 1635 "by unlawful means" and contrary to the customary practice of 300 years. In 1641, Charles agreed to circumscribe royal forests within boundaries accepted in the twentieth year of his father's reign. See Rushworth, *Historical Collections*, 4: 136–39; 16 Car. I, c. 16, in *SR*, 5: 119–120; GRO: D 2700, Berkeley Mss, K1, 504.M14.31, No. 19.

[127] CKS: U 269, Sackville Mss/4/2/1: William Underhill to Middlesex, 8 May 1643, 26 September 1643.

[128] The concentration of "disorder," defined narrowly in terms of riot, in the early and late 1640s is explored in J. S. Morrill and J. D. Walter, "Order and Disorder in the English Revolution," in Fletcher and Stevenson, *Order and Disorder*, 137–65.

Conclusion: Royal symbols, forest politics, and popular politics in early modern England

ALDERMAN It seems there is a commonwealth in a park...

KEEPER   The king's majesty's parks, chases, and forests are liberally bestowed. But they that steal a deer off the king's ground, the horns may hereafter chance to choke them. They that steal deer, trees, lands, and all, the very stones will fly in their faces...

Man in the Moon [John Crouch], *Second Part of Newmarket Fair* (1649)

The symbolism of hunt and forest became significant partisan political markers following the Civil War and Revolution. Knowledge and expertise in the hunt, and respect for its exclusions, became a test of reverence for a monarchy restored in part on the ineffable distinction of nobility and commons in a hierarchic social and political order. In 1664, even the hunt's cuisine became a political site, as restoration cookbook writers reviled republican pretensions. The anonymous writer of *The Court and Kitchen of Elizabeth, Commonly Called Joan Cromwell* celebrated "a haunch of venison" as a "truly royal and constant dish in its season at court, when it was so really," but kept only as a "curiosity" and "dish of state" under the Commonwealth and Protectorate. The formerly "extraordinary" qualities of venison vanished, "since the times destroyed the game, yet cheapened and aviled the venison, making it everyone's meat." A venison pasty had been "a king of dainties, which Oliver stole by retail, as he did a more real regality." Cromwell had shared this "sovereign delicacy" among his "accomplices" as a "deer stealer," as "lord and avowed master of the game, more than Robin Hood, dressing their prey *a la mode Cromwellian*."[1] In this view, the Republic had rendered the virtues of both venison and regality as retail commodities, available for a price.

The use of hunting rites and related notions of gentility as a test of political legitimacy had become a theme of royalist polemic during the late

---

[1] Anonymous, *The Court and Kitchen of Elizabeth, Commonly Called Joan Cromwell* (London, 1664), 123, 125.

1640s. John Crouch employed these tactics and exploited the rich symbolism of the hunt in *Newmarket Fair*, a play published in 1649.[2] Crouch took revolutionary disafforestation as his premise, announcing in the first part of his play the sale of "a gold crown, worth many a hundred pound, and a scepter for to sway a kingdom," alongside a scene of the king's "parks, chases, and forests, with horses and deer feeding," being measured by a surveyor in preparation for division and sale.[3] In February 1649 the House of Commons had appointed a committee to clear the way for surveys of "parks, chases, and forests" and other properties of the crown as a prelude to their improvement and sale. In April, a second committee began to consider the best way to dispose of the deer in the interests of the state, now desperate for the means to pay its soldiers. In July, a law for the sale of crown property, among its many other provisions, effectively disafforested the Great Park in Windsor Forest. A new survey in February 1650 led quickly to the division and sale of this greatest of the royal hunting preserves, "the park being already commodiously severed into four walks with very convenient houses or lodges for the accommodation of the purchaser or purchasers."[4] Crouch used his play to deride this profane use of the forests and to mock those responsible. The second part of *Newmarket Fair* scripted the hunt as a school of honor and conveyed the primary meaning of a forest in a scene devoted to the mishaps suffered by a group of London aldermen, hunting under a parliamentary license in a disafforested royal park. One of the aldermen describes this New Park as "a commonwealth," but does not know the terms for different kinds of deer, such as "teggs, brockes, sores, and prickets," and so fails to understand the order of the "commonwealth" and shows himself unfit to rule. Themes of unfitness and usurpation pervade both the scene and state, as Crouch shows the Council of State dishonoring the noble currency of "deer such store" to bribe the aldermen, a corrupt tactic to secure London's financial support. But the failure of upstart commoners even to navigate the landscape of the park on horseback attests to larger moral and political shortcomings. Ultimately, the mayor accidentally "hanged himself in a tree," an alderman "broke his neck," and the keeper of the park disdainfully "held it reason not

---

[2] There are discussions of Crouch and further examples of his work in Raymond, *Making the News*, 20, 24, 124, 138–139, 149–151, 181, 252; and Underdown, *A Freeborn People*, 95–111.

[3] Man in the Moon [John Crouch], *A Tragicomedy Called Newmarket Fair, or A Parliament Outcry of State Commodities Set to Sale* (London, 1649), 3, 7.

[4] Both Windsor Castle and the Little Park were exempted for "the public use of the commonwealth." See Tighe and Davis, *Annals of Windsor*, 2: 240–260 for the parliamentary surveys; 2: 241, 242 for quotations.

to serve [them], for fear I commit treason."[5] This inclusion of the hunt's symbolism in a language of loyalty to the crown proved a successful formula, and in 1661, Crouch's brother Edward reprinted *Newmarket Fair* "at the request of some young gentlemen, to act in the Christmas holidays."[6] As the history of this text suggests, the "great man" and "country" understandings of forest that had long figured in forest politics had themselves become politicized in the course of war, regicide, and revolution.

The commonwealth notion of forest as a species of public property in republican political culture stood in sharp contrast to this royalist view of forest and hunt as sources of political virtue. If the constitutive violence of the hunt – its significance in the making of the social order – became a mark of militant royalism, however, the republic drew successfully on traditional notions of martial virtue and masculine honor to fashion its own distinctive political culture.[7] An element of violence remained vital to the symbols of political order. Although it is considerably removed from the evidence considered in this book, some reflection on the broader political history of constitutive violence is warranted here. After the restoration of monarchy in 1660, the persistence of the hunt and forest law as symbols of the "honor and power of the crown" tended to invest royal authority, and thus the authority of the state, in the sanctity and security of specific sites and properties. As late as the 1720s E. P. Thompson noted among the conditions that preceded the Black Act "a sorry state of affairs when the king could not defend his own forests and parks, and when the acting commander in chief of the armed forces could not prevent his own park from being driven for deer."[8] As a mode of violence, the hunt and forest regime made symbols of difference in a hierarchic order, dividing gentle and common qualities in social, political, and spatial terms. The power to shed the blood of a noble animal was instrumental in the differentiation of rank and in the constitution of order, and the forest existed to protect this power. The evidence of this process from Windsor and Waltham forests has revealed the political conflict that resulted from this interrelationship of royal authority and local communities in forests and parks. Thompson's work has made familiar the brutal sanctions imposed

---

[5] Man in the Moon [John Crouch], *Second Part of the Tragicomedy Called Newmarket Fair, or Mrs. Parliament's New Figgeries* (London, 1649), 11–15. In the jargon of hunters, teggs were does in their second year; prickets, brockes, and sores were male deer in their second, third, and fourth years, respectively.

[6] Man in the Moon [John Crouch], *A Tragicomedy Called Newmarket Fair, or A Parliament Outcry of State Commodities Set to Sale* (London, 1661).

[7] Sean Kelsey, *Inventing a Republic: The Political Culture of the English Commonwealth, 1649–1653* (Stanford University Press, 1997), 53–84, 119–150.

[8] Thompson, *Whigs and Hunters*, 191.

under the Black Act to protect forests and parks as symbols of royal authority and as expressions of absolute property. There is a striking contrast between this explicit use of sacrificial violence and the natural symbolism of blood, making the social order part of a natural order, and modern views of authority and order as human inventions, the result of rational human processes and actions. After all, the forest as a domain of the dynastic state, as a hunting preserve, and as a school of gentility and political virtue did not survive the abolition of forest law during the 1850s. Since the nineteenth century, modern nations have shifted constitutive violence from the familiar spaces of everyday life and activity to the shadowy linguistic space of metaphor, where the symbols of nation are fashioned from tropes of sacrifice and the sites dedicated to those killed in their service.[9] Although few now are blooded as James marked his favorites, many are touched by this violent rhetoric from the pulpits of nationalist politics.

Despite important local variations, the politics of hunting and its related territories in early Stuart England reveal distinct patterns. The assumptions, beliefs, and practices that comprise these patterns were sufficiently coherent and consistent to suggest political traditions, especially in the "special localities" of the forests. Despite inevitable problems of evidence, the micro-histories in this book afford a composite sketch of these patterns. Many gentlemen perceived forests, chases, and parks as arenas in which to compete for honor and reputation. Sir Peter Temple and Abel Dayrell in Stowe, Robert Quarles and Edward Carrowe on the border of Waltham Forest, Richard Hanbury of Datchet near Windsor, and Edmund Harris of Deerhurst Walton on the border of Corse Lawn Chase, as well as their servants and friends, competed for honor and status as uninvited but regular visitors to the forests, chases, and parks in their neighborhoods. Although honor often reflected expertise in the hunt, both gentlemen and commons frequently justified their behavior in these arenas in terms of important political principles. Abel and Peter Dayrell defended the "ancient liberty of purlieu" on the border of Whittlewood Forest, where "freeholders had liberty to hunt and chase." Quarles and Carrow asserted "ancient liberties and inheritances" in Waltham Forest, where John Tay of Nazeing made a stand for the commonwealth and body politic. Both the

---

[9] Benedict Anderson, *Imagined Communities: Reflections on the Origin and Spread of Nationalism* (New York: Verso, 1983, 1991), 144; George L. Mosse, *Fallen Soldiers: Reshaping the Memory of the World Wars* (Oxford University Press, 1991); Ivan Strenski, *Contesting Sacrifice: Religion, Nationalism, and Social Thought in France* (Chicago: University of Chicago Press, 2002); Greg Eghigian and Matthew Paul Berg (eds.), *Sacrifice and National Belonging in Twentieth Century Germany* (College Station, TX: Texas A&M University Press, 2002).

forest courts and the manor courts served political ends in their contribution to a general awareness of law and custom and as sites for political action. In 1622, the manor court in Nazeing became a focal point for resistance to lord Denny's plans for the wood common. In Windsor, the complex intercommons of Arborfield, Barkham, Hurst, and Wokingham parishes in Bearwood Walk clearly underlay the local action in defense of "diverse privileges and immunities" under the law. When the debate over local customs became too difficult in his lordship near Corse Lawn Chase, the Earl of Middlesex suspended the sessions of the manor court in Forthampton. Moreover, as the massacre in Corse Lawn Chase reveals, success in forest politics demanded a process of negotiation essential to the survival of the deer. In 1630, Sir Peter Temple tried to persuade Edmund Dayrell to exchange his lands and rights of common near Stowe Park. In Windsor, James understood the forest could not endure as a hunting preserve in the face of local hostility. As a result, he granted "privileges and immunities" to Bearwood and Surrey walks "on condition of preserving the king's deer in the forest."[10] These patterns indicate the presence in these "special localities" of political principles and tactics, leadership, institutions, and a tradition of local action in the service of law.

Patterns also suggest a systematic quality, but ultimately the microhistories of Stowe Park, Waltham and Windsor forests, and Corse Lawn Chase affirm the importance of agency in politics beyond parliament. Although the patterns of forest politics necessarily limited the field of action, individual decisions had a major impact on local situations. Abel Dayrell scorned the passivity of his father's acceptance of Sir Peter Temple's park and fought for his inheritance. Bennett Turner, Sarah Grave, and their friends stymied lord Denny's plans for Nazeing wood by attacking William Gardiner, acting on their conviction that this diseased servant of a corrupt lord had no authority to impound their animals. When the Earl of Middlesex and his servant Richard Dowdeswell decided to revive the forest law in Corse Lawn Chase, their action fostered the coalition of woodcutters and hunters that destroyed 600 deer in a matter of days. Because the Earl of Holland chose to drive the Great Park in Windsor Forest, the village of Egham divided between the supporters of a petition to negotiate their commons and the advocates of violent disafforestation. All of these actions make sense in the broader context of forest politics, but none of them were determined or forced from the actors by the demands of

---

[10] See Braddick and Walter, *Negotiating Power in Early Modern Society*, for more extensive treatments of the politics of negotiation.

a broader system. In this way, popular politics resembled more closely the familiar politics of high office under the Caroline regime, as crucial decisions by powerful officers affected the perception of the forest eyres during the 1630s. The micro-histories have indicated initial support and even enthusiasm for the revival or reform of forest law in Windsor, Dean, and Waltham. But decisions by the Earl of Holland, Sir John Finch, and presumably Charles himself, to enlarge the boundaries of the forests and to broaden the prosecutions in these high courts, especially after the eyre for the Forest of Dean in 1634, made the "rigid execution of the forest laws" into a national grievance in 1640 and set in motion the violent politics of disafforestation evident in Windsor and in Corse Lawn Chase.[11]

This forest politics offers no easy solutions to the problems posed by the English Civil War and Revolution. As the symbols of hunt and forest could express different political styles, discussed here in terms of "great man" and "country" meanings of forest, the actions performed through these symbols could not escape their ambiguities.[12] Despite their evident political qualities, the attacks on forests, chases, and parks in 1642 were not easily scanned as statements of support for crown or parliament. Perhaps for this reason, the incidents reveal important aspects of political choice during these crucial months. Those who took part in the violence, as well as those who attempted to restrain them, tended to justify their decisions in terms of clearly defined, opposed views of the forest. It is difficult to reconcile their statements and actions with John Morrill's view of political choice as unfamiliar and foreign to most experience in 1642, encouraging the kind of "passive" obedience to orders that lay at the heart of "localism." The distinction in his account between "local groupings" and "ideological differences" does not make sense of the forest evidence.[13] Just as importantly, the dynamics of forest politics in 1642 do not appear to confirm the notion that political choice reflected other influences, apart from political beliefs, in the way David Underdown and Mark Stoyle have mapped religious differences and political loyalties on variations in the ecology and environment of local communities.[14] The forest regime cultivated a distinctive political culture,

---

[11] Hammersley, "Revival of the Forest Laws," 93–95, 100–102. This view of agency has much in common with the analysis of contingency in John Morrill, *Revolt in the Provinces: The People of England and the Tragedies of War, 1630–1648* (London: Longman, 1976, 1999), 68.

[12] James Fernandez, "The Dark at the Bottom of the Stairs: The Inchoate in Symbolic Inquiry," in James Fernandez, *Persuasions and Performances: The Play of Tropes in Culture* (Bloomington, IN: Indiana University Press, 1986), 214–238.

[13] Morrill, *Revolt in the Provinces*, 64.

[14] Underdown, *Revel, Riot, and Rebellion*; Mark Stoyle, *Loyalty and Locality: Popular Allegiance in Devon During the English Civil War* (Exeter University Press, 1994).

but this did not allow an easy translation of forest ecology into the political terms of support for crown or parliament in the Civil War. The choices made in the forests in 1642 nevertheless reflected the political experience of their makers, an experience of negotiation equally familiar in other English localities.[15] To say that such choices were not unprecedented or traumatic is not to say that they were welcomed by those who had to make them. But the complex local experience of the early Stuart forest regime, the accumulation of local knowledge concerning the institutional sources and uses of its authority, had accustomed those who lived their lives within its power to the practice of politics.

The attacks on deer and woods in 1642 did not signal clear popular allegiances in the escalating crisis dividing crown and parliament. But even in the absence of such a concise partisan political meaning, the extreme violence of the episodes, and their recurrent appeals to the authority of law and defense of custom, helped to create an environment that lent an urgency to political choices and actions. In October, Richard Dowdeswell alluded to the threatening presence of both "volunteers and cavaliers" in the neighborhood of Corse Lawn Chase. He did not attribute the attack on the chase to the politics of one camp or the other, but Dowdeswell feared "this time of liberty" and viewed the violence in the chase as "the turning of a straw" that would induce the paramilitaries of crown and parliament to "set a whole county in a flame." The idiom of forest politics could join other political discourses to support an array of responses to the crisis. In January 1643 the Dayrells acted on the reverence for "ancient liberties" declared in their parliamentary petition by raising soldiers for the king in Stowe, including the successful recruitment of several of Sir Peter Temple's tenants.[16] Temple's anxious concern to protect "his majesty's game" beyond the pale of Stowe Park did not extend to the recruits named in this list, compiled by Temple for the uses of the parliament. Many hundreds of foresters, like thousands of their compatriots, made difficult political decisions of this kind in 1642. As this book has attempted to show, however, these choices were based on experience and were hardly the first political decisions of their lives.

---

[15] Andy Wood, "Beyond Post-Revisionism? The Civil War Allegiances of the Miners of the Derbyshire 'Peak Country'," *Historical Journal*, 40 (1997): 23–40.

[16] HL: STT Military Box 1: 26, A Note of Names as Went to Brill from Stowe Parish, 10 January 1643. Of the twenty-one recruits in Edmund Dayrell's company, Tristram Busby, Henry Davy, John and Thomas Jeffes, Matthew and Richard Robins, Thomas Sayer's servant, John Spatcher, Edward Stevens's servant, and John Walcott were Temple's tenants or their relatives or servants.

BIBLIOGRAPHY

PRIMARY SOURCES

MANUSCRIPTS

Centre for Kentish Studies

Sackville Manuscripts

Gloucester City Library

Gloucestershire Collection
Survey of Tewkesbury Abbey Lands, 1632

Gloucestershire Record Office

Berkeley Manuscripts
Gloucester Diocesan Records
Wills

House of Lords Record Office, London

Main Papers, 1509–1700

Huntington Library, San Marino, California

Ellesmere Manuscripts
Stowe Temple Papers
Stowe Temple Legal Papers
Stowe Temple Manorial Papers
Stowe Temple Military Papers
Stowe Temple Miscellaneous Legal Papers

Northamptonshire Record Office

Wake Collection

Public Record Office, London

Chancery
C99, Chief Justice of the Forests South of Trent: Records of Forest Eyres, Charles I, 1632–1640
C 154, Proceedings and Presentments of Forest Courts, James I and Charles I
Star Chamber, James I
State Papers

PRINTED SOURCES

Anonymous, *Haec Vir or the Womanish Man: Being an Answer to a Late Book Entitled Hic Mulier* (London, 1620).
Anonymous, *Hic Mulier* (London, 1620).
Anonymous, *Muld Sacke* (London, 1620).
Anonymous, *The Court and Kitchen of Elizabeth, Commonly Called Joan Cromwell* (London, 1664).
Burton, Robert, *Anatomy of Melancholy* (London, 1621).
Calendar of Proceedings of the Committee for Advance of Money, 1642–1656, 3 vols. (London: Her Majesty's Stationery Office, 1888).
Calendar of Proceedings of the Committee for Compounding, 1643–1660, 5 vols. (London: Her Majesty's Stationery Office, 1889).
Calendar of State Papers, Domestic Series, of the Commonwealth, 13 vols. (London: Longman, 1875–1880).
Calendar of State Papers, Domestic Series, of the Reign of Charles I, 23 vols. (London: Her Majesty's Stationery Office, 1858–1893).
Calendar of State Papers, Domestic Series, of the Reign of James I, 12 vols. (London: Longman, 1856–1872).
Calendar of State Papers, Venetian, 38 vols. (London: Longman Green, 1864–1947).
Cavendish, Margaret, marquionesse of Newcastle, *Philosophical and Physical Opinions* (London, 1655).
Cockayne, Sir Thomas, *A Short Treatise of Hunting* (London, 1591).
Drayton, Michael, *Works of Michael Drayton*, 5 vols. (Oxford: Basil Blackwell, 1933).
Erasmus, Desiderius, *Praise of Folly*, trans. Sir Thomas Chaloner (Oxford University Press, [1549] 1965).
Fabyan, Robert, *Chronicle*, 4th edn. (London, 1559).
[Gascoigne, George], *The Noble Arte of Venerie or Hunting* (London, 1575).
Harrington, James, *The Commonwealth of Oceana* (Cambridge University Press, [1656] 1992).
Harrison, William, *Description of England* (New York: Dover, [1587] 1994).
Hobbes, Thomas, *Behemoth or the Long Parliament* (Chicago: University of Chicago Press, [1682] 1990).
Historical Manuscripts Commission, *Fifth Report of the Royal Commission on Historical Manuscripts, Part I: Report and Appendix* (London: Her Majesty's Stationery Office, 1876).

Hyde, Edward, Earl of Clarendon, *History of the Rebellion and Civil Wars in England*, ed. W. D. Macray, 6 vols. (Oxford: Clarendon Press, 1888).

Journals of the House of Lords, 1509–1714, 19 vols. (London: His Majesty's Stationery Office, 1802).

Letters and Papers, Foreign and Domestic, of the Reign of Henry VIII, 21 vols. (London: Her Majesty's Stationery Office, 1864–1920).

Man in the Moon [John Crouch], *A Tragicomedy Called Newmarket Fair, or A Parliament Outcry of State Commodities Set to Sale* (London, 1649, 1661).

Man in the Moon [John Crouch], *Second Part of the Tragicomedy Called Newmarket Fair, or Mrs. Parliament's New Figgeries* (London, 1649).

Manwood, John, *A Treatise of the Laws of the Forest* (London, 1598, 1615).

Markham, Gervase, *Country Contentments* (London, 1615).

Matthews, A. G. (ed.), *Walker Revised* (Oxford: Clarendon Press, 1948).

Nichols, John (ed.), *Progresses, Processions, and Magnificent Festivities of King James I*, 4 vols. (London, 1828).

Raymond, Joad (ed.), *Making the News: An Anthology of the Newsbooks of Revolutionary England, 1641–1660* (New York: St. Martin's Press, 1993).

Rushworth, John (ed.), *Historical Collections*, 8 vols. (London, 1721).

Rylands, W. Harry (ed.), *The Four Visitations of Berkshire* (London: Harleian Society, 1907).

Rylands, W. Harry (ed.), *The Visitation of the County of Buckingham, 1634* (London: Harleian Society, 1909).

Smyth of Nibley, John, *The Berkeley Manuscripts*, 3 vols. (Gloucester, 1885).

Statutes of the Realm, 11 vols. (London: Dawsons of Pall Mall, 1810–1828).

Whiteman, Anne (ed.), *The Compton Census of 1676: A Critical Edition*, (Oxford University Press, 1986).

Willis-Bund, J. W. (ed.), *Worcestershire County Records: Calendar of Quarter Sessions Papers*, 2 vols. (Worcester, 1900).

Wilson, John (ed.), *Buckinghamshire Contributions for Ireland* (Buckinghamshire Record Society, 1983).

SECONDARY WORKS

Anderson, Benedict, *Imagined Communities: Reflections on the Origin and Spread of Nationalism* (New York: Verso, 1983, 1991).

Bakhtin, Mikhail, *Rabelais and His World* (Cambridge, MA: MIT Press, 1968).

Beaver, Dan, "Conscience and Context: the Popish Plot and the Politics of Ritual, 1678–1682," *Historical Journal*, 34 (1991): 297–327.

Beaver, Dan, "The Great Deer Massacre: Animals, Honor, and Communication in Early Modern England," *Journal of British Studies*, 38 (1999): 187–216.

Beaver, Daniel C., *Parish Communities and Religious Conflict in the Vale of Gloucester, 1590–1690* (Cambridge, MA: Harvard University Press, 1998).

Berry, Edward, *Shakespeare and the Hunt: A Cultural and Social History* (Cambridge University Press, 2001).

Blackstone, Sir William, *Commentaries on the Laws of England*, 4 vols. (Oxford, 1765–1769).

Bloch, Maurice, *Prey into Hunter: The Politics of Religious Experience* (Cambridge University Press, 1992).

Brand, John (ed.), *Observations on the Popular Antiquities of Great Britain*, 3 vols. (London: George Bell and Sons, 1877).

Braddick, Michael, "State Formation and Social Change in Early Modern England: A Problem Stated and Approaches Suggested," *Social History*, 16 (1991): 1–17.

Braddick, Michael J., *State Formation in Early Modern England* (Cambridge University Press, 2000).

Braddick, Michael J., and John Walter (eds.), *Negotiating Power in Early Modern Society: Order, Hierarchy, and Subordination in Britain and Ireland* (Cambridge University Press, 2001).

Burgess, Glenn, *The Politics of the Ancient Constitution: An Introduction to English Political Thought, 1603–1642* (University Park, PA: Pennsylvania State University Press, 1993).

Burke, Peter, *Popular Culture in Early Modern Europe* (London: Temple Smith, 1978).

Colvin, H. M. (ed.), *History of the King's Works*, 6 vols. (London: Her Majesty's Stationery Office, 1963–1982).

Corbin, Alain, *Village of Cannibals: Rage and Murder in France, 1870* (Cambridge, MA: Harvard University Press, 1992).

Cox, J. Charles, *The Royal Forests of England* (London: Methuen, 1905).

Cressy, David, *England on Edge: Crisis and Revolution, 1640–1642* (Oxford University Press, 2006).

Cust, Richard, "News and Politics in Early Seventeenth Century England," *Past and Present*, 112 (1986): 60–90.

Cust, Richard, and Ann Hughes (eds.), *Conflict in Early Stuart England: Studies in Religion and Politics, 1603–1642* (London: Longman, 1989).

Darnton, Robert, *The Great Cat Massacre and Other Episodes in French Cultural History* (New York: Basic Books, 1984).

Douglas, Mary, *Natural Symbols: Explorations in Cosmology* (New York: Pantheon, 1982).

Eghigian, Greg, and Matthew Paul Berg (eds.), *Sacrifice and National Belonging in Twentieth Century Germany* (College Station, TX: Texas A&M University Press, 2002).

Elrington, Christopher (ed.), *Victoria County History of Gloucester*, 9 vols. (Oxford University Press, 1968).

Fernandez, James, *Persuasions and Performances: The Play of Tropes in Culture* (Bloomington, IN: Indiana University Press, 1986).

Fisher, William Richard, *The Forest of Essex* (London: Butterworths, 1887).

Fletcher, Anthony, *The Outbreak of the English Civil War* (New York: New York University Press, 1981).

   Reform in the Provinces: The Government of Stuart England (New Haven: Yale University Press, 1986).

Fletcher, Anthony, and John Stevenson (eds.), *Order and Disorder in Early Modern England* (Cambridge University Press, 1985).

Frazer, James George, *The Golden Bough: A Study in Magic and Religion* (Oxford University Press, 1915, 1994).

Gardiner, Samuel R., *History of England from the Accession of James I to the Outbreak of the Civil War, 1603–1642*, 10 vols. (London: Longmans, 1894).

Girard, René, *Violence and the Sacred* (Baltimore: Johns Hopkins University Press, 1972).

Griffiths, Paul, Adam Fox, and Steve Hindle (eds.), *The Experience of Authority in Early Modern England* (New York: St. Martin's Press, 1996).

Hammersley, George, "The Revival of the Forest Laws Under Charles I," *History*, 45 (1960): 85–102.

Hay, Douglas, Peter Linebaugh, John G. Rule, E. P. Thompson, and Cal Winslow (eds.), *Albion's Fatal Tree: Crime and Society in Eighteenth-Century England* (New York: Pantheon, 1975).

Heal, Felicity, and Clive Holmes, *The Gentry in England and Wales, 1500–1700* (Stanford University Press, 1994).

Helgerson, Richard, *Adulterous Alliances: Home, State, and History in Early Modern European Drama and Painting* (Chicago: University of Chicago Press, 2000).

Hindle, Steve, *The State and Social Change in Early Modern England, c. 1550–1640* (New York: St. Martin's Press, 2000).

Hubert, Henri, and Marcel Mauss, *Sacrifice: Its Nature and Functions* (Chicago: University of Chicago Press, 1898, 1964).

Hughes, Ann, *The Causes of the English Civil War*, 2nd edn. (London: Macmillan, 1998).

Hutton, Ronald, *The Rise and Fall of Merry England: The Ritual Year, 1400–1700* (Oxford University Press, 1994).

  The Stations of the Sun: A History of the Ritual Year in Britain (Oxford University Press, 1996).

Ingram, Martin, "Ridings, Rough Music and the "Reform of Popular Culture" in Early Modern England," *Past and Present*, 105 (1984): 79–113.

James, Mervyn, *Society, Politics, and Culture: Studies in Early Modern England* (Cambridge University Press, 1986).

Justice, Steven, *Writing and Rebellion: England in 1381* (Berkeley: University of California Press, 1994).

Kearney, Hugh, *Strafford in Ireland, 1633–41: A Study in Absolutism* (Cambridge University Press, 1959).

Kelsey, Sean, *Inventing a Republic: The Political Culture of the English Commonwealth, 1649–1653* (Stanford University Press, 1997).

Kishlansky, Mark, *A Monarchy Transformed: Britain, 1603–1714* (London: Penguin, 1996).

Lake, Peter, with Michael Questier, *The Antichrist's Lewd Hat: Protestants, Papists, and Players in Post-Reformation England* (New Haven: Yale University Press, 2002).

Lindley, Keith, *Fenland Riots and the English Revolution* (London: Heinemann, 1982).

Lipscomb, George, *The History and Antiquities of the County of Buckingham*, 3 vols. (London: Robins, 1847).

Malden, H. E. (ed.), *Victoria County History of Surrey*, 4 vols. (London: Archibald Constable and Company, 1905).

Manning, Brian, *The English People and the English Revolution* (Harmondsworth: Penguin, 1976).

Manning, Roger, *Village Revolts: Social Protest and Popular Disturbances in England, 1509–1640* (Oxford: Clarendon Press, 1988).

Hunters and Poachers: A Social and Cultural History of Unlawful Hunting in England, 1485–1640 (Oxford: Clarendon Press, 1993).

McIntosh, Marjorie, *A Community Transformed: The Manor and Liberty of Havering, 1500–1620* (Cambridge University Press, 1991).

McIntosh, Marjorie, *Controlling Misbehavior in England, 1370–1600* (Cambridge University Press, 1998).

Morant, Philip, *History and Antiquities of the County of Essex*, 2 vols. (London, 1768).

Morrill, John, *The Nature of the English Revolution* (London: Longman, 1993).

Morrill, John, *Revolt in the Provinces: The People of England and the Tragedies of War, 1630–1648* (London: Longman, 1976, 1999).

Mosse, George L., *Fallen Soldiers: Reshaping the Memory of the World Wars* (Oxford University Press, 1991).

Munsche, P. B., *Gentlemen and Poachers: The English Game Laws, 1671–1831* (Cambridge University Press, 1981).

Page, William (ed.), *Victoria County History of Buckingham*, 4 vols. (London: Dawsons, 1927, 1969).

Page, William, and J. Horace Round (eds.), *Victoria County History of Essex* (London: Archibald Constable, 1907).

Page, William, and P. H. Ditchfield (eds.), *Victoria County History of Berkshire* (London: St. Catherine Press, 1923).

Pettit, Philip A. J., *The Royal Forests of Northamptonshire: A Study in Their Economy, 1558–1714* (Gateshead: Northumberland Press, 1968).

Powell, W. R. (ed.), *Victoria County History of Essex*, 10 vols. (London: Oxford University Press, 1966, 1973).

Prestwich, Menna, *Cranfield: Politics and Profits Under the Early Stuarts* (Oxford: Clarendon Press, 1966).

Questier, M. C., "Sir Henry Spiller, Recusancy, and the Efficiency of the Jacobean Exchequer," *Historical Research*, 66 (1993): 251–266.

Rival, Laura (ed.), *The Social Life of Trees: Anthropological Perspectives on Tree Symbolism* (Oxford: Berg, 1998).

Ruff, Julius R., *Violence in Early Modern Europe, 1500–1800* (Cambridge University Press, 2001).

Sahlins, Peter, *Forest Rites: The War of the Demoiselles in Nineteenth-Century France* (Cambridge, MA: Harvard University Press, 1994).

Scott, James C., *Domination and the Arts of Resistance: Hidden Transcripts* (New Haven: Yale University Press, 1990).

Seeing Like a State: How Certain Schemes to Improve the Human Condition Have Failed (New Haven: Yale University Press, 1998).

Scott, Jonathan, *England's Troubles: Seventeenth-Century English Political Instability in European Context* (Cambridge University Press, 2000).

Sharp, Buchanan, *In Contempt of All Authority: Rural Artisans and Riot in the West of England, 1586–1660* (Berkeley: University of California Press, 1980).

Sharpe, Kevin, *The Personal Rule of Charles I* (New Haven: Yale University Press, 1992).

Skipp, Victor, *Crisis and Development: An Ecological Case Study of the Forest of Arden, 1570–1674* (Cambridge University Press, 1978).

Stallybrass, Peter, "'Drunk With the Cup of Liberty': Robin Hood, the Carnivalesque, and the Rhetoric of Violence in Early Modern England," *Semiotica*, 54 (1985): 113–145.

Stewart, Frank Henderson, *Honor* (Chicago: University of Chicago Press, 1994).

Stone, Lawrence, *The Causes of the English Revolution, 1529–1642* (London: Routledge, 1972, 1986).

Stoyle, Mark, *Loyalty and Locality: Popular Allegiance in Devon During the English Civil War* (Exeter University Press, 1994).

Strenski, Ivan, *Contesting Sacrifice: Religion, Nationalism, and Social Thought in France* (Chicago: University of Chicago Press, 2002).

Theis, Jeffrey, "The 'Ill Kill'd' Deer: Poaching and Social Order in *The Merry Wives of Windsor*," *Texas Studies in Literature and Language*, 43 (2001): 46–73.

Thomas, Keith, *Man and the Natural World: Changing Attitudes in England, 1500–1800* (Oxford University Press, 1983).

Thompson, E. P., "The Moral Economy of the English Crowd in the Eighteenth Century," *Past and Present*, 50 (1971): 76–136.

Whigs and Hunters: The Origin of the Black Act (New York: Pantheon, 1975).

Customs in Common (New York: New Press, 1991).

Tighe, Robert, and James Davis, *Annals of Windsor*, 2 vols. (London: Longman, 1858).

Underdown, David, *Revel, Riot, and Rebellion: Popular Politics and Culture in England, 1603–1660* (Oxford: Clarendon Press, 1985).

A Freeborn People: Politics and the Nation in Seventeenth Century England (Oxford: Clarendon Press, 1996).

Valeri, Valerio, *Kingship and Sacrifice: Ritual and Society in Ancient Hawaii* (Chicago: University of Chicago Press, 1985).

Forest of Taboos: Morality, Hunting, and Identity among Huaulu of the Moluccas (Madison: University of Wisconsin Press, 2000).

Verey, David, and Alan Brooks, *Gloucestershire: The Vale and the Forest of Dean* (New Haven: Yale University Press, 2002).

Walter, John, *Understanding Popular Violence in the English Revolution: The Colchester Plunderers* (Cambridge University Press, 1999).

Watt, Tessa, *Cheap Print and Popular Piety, 1550–1640* (Cambridge University Press, 1991).

Weber, Max, *Economy and Society: An Outline of Interpretive Sociology*, ed. Guenther Roth and Claus Wittich, 2 vols. (Berkeley: University of California Press, 1978).

Willis-Bund, J. W. (ed.), *Victoria County History of Worcester*, 4 vols. (London: Dawsons, 1971).

Wood, Andy, "Beyond Post-Revisionism? The Civil War Allegiances of the Miners of the Derbyshire 'Peak Country'," *Historical Journal*, 40 (1997): 23–40.

  The Politics of Social Conflict: The Peak Country, 1520–1770 (Cambridge University Press, 1999).

Woolrych, Austin, *Britain in Revolution, 1625–1660* (Oxford University Press, 2002).

Young, Michael B., *King James and the History of Homosexuality* (New York: New York University Press, 2000).

INDEX

Titles in the series